IMAGE MAKING

First Warbler Press Edition 2024

Image Making: Essays on Visual Culture (1978–2018) © 2024 Shelley Rice

Cover illustration: Francesca Woodman, *Untitled,* c. 1977–78, Gelatin silver print 5$^{3/4}$ x 5$^{3/4}$ in., © Woodman Family Foundation/Artists Rights Society (ARS), New York. Printed with permission.

All rights reserved. No part of this book may be reproduced in any form or by any means, electronic or mechanical, including photocopying, recording, or by any information storage and retrieval system, without permission from the publisher, which may be requested at permissions@warblerpress.com.

ISBN 978-1-962572-82-8 (paperback)
ISBN 978-1-962572-83-5 (e-book)

Library of Congress Control Number: 2024942005

warblerpress.com

IMAGE MAKING

ESSAYS ON VISUAL CULTURE (1978–2018)

SHELLEY RICE

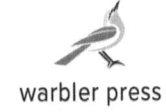

warbler press

Praise for *Image Making: Essays on Visual Culture (1978–2018)*

"While gathering her critical essays for *Image Making*, Shelley Rice recognized that 'intelligence, curiosity, and respect' were her mainstays as she built a global view of art. Her perspectives were and are still uniquely fresh and insightful."
—Anne Tucker, curator and essayist for fifty years

"I remember reading *Parisian Views* over twenty years ago and immediately being struck by Shelley Rice's beautiful prose and thought-provoking insights. I had been thinking about the photographers she engaged—Marville, Le Secq, Baldus, and Le Gray, and wondering why I found their works so dear and familiar. Little did I know, until reading Rice's book, that her book was as much about nineteenth-century Paris as it was about Beirut and many twentieth-century cities that were in the midst of massive social, cultural, architectural, and economic transformation. From that moment on, I knew that I would follow her time and again, down her various rabbit holes. And she did not disappoint as she opened doors to various known and unknown artistic, historical, and critical universes."
—Walid Raad, artist and Professor of Photography, Bard College

"Shelley Rice is an incisive, sagacious, and unafraid observer of the field of photography. Although she got in fights with some prominent artists, she remained unafraid. Over forty years, her scope expanded from the downtown New York scene to the international stage. *Image Making: Essays on Visual Culture (1978–2018)* is an essential survey of our visual world."
—Martha Wilson, artist and Founding Director Emerita of Franklin Furnace Archive, Inc.

"The photo criticism of Shelley Rice evolved in the space that was once called New Journalism and is now a venerable and still exciting, hybrid place of the objective (for want of a better word) and the personal. In *Image Making: Essays on Visual Culture, 1978–2018*, Rice's wide-ranging observations about the art of creating photographs and its relationship to her own life are vivid, original, and profound."
—Kenneth E. Silver, Silver Professor of Art History Emeritus, New York University

"A joy to read. Each essay is a force field, a graven memory, philosophy as fresh as day. Reading this book is like walking through a portal, a different one, time after time; an adventure in high seriousness."
—Alexander Nemerov, author of *Fierce Poise: Helen Frankenthaler and 1950s New York*

"Shelley Rice's brilliant essays on image making tell it like it is in forty years of commentary from the art world or worlds. An integral voice in the course that finally anointed photography as an art form, her erudite and readable prose is global in scope and critical in the best sense. Rice is an important ally to artists while holding them to high standards, political and aesthetic, opening herself to the art, and growing and changing (her words) in the process."
—Lucy R. Lippard, activist, curator, and the author/editor of *Partial Recall: Photographs of Native North Americans*

"While books such as *Parisian Views* and *Inverted Odysseys* (both 1999) established Shelley Rice's reputation as a ground-breaking historian of photography, her direct engagement with the medium as a critic and her sustained bursts of writing about the many other forms that visual culture takes may be less known. This book remedies that loss, in spades. Her "Image Making" columns in the *Soho Weekly News* during the 1970s, collected here, are a vivid, highly personal, yet critically acute snapshot of a decisive moment in photo history—the widespread use of photography as a leading medium for contemporary art—in the work of artists such as Barbara Kruger and Robert Mapplethorpe. Rice insisted on holding these works to moral, as well as aesthetic, account, stirring controversy in the process. Forty years later, her blogs for the Jeu de Paume, Paris, immerse us in practices of artmaking and curating that were emerging from all over the world and remaking worlds in the process. She encounters the work of pivotal artists such as Juan Downey, Cindy Sherman, Ana Mendieta, Duane Michals, Rotimi Fani-Kayode, and Walid Raad, and exhibitions such as Okwui Enwezor's *La Triennale 2012: Intense Proximity*, and Kara Walker's staging of Bellini's *Norma*, with the attention, respect, and love, they deserve."
—Terry Smith, Andrew W. Mellon Emeritus Professor of Contemporary Art History and Theory, University of Pittsburgh

"*Image Making* is a testament to Shelley Rice's enduring influence and the vital role she plays in shaping how we see and understand the world. It offers a guiding light for those of us navigating the complexities of visual expression. I first encountered Shelley's work as a student and since then my thinking about images has never been the same. It is exciting to see this culmination of her decades of work in one place where current and future scholars can access it."
—Hank Willis Thomas

My love and gratitude to those—like Jacki Apple, Martha Wilson, and Lucy Lippard—who set me on my life path and to the many others—like Ulrich Baer and Rob Perrée—who walked beside me as I forged my way forward.

CONTENTS

Introduction Why Now?... xiii

PART 1: IMAGE MAKING COLUMN 1
Preface 3
On Curation 7
Images of Women..12
Photography, Power, and Oppression (Part 1).......................17
Photography, Power, and Oppression (Part 2).......................20
Visual Consciousness: Aaron Siskind and Andrea Kovacs..............25
Barbara Kruger Goes to the Bathroom: Self and World...............30
Solitude, Privacy, Culture: Manuel Álvarez Bravo...................33
A. D. Coleman: Light Readings 37
Altered Photographs 41
The Male Nude 44
Living in a Mediated World: Erving Goffman and Eileen Berger........47
On Violence in the Arts..51
Success, Rigor Mortis, Experimentation...........................57
Two Ways of Picturing Death.....................................60
Postscript: Part 1 63
    The Flip Side of Glitter—Political Photography 63

PART 2: IMAGE MAKING IN THE EXPANDED FIELD 73
Preface 75
Reflections on the Wind 77
Short Takes: Reviews (March 20, 2012) 82
    The Radical Camera: New York's Photo League, 1936–1951 82
    Juan Downey: The Invisible Architect 84

Doug Wheeler, SA MI 75 DZ NY 12 85
Observed: Milagros de la Torre...................................86
Whitney Biennial (March 1–May 27, 2012) by Shelley Rice
and Rob Perrée 88
On Aging, Absence, and Angels: Cindy Sherman and
Francesca Woodman 91
Digital Images: The Short and the Long View by Verna Curtis...........97
Invisible Borders: Trans-African Photography Project by Shelley Rice,
Jennifer Bajorek, and Erin Haney................................100
Short Takes: Reviews (Spring 2012)................................103
   Men on the Edge (and Vibha Galhotra) 103
Eighty Years Young: Duane Michals—The Man Who Invented Himself by
Duane Michals, Shelley Rice, Véronique Bernard, Anne Morien, and
France Saint Léger...108
Here is the World: The New (Old) Art Photography (Paul Graham and
Mitch Epstein) by Shelley Rice and Rob Slifkin 115
Dak'Art Needs a New Face! by Rob Perrée............................122
Lorraine O'Grady: New Worlds 125
The 2012 PEN World Voices Festival: "Good Literature is Liberating" ...128
Photography at the Arab Crossroads: Postcard from Abu Dhabi 133
Intense Proximity: An Archaeology of Space and Time................136
Documenta 13: Walid Raad, Arabian Nights, and the
Pitfalls of Pilgrimages...140
Welcome to Photoville! by Shelley Rice and Lorie Novak 145
Just (a Few More) Kids: George Dureau, Robert Mapplethorpe,
and Company 148
Found Memories: The Quick and the Still 151
People in Glass Houses…by Shelley Rice and Pepe Karmel............154
Stories Played on the Same Keyboard: La Jeunesse D'Alan
An Interview with Emmanuel Guibert 157
Anne Sinclair, Diane Arbus, and Me................................164
Gerhard Richter: Through a Glass, Darkly.........................169
On Meaning, Chris Killip and a Girl Chewing Gum 173
The View from Left Field..177
Home Again!...181
Domestic Tension: An Interview with Wafaa Bilal 185

Life Worlds 191
Farewell from the Big Apple! 197
Postscripts: Part 2 198
    Gifts, Misappropriated: Kara Walker's Norma 198
    Shifting Spaces, Impossible Borders: Ana Mendieta, Liliana Porter, and Cecilia Vicuña 204

Acknowledgements 215

INTRODUCTION
WHY NOW?

For several years, I have been thinking about collecting my art critical columns from the 1970s and 2010s into a book. I was very excited when Warbler Press proposed the possibility of this book, until I began to think about the existential questions inherent in such a collection. What, precisely, would I be offering to readers of this volume? Why should they be interested in long-ago shows and old commentaries? On the most basic level, I needed to indulge my strong sense that there is something to be learned from my fifty years of experience as a critic that might be helpful to my colleagues and students, and really to anyone in the fields of art, photography, and criticism today. I am, perhaps, best known as a historian of photography, but throughout my career I have devoted myself—in addition to writing for academic and scholarly audiences, and teaching—to publishing essays aimed at broader audiences. I've always felt that this practice allows me to participate more fully in the ongoing life of the art world. During these years, I have written two extended columns over thirty years apart. The first, for the *Soho Weekly News*, covered photo-based works being shown in galleries and alternative spaces—or published in magazines, newspapers, and books—during the late 1970s, chiefly in New York City. The second, an online blog connected to the Jeu de Paume Museum in Paris, focused on global contemporary art and its international audience. It seems to me that these two streams of journalism raise useful questions—and suggest tentative answers—about the role and purpose not only of the critic but, more importantly, of art in the modern world.

The *Soho News* column and the Jeu de Paume blog represent two challenging and engaging assignments in my career that coincided with periods of momentous cultural change. Both columns trace the expansion of art at the turn from the twentieth to the twenty-first century: the changes in audiences and platforms that have contributed to the diversity of visual culture and its role in contemporary life—from high culture to popular image forms, from prescribed aesthetics to pluralism in the 1970s, and from local to global networks in the 2010s. These are moments when the restrictive confines of the white/male/Western precepts of elite art began crumbling, moments when a critic was obliged to use imagination, intelligence, and flexibility in reacting to rapidly changing social, political, geographic, and technological landscapes.

There are two consistent threads that link my early writings to my later publications which have become fully apparent only with hindsight. The first is an unshakeable commitment to the idea that art is a vessel for human experience, a vehicle for the transmission of information and understanding. The second is my certainty that this experiential expression can be mediated through the mind and eye of one critic: me. Whether I am beating the pavement in New York or the surfing digital highways of the Internet, I see my job in the same way. I am tasked with using my critical perceptions to interpret an evolving visual language and translating that aesthetic experience into words for the benefit of others. My point of view, filtered through the lens of writing for the general public, offers an immediacy not available in my academic writing. Full of (relatively) unmediated judgments and first stage analyses, these essays are based on reactions, feelings, and even mistakes that would be refined later by me and others. Tentativeness and incompleteness are always part of the journalistic mix, but these contingent traits are colored by a personality, a brain, an education. The philosophy of art in all fine criticism grows from the subjectivity of the writer—a truism that seems more and more unattainable in recent years, when critics are treated like so much copy filler, their role as mediators and thinkers downplayed and devalued.

My feelings about this show my age, clearly; they are part of a generational idea that seems increasingly remote today. When I was young, in the 1970s, people like Clement Greenberg, Harold Rosenberg, and Lawrence Alloway were publishing their writings in magazines. This was a golden age of criticism, whether or not one agreed with the conclusions of the writers, because each of these critics came to their job with a position, a philosophy, a worldview—whose passionate explication gave them a reason for devoting their lives to the understanding of art. Greenberg, anxious to differentiate fine art from the kitsch of popular culture, devoted himself to formalism and a Darwinian attitude toward progress in the arts. His writing was analytical and prescriptive; he excluded much more than he included and took upon himself the task of marching painting forward toward its inevitable future. Rosenberg saw the artist as a man who painted in order to *perform* his relationship with the social and political dilemmas posed by modern life. And Alloway, who equated the critic with an anthropologist, set out to describe the expanded field of visual culture. These men set a high bar for a young critic like me: they proposed that an art writer was a thinker, not a PR lackey creating generic and endlessly adaptable copy cribbed from a gallery's or museum's press release. Their lives were engaged with the task of defining the meaning and importance of visual expression. Their contrasting positions and points of view, which they crafted, honed, and refined with the same care and nuance that artists lavished on objects, were argued, discussed, and altered by their public, including artists, museum goers, and anyone interested in the meaning, purpose, and aspirations of art-making in our world; each had followers, committed to their way of describing the role of art in modern life. They were, frankly, intellectual giants, pioneers of vision, nothing less than philosophers. By translating their experiences with particular artworks into writings and ultimately theoretical models for understanding art and ourselves, they provided foils and framings for others to orient and deepen their experiences in turn. For better or worse, I inherited that heroic model of the critical vocation.

    I entered the fray when Clement Greenberg ruled; his disciples were Michael Fried, Rosalind Krauss, and William Rubin of MOMA, who was my teacher at the Institute of Fine Arts. Harold Rosenberg was my favorite writer; his impassioned political stances thrilled me. But my mentor, at SUNY Stony Brook where I earned my BA, was Lawrence Alloway, whose worldview—optimistic, open, inclusive, generous, and constantly expanding—pointed in the direction I wanted my life and intellect to go. His influence buttresses all the essays in this volume, underpinning my judgments and analyses with an unwavering commitment to describing the present—rather than prescribing the future.

Working against the prevailing wisdom of the time, Alloway rejected linear notions of historical evolution, which saw all of history as a Darwinian march toward cultural progress. In his essay "The Complex Present," he saw "the cross section as an art historical method of enquiry."[1] He was interested in preserving what he called "multiplicity," the various styles and symbols coexisting at any historical moment. He saw this description of the present (which he called "actuality") as an "approach that does not depend for its existence on the exclusion of most of the symbols that people live by. Now when I write about art (published) and movies (unpublished), I assume that both are part of a general form of communication. All kinds of messages are transmitted to every kind of audience along a multitude of channels. Art is one part of the field; another is advertising. We begin to see the work of art in a changed context freed from the iron curtain of traditional aesthetics separating absolutely art from nonart. In the general field of visual communications, the unique function of each form of communication and the new range of similarities between them is just beginning to be charted. It is part of an effort to see art in terms of human use rather than in terms of philosophical problems."[2]

For Alloway, the present represented not only an "expanded field,"[3] an inclusive temporal field, full of agreements and parallels but also contrasts, complexities, and contradictions. He visualized this field by comparing the idea of a pyramid of culture—with elite definitions of high art at the top—with a line, a continuum, where all the different forms of visual communication were equally represented. He saw contemporary pluralism and the global profusion of styles as "multiple points of view…the form of liberty, not the collapse of standards."[4] Unlike most of his colleagues, this critic was willing to expand his field to include not only films and photography—still walled off from serious high art at that time—but also billboards and highway signs and Chinese porcelain, understanding that the modern pluralism of

---

[1] Lawrence Alloway, "The Complex Present," in *Art Criticism* 1:1, Spring 1979, reprinted in Richard Kalina (ed.), *Imagining the Present: Context, Content and the Role of the Critic. Essays by Lawrence Alloway* (New York and London: Routledge), p. 244.
[2] Ibid., pp. 244–5.
[3] Alloway, "Systems of Cross-Reference in the Arts: On Translation," in Kalina, op. cit., p. 179.
[4] Alloway, "The Complex Present," p. 242.

visual media had its roots not only in eighteenth century salons but in the massive changes brought about by the new modes of transportation and imperialism in the nineteenth century, best exemplified by the Universal Expositions. "Spectator mobility"[5] was one of his favorite concepts: the mobile viewer with diversified tastes, free to cross national borders, and sample different cultures just as he or she is free to traverse the lines between high and low art. From Alloway's point of view, the expansion of art's audience—either through large international exhibitions or mechanical reproductions—since the nineteenth century made it impossible to sustain control over its reception or interpretation. "The global scale of art today weakens the consensual effect of national groups of critics anxious to define their own country's art as normative."[6] In the vacuum left by aristocrats and the imperialist tastemakers after the ongoing social transformations started in the early nineteenth century, Alloway saw the possibility of a flow of information that could lead to a real expansion and democratization of culture.

I have expanded on my mentor's key ideas at length to make clear, not only his relevance for my work but also his prescience in pointing to precisely the issues that would be central to cultural definitions in the late twentieth and early twenty-first century. He defined the field of "visual culture" long before it was enshrined in the academy under the rubrics of cultural and visual studies, focusing not on medium, style, privileged, and powerful classes or races but on the networks and relationships inherent in the continuum of social communications. One of the earliest champions of Pop Art, one of the first historians of the Venice Biennale, and one of the few art critics to write a book about popular film, Alloway paved the way for the essays you will read here. My journalism and insistence on the relevance of photography (high and low) is, in fact, "applied Alloway"; my awareness of cultural difference and its importance, low key in the 1970s but central to my criticism of the 2010s, was an issue raised in his writing by the 1960s and 1970s. And the untenability of elitist, colonial, "universal" judgments on art in a world of "spectator mobility"—a world where people "below" and "outside" (sic) of the Western hierarchies keep on

---

5   Alloway, "Artists as Consumers," in Kalina, op. cit., p. 72.
6   Alloway, "Art and the Expanding Audience," in Kalina, op. cit., pp. 141–2.

breaking down the doors and expanding the horizons[7]—is one of my mantras.

Active on all levels of the cultural pyramid globally, photography became my ideal (and endlessly expansive) focus. In the *Soho News* column, written from 1978 to 1979, the tangled interconnections of photographic usage in the United States preoccupied me and focused my writing; the forms, functions, and audiences for this ubiquitous medium allowed me to literally map the brave new world that Alloway had described. This was a deeply radical position in those days. The medium's history and interpretation had been defined in our country by Alfred Stieglitz and followers committed to elevating photography to an art. Its analysis in relation to painting, its presence in museums and galleries, and its economic viability in relationship to other art forms: these were the goals set out by prevalent art historians, curators, and critics of the time like John Szarkowski and Peter Bunnell, and taught with great fervor at Princeton University, where I did my PhD work. The contradiction between the omnipresence of the medium in Western culture, its ubiquity in all aspects of our modern life, and its exclusive and limited acceptance as an art form was central to my analyses. The absurdity of a hierarchical system of judgments which aggrandized a small number of precious images, whose references were frequently European, at the expense of the medium's vast and international visual reach, was a constant theme in my writings. Because of my positions, and my insistence on discussing artistic images within the broader arena of popular culture, the *Image Making* column was both quite controversial and quite influential. I began publishing criticism, at that time dominated by painting and formalist analysis, to propose a new, more inclusive, and, frankly, more realistic vision of the medium dedicated to reproduction, mobility, and outreach. The column played a role in the hearts and minds of the emerging postmodern generation—Laurie Simmons, Richard Prince, and others—whose investigations signaled a groundbreaking integration of popular visual culture into art.

This Alloway-influenced expansion was birthed in the pages of the *Soho News*. This weekly was a very important participant in the

---

7   Lawrence Alloway, "The Uses and Limits of Art Criticism," in *Topics in American Art* since 1945 (New York: W.W. Norton, 1975), p. 266.

downtown scene of New York City in the 1970s. A resolutely local, proudly neighborhood newspaper, it was essential reading for the impassioned discussions that took place in the lofts and alternative spaces below 14th Street. My colleagues included John Perrault, Sally Banes, Jill Johnston, Noel Carroll, and Gregory Battcock, among others—knowledgeable and experimental critics eager to describe a vibrant art scene coming into being. The wonderful thing about journalism is, in fact, that one can develop ideas, make mistakes, shape radical points of view, piss everyone off, and break new ground. Liberated from the "seriousness," (sic) intended longevity, and conservatism of academic writing, away from the frowning judgments of those who prize the enshrinement of *idées recues* over cutting edge analysis, a newspaper critic is free to try on new clothes with each column, to see if "actuality,"[8] well described, elicits new forms of both art and writing. This was the context for my decision to base most of my columns on comparisons between contemporaneous art photography and popular image forms. It allowed me to describe a specific and immensely productive and exhilarating moment in culture while simultaneously proposing that photography's networks of communication were central to the shaping of that culture.

Please note that one could easily define "that culture" in the 1970s, in spite of the pluralism of media and the radical introduction of diverse audiences and feminists during the decade. The reference was Western, American/European, upper class, and male, but ever-widening cracks were showing in the edifice. By 1973, Alloway began to define what we now call identity politics and parse its relationship to both artistic creation and reception. In a series of lectures given at the Art Students League (located in Greenwich Village and offering classes and workshops for aspiring artists and an interested public) and later published in his collection *Topics in American Art*, he called for the separation of the concept of social change from stylistic change. This was a time of vast social transformation in the United States and the world due to various civil rights movements, but the Darwinian (Greenbergian) march of formal progress dominated most discussions of artistic evolution. Citing black, Puerto Rican, and women artists putting revolutionary

---

8 George Kubler, *The Shape of Time: Remarks on the History of Things* (New Haven and London: Yale University Press, 1970), p. 16.

pressure on society, Alloway wrote, "It is central to a new condition in the art world that the content of art can be a group's awareness of its identity over and above stylistic differences in the works themselves… The fact that these artists are producing art and forcing its recognition is socially of prime importance, and it makes the often recited inventory of formal breakthroughs—that is, the procession of stylistic revolution without sociological impact—seem remote and idle."[9] This shift in critical perspective was foundational, and would be expanded later, in the 1980s, when he began to add global artworks to the mix, to extend his range beyond Europe and America in order to understand a broader and more complex range of human expressions.

This global shift was the *raison d'être* of my Jeu de Paume blog: it represented my exploration of a brave new world of vision, of culture, and of theory. Born years after Alloway's passing on another continent, during a decade of massive expansion of international travel, exchange, and expositions, it allowed me to beat a virtual pavement, to interact digitally with an endless range of people, perspectives, and artistic forms and functions. This new mindset has become nearly quotidian for many of us; it is reflected, for instance, in a quote I encountered on the blackboard of the Jefferson Market Library on a summer day: "In the world through which I travel, I am endlessly creating myself."[10] I realized that this *Quote of the Day* by Frantz Fanon perfectly describes my attitude toward my journalistic experiment. Never intended as extended objective description of "actuality," my criticism has always been a voyage into other ways of seeing the world. It was and is intended to be a celebration of cultural differences, a learning curve that allows me to continually expand my definition of the "human." Seeing artworks—their forms, functions, and audiences—as communication, as messages in various shaped bottles that are designed to reach out and tell us what life is like in Mongolia, São Paulo, Beirut, or South Africa, I couldn't help thinking that the blog assignment was a gift—an opportunity to travel the world, sometimes in my body but always with my mind.

This may seem trite and self-evident—possibly to a generation of

---

9   Alloway, "The Uses and Limits of Art Criticism," p. 266.
10 Frantz Fanon, *Black Skin, White Masks* (New York: Grove Press, 1967), p. 229. Trans. Charles Lam Markmann.

readers who grew up in a world where long-haul travel is affordable and common, and where any bit of information generated anywhere can be accessed from any other place—but it is not. The first thing that became evident to me when I branched out beyond my geographical and national comfort zone was my ignorance. Back in 1979, confronted with the amazing Manuel Álvarez Bravo show at the Americas Society in New York City, I uncomfortably found the works opaque, indecipherable, impervious to what I considered my considerable analytic and critical tools. My fancy education, honed in seminar discussions and lectures by some of the preeminent art historians and critics in the world at the time, couldn't save me. I described my discomfort in my *Image Making* column and recognized that outreach into other lands meant outreach of the heart and the intellect, too—and that this latter kind of outreach was different in nature and degree than even the furthest and most complicated trip. Research was necessary; discussion imperative too, so I could pierce and comprehend the ways in which Álvarez Bravo was visually describing the lives of his countrymen. By the time I began to write the Jeu de Paume blog in 2012, I had been able to integrate these international tools into my vocabulary—and each challenging global assignment forced me to expand my range of experience. By this time, I had seen a lot of the world and a lot of the world's art; I had traveled to many countries and been a "mobile spectator" in many global expositions. Importantly, I had also had the privilege of befriending and teaching with Okwui Enwezor, the global curator whose brilliant grasp of the "postcolonial constellation"[11] remains a guiding light for me.

I wrote about several Enwezor shows in the blog, most notably *Intense Proximity*, which he curated for the Palais de Tokyo in Paris. The exhibition's insistence on seeing art curatorship as a form of ethnographic research, a foray into many cultures for the purpose of bringing back information and describing other modes of communication, was determinative for me. Creating an exhibition full of surprising juxtapositions and harmonies, cacophonies and clashes, dissonances and crescendos, messages from near and far (both geographically and

---

11 Okwui Enwezor, "The Postcolonial Constellation," in Terry Smith, Okwui Enwezor and Nancy Condee (eds.), *Antimonies of Art and Culture* (Durham and London: Duke University Press, 2008), pp. 207–34.

historically) allowed this curator to shape his presentation like an artwork, to allow its sheer scale to help visitors experience the amazing pluralism of the global environment within which we live. Curatorship as performance: Enwezor's brilliant and sensitive interpretations, especially of African artists and art worlds, did much to shape my respect for the complex dynamics of Others and Elsewheres. Alloway thought art critics should aspire to be like anthropologists; Enwezor saw them as ethnographers. Both of them celebrated the objects and images created by diverse cultures, describing expanded fields of creation and usage; in order to do so, both of them rejected the judgments of the academy, leaving Western aesthetic hierarchies and assertions of privilege in the dust as they raised descriptive, comparative, and interpretive points about the cornucopia of art they experienced.

I like to think that I learned well from these mentors, colleagues, and friends. The readers can, of course, decide for themselves on this score. But one thing I will say for certain: global knowledge is now a prerequisite for this job, in a way that it never was in my youth. The sidewalks of Soho in 1970 were full of foreigners, immigrants, and a wide range of creative types, but this melting pot demanded less understanding of Others than our mobile spectatorship does now. We were, after all, in the United States, and the mores of the natives remained the dominant ones. My friend, Ana Mendieta, for instance, was well assimilated into the downtown art scene in the 1980s, even though she had much to say to us then about her experience as an exile from Cuba, a woman, and an artist. Speaking for myself, I could not hear her lone voice as I can hear it now, after many years of global travel, conversations, and experience. (See *Shifting Spaces, Impossible Borders* from 2018, included in this volume.) By the time I began the blog, the art world had transformed itself from a local, albeit pluralistic place to a communication network of great sophistication and cultural range—an open, virtual space, a "chat room" where international artists meet to share their varied experiences of the world with each other and their audiences.

What is needed is a sensitive and nuanced vision of the expanded field today, one that will allow for the circulation and mobility of images while at the same time respecting the manifold "relationships between signs and their users,"[12] as Alloway said. Such a vision will maintain

---

12 Alloway, "Art and the Expanding Audience," pp. 137–45.

diversity; but it will also respect all the players in the Postcolonial Constellation, our brave new world where the center and the periphery are continually meeting and merging in magazines, museums, international art fairs, and on the web. A good example: one day in 2007, the African photographer Philip Kwame Apagya presented his work in a crowded lecture hall at New York University. Apagya spoke with enthusiasm about the people he defined as his clients: his neighbors in a small fishing village in Ghana, who have been supporting the family studio since it was established decades ago by Philip's father. Striving to attract customers by providing them with painted backdrops (of Mecca, of air travel, of technological and architectural wonders unavailable in the village) that transform portrait photographs into fields of dreams, Apagya declared that his success as an imagemaker is dependent on his sensitivity to his neighbors' desires. Photographer Lyle Ashton Harris, a professor at the university, took exception to Philip's understanding of his accomplishments and his audience. More focused on Apagya's recent reception in the global marketplace, Harris insisted that Philip's primary customers are no longer his local patrons but the movers and shakers of the international art world. The good-natured dispute was amusing and telling: Philip does have both a local clientele and a global one, simultaneously, and they buy the same pictures, albeit in different sizes. In this he is like Seydou Keïta from Mali, whose portrait studio provided friends and neighbors with small and inexpensive images of themselves, loved ones, friends, and associates in the 1950s. Those same black-and-white negatives are now being reprinted by gallerists; large, costly, and precious, the new prints hang in foreign collectors' homes and major museums, where the originally beloved individuals are transformed into anonymous African types for the rest of us.

There are those who feel that images like these by photographers such as Apagya and Keïta and others should have some kind of "authentic" meaning and context—but such an idea is ultimately essentialist and irrelevant. The audiences and usages of Apagya's and Keïta's images can and should coexist, but—and this is important—both of them should be part of the discourse. As it stands now, the art world and its elitist attributions of meaning and value overwhelm the original context of production. We see yet another expensive photograph, but its similarity—most often in scale and price tag—to all the other photographs on the circuit, in art fairs, galleries, photo books and museums, deprives us of the knowledge we could gain of life in Africa, Korea, or Brazil. There is no reason why we can't live in a world where the same images are shown at the Centre Pompidou and in a grandmother's home. Such an open-ended understanding of the flexibility of image-functions will allow us to avoid superimposing a Theoretical Colonialism on our artist friends. Universality comes at a cost when cultural usage and communication is downplayed in favor of one elitist international language.

A multilayered understanding of image production, dissemination, and receptions, on the other hand, can expand the capacity for international communication. Shirin Neshat, in a presentation at New York University in 2000, emphasized the urgency of artistic expression. She was speaking of herself, and other expatriate Iranian artists, who have the freedom to describe and thus resist situations their compatriots back home are forced to endure. She believes, like the Haitian writer Edwige Danticat, that it is her responsibility as an immigrant artist to "create dangerously...as a revolt against silence, creating when both the creation and the reception, the writing and the reading, are dangerous undertakings."[13] That urgency is simultaneously transmitted and suppressed by the hegemony of the art market and its various discourses, and artists from all countries are learning to manipulate the different meanings, uses, and values of their works. They have learned, shrewdly and by necessity, to speak art's international language—and they see it as just that, a linguistic platform that can be altered by the initiate, not a cultural endowment that belongs to and is controlled by a specific race, gender, or nationality. For many global artists, putting themselves in the Big Picture of culture means, simply, mastering its tools: not only the language of art, but also the diverse image streams on the international information highway.

Increasingly, in fact, contemporary art is less about a specific subject than it is about these image streams and their interpenetrations. In a lecture at a meeting of the College Art Association in 2011,[14] David Joselit remarked that more and more artists have decided to *aggregate*

---

13   Edwidge Danticat, *Create Dangerously: The Immigrant Artist at Work* (New York: Vintage, 2011), p. 18.
14   "The Crisis in Art History," a session at the CAA conference held in New York City in 2011.

existing images rather than *create* new ones. Such a stance on the part of global artists makes it imperative that viewers position themselves within Alloway's "expanded field" of media if they wish to understand contemporary expression. Artists like Tacita Dean and Susan Hiller, following in the footsteps of Andy Warhol and Gerhard Richter in their use of popular imagery as primary aesthetic material, are virtually incomprehensible without a sophisticated awareness of the image landscape that serves as their primary creative environment. Recent changes in our occupation of both time and space are signaled by aggregations of pictures, virtual museums without walls. Images simultaneously provide information about the world and our mediation of it; they can signal changes and juxtapositions in culture, in class, in temporality and subjectivity without making reference to concrete situations. From this vantage point, even art's traditional history becomes a treasure trove of expressive possibilities for the contemporary artist.

In 1849, for instance, viewers and critics believed they were shocked by Gustave Courbet's rendition of the *Stonebreakers*. Now we can suggest that, in fact, it was the scale of the painting that bothered them rather than the subject matter. A small and romanticized Millet peasant stayed in his image-place; by enlarging the canvas, Courbet "changed the profile" of his subject. He manipulated the established image-codes by monumentalizing the poor, thereby inverting the cultural pyramid and, of course, inciting revolution in life and art. Seen in this way, even Realism becomes a postmodern predecessor, with lessons to learn about the potentially explosive relationships between iconography and iconology, between signifier and signified.[15] Today, artists from all over the world create in the interstices between signifier and signified, using diverse image-forms from the past and present to position themselves within and between cultural experiences. Manipulating the myriad media possibilities of the contemporary environment, they are inventing new ways of describing the multiplicities of their lives.

The work of South Korean artist Nikki Lee, and its reception in the New York art world, is a good case in point. Lee has too often been described by critics as an Asian version of Cindy Sherman—an assessment that makes little sense if one sees her art in the context of her background and experience rather than simply within the context of

---

15 Lawrence Alloway, "Photo-Realism," in *Topics in American Art,* op. cit., p. 191.

contemporary Western art. Lee began to "perform" her photographic series when she was a graduate student in New York, a foreigner committed to using visual imagery to both explore and participate in a new environment. Fascinated by the many subcultures she encountered in her adopted city and country, Lee decided to merge with them by careful observation, dress, and behavior. She spent months shopping for clothes and accessories, adjusting her weight and practicing skills prized within each group, whether Puerto Ricans, yuppies, exotic dancers, or senior citizens. Transforming herself into the strangers she beheld, she joined their communal gatherings and—always announcing first that she was an artist doing a project—had informal color snapshots taken of her participation in their social rituals.

Historically, it has not been uncommon for artists to use their cameras to bridge chasms of culture. André Kertész, Lisette Model, Robert Frank, and Sylvia Plachy were all foreigners who arrived in New York and created images that would help them make sense of a foreign land. But Nikki Lee arrived on the scene after Cindy Sherman, and she understood that she had another option: she was free not only to observe others but also to insert herself in the picture with the natives, to use her own body to make a visual link between the East and West. Merging the Korean insistence on group identity and belonging with the snapshot style Americans recognize as indicative of individual experience and memory, she visualized both the personal and the political meanings of cultural exchange. Understanding the expressive possibilities of joining "Eastern social practices with Western imageforms,"[16] Lee made that merger the real subject of her art. Seeing her as yet another Cindy Sherman not only maintains the hegemony of Western art but also misses the point (and the importance) of her statement entirely.

Which leads me to my main focus: the intelligence, curiosity, and respect required to write criticism in a global world. Taking Enwezor at his word, functioning as an ethnographer, the critic is obliged to take the stance of a researcher observing the treasures inherent in new horizons. Too often, my colleagues take the easy way out, using their normal tools to discuss form and content, neglecting entirely the

---

16 Nikki Lee, conversation with Shelley Rice, Carlos de Jesus and students, New York University, Tisch School of the Arts, 2001.

heavy lifting required of those whose investment is in understanding and communication with Others, whose worldview might be quite different from ours. Some criticism of the Myrlande Constant show at Fort Gansevoort, in New York City, is a good case in point. That show was one of the gems of 2023; an entire universe of Haitian mysticism and Voudou surrounded the viewer. There is no way to discuss the textiles, the beads, the astonishing variety of colors, materials, and reflective light without understanding this immersive universe, so real for the artist (and so amazingly beautiful as a cosmology). But some (not all!) of my colleagues did try to simply assess her iconography, praise her still lives, or applaud her use of fabrics and materials. Unlike Fanon, they were not recreating themselves in relation to the world in which they traveled; they were shrinking the world by imposing their own critical language and values on it. And perhaps I write criticism to insist that we grow and change in relation to the art that we view— to experiment with descriptions and interpretations that can help us move out of our comfort zones and meet our artist friends halfway: to see them, really, and respect the great task they fulfill. For they are building the world anew for us, every time.

What a privilege it is to participate in this Mind Building Project. I don't want anyone to miss out on it! And maybe, just maybe, that is why I write, and why I think it is important to collect these essays now.

PART 1: IMAGE MAKING COLUMN
THE SOHO WEEKLY NEWS (1978–1979)

PREFACE
(October 12, 1978)

I BEGAN WRITING PHOTOGRAPHY criticism four years ago, at a time when the photographic community in New York was still small, and critical and aesthetic guidelines were still, for the most part, unformed. My job was exciting then: There were lots of new images coming into view, lots of new processes being explored, lots of new faces joining the crowd, and lots of new ideas and issues being bantered around. The field was wide open, and energy levels were high because all of us working in New York had the sense that we were building a foundation that would be important for photography's future.

Well, that future has now arrived. In the four years since I first sat down at my typewriter to assist in the promotion of photography, the medium has been recognized as an "art" form by the art world establishment and the public. More and more galleries now show photography; more and more media space is devoted to aspects of the medium; and more and more photographers are able to cash in on the economic benefits of artistic success. But the celebrations announcing the arrival of photography on the art scene were brief, and our "highs" were quickly followed by some dreadful "lows," because the "museumization of photography" (to quote Hilton Kramer) brought on the ossification of photography, and we're now all living in its wake.[1]

This ossification has seriously impeded my viewing pleasures in recent times. I remember when I began to notice a marked decline in the quality of images on gallery walls—it must have been around a year and a half ago. I had been involved with the art world for too long by that time not to recognize the patina of pretension that was beginning to form on the surface of silver prints. Artistic trends and attitudes, long since *passé* in the art world, began to show up on, and

---

1 Hilton Kramer, "Anxiety about the *Museumization of Photography*," *New York Times*, July 4, 1976, p. 113.

then to dominate, the walls of photographic exhibition spaces. Second generation formalism and conceptualism spread through New York like contagious diseases, and these derivative styles were quickly "recognized" and rewarded by conservative art world officials. Worn-out street and topographic photography, long time Szarkowski favorites, began oozing outward from MOMA and sticking to the walls of museums and galleries interested in aligning themselves with more powerful economic institutions. And the situation has worsened considerably in the past year. By last spring, I began to realize that gallery-hopping, an occupation that used to be a joy for me, had become a tedious chore, a responsibility to be shirked like dishwashing and housecleaning. I had to face the truth: I was bored stiff by art photography.

This chronic *ennui* reached the crisis stage for me this summer, at the opening of the "Mirrors and Windows" exhibition at MOMA.[2] I've been criticizing Szarkowski's narrowness and lack of imagination for several years, but I must confess that I wasn't prepared for this show, which purported to be a survey of trends in photography since 1960. As I recall, there was a lot of interesting work done by photographers in the 1960s and 1970s. But obviously Szarkowski and I perceive the world differently, because rarely have I seen an exhibition so lifeless, so self-referential, and so ultimately meaningless as this one; rarely have I seen several hundred images on a wall that displayed so little vitality, and so little connection to the contemporary life that, ostensibly, spawned them. So when I received a phone call asking me if I'd be interested in reviewing the show, I thought about it at length—after all, I reasoned, here was the perfect opportunity to rage and scream (again) about the Museum of Modern Art's destructive influence on photography. But ultimately, I said "no" to the assignment because I knew there was nothing for me to say. I realized then that I'd said everything I had to say at least five times before and that was going to have to be enough. I refuse to spend the rest of my life wallowing in everyone else's shit.

And this realization left me in a bind—a critical identity crisis, I usually call it. I started asking myself a lot of tough questions. What can you, as a critic, do if you can't respond to the dominant trends in

---

2 "Mirrors and Windows: American Photography since 1960," Museum of Modern Art, New York City, July 26–October 2, 1978.

art today? What can you write about if you can't even bear to look at the contemporary work on the walls? Why should you write at all? After mulling over these questions for a few months, I realized that, under these circumstances, I had exactly three choices: I could either pan everything in sight for an indefinite period of time, stop writing altogether, or attempt to build a body of criticism that would provide alternatives to the dominant modes of art and thought that currently exist.

And obviously, by starting this biweekly column, I'm signaling that I'm opting for the third choice. Luckily, an alternative form of criticism is a possibility (indeed, a necessity) today, since there is a great deal of fine photographic work that never makes it to the forefront of the New York scene. As the title suggests, the column will not be devoted uniquely to photographic exhibitions; it will, instead, deal directly with artists and artworks that for one reason or another have been excluded from the mainstream circuit in New York. I'll pose new questions about subject matter, form, and technique; I'll discuss multimedia and performance works that utilize photographic images and try to understand how these artistic forms extend the boundaries of the medium. I'll also seek out and air the philosophic questions of context, of audience, and of alternatives to the current systems of distribution. In short, I'll try to use this column, at least in part, as a sounding board for photographic artists and their works—and as a space where I can develop new, and broader, methods of critical discourse and analysis that will be more responsive to the wide range of contemporary art than the established art world system currently is.

But the column will not focus simply on aspects of "art" photography because I cannot concur with the presently accepted distinctions between "fine art" and "popular" photography. Hierarchies of "high" and "low" make no sense when they are applied to a medium as broad ranging, and as democratic in its uses, as photography. Fine art may be more sophisticated and more subtle than other forms of photography (though nowadays that is questionable), but popular imagery has far more influence on our cultural life as a whole. Photography critics who ignore that fact and concern themselves solely with the formal problems raised by contemporary art are closing their eyes to the impact that "mythologies" (Roland Barthes' term) have on the social and political structures of modern life.³ I've had enough of this exclusionary type of criticism. There's a big world out there, and I want to be able to connect to it in my writing. I want to develop a body of criticism that places "fine art" and "popular imagery" within a continuous framework, that acknowledges and explicates the differences in their forms, functions, and audiences, and that examines their interlocking roles within the culture as a whole. So, I am going to use this column as my vehicle for formulating a holistic, inclusive, and multifaceted vision of contemporary photography—a vision that may point the way toward a more complex understanding of the uses of photography in the modern industrial world.

---

3   Roland Barthes, *Mythologies* (New York: Farrar, Straus, Giroux, 1972), trans. Annette Lavers.

ON CURATION
(October 26, 1978)

I'VE BEEN THINKING a lot about curatorship lately, primarily because I'm convinced that the people who should be thinking about this issue (i.e., curators) rarely do. Of course, every curator of photography thinks about selecting strong single images—but few of them realize that they are, at the same time, structuring a context that will influence the way the artist is perceived by the viewing public. Curating an exhibition is an interpretive act, and too often this mediating act works against the best interests of the artist and the art. So, I believe it might be time to examine the attitudes underlying the selection and arrangement of photographs in exhibitions, and the effect that these attitudes have on our perception of the creative process.

I saw two exhibitions last week that got me thinking along these lines. The first was the Ray Metzker retrospective, curated by Bill Ewing, at the International Center of Photography. Metzker's concerns have remained fairly consistent in the roughly twenty-five years that he's been working. He's been interested in recording and manipulating the visual patterns, the black-and-white tonal contrasts, and the formal interrelationships that he "finds" as he roams through city streets, suburban areas, and crowded beaches. Yet the artist has carried these simple formal problems to their extremes and has created an enormously complex, enormously varied, and often brilliant body of work. Single prints, couplets, collages, and composite images ranging wildly in size, shape, scale, and format complement each other within his *oeuvre*, and work together to express a multifaceted vision that links diverse photographic styles, techniques, and formats into a highly personal system.

But I wouldn't have known this from looking at the ICP show, which emphasized the single-image photographs taken in the 1950s and 1960s. The pictures on view are, with a few exceptions, almost uniform in size and sensibility; they all explore similar formal problems in similar ways, and the interconnections that Ewing stresses often represent the shallowest aspects of Metzker's photographic explorations. The few collages, couplets, and composite images that are included appear like afterthoughts and are never satisfactorily integrated into the artist's development. As a result, the exhibition falls flat; its repetitions begin to appear obsessive, its discoveries seem banal and superficial. And Metzker comes off looking like just another boring formalist.

Ewing was quick to point out, in the wall hanging accompanying the show, that he was interested in representing both the diversity and the consistency of the artist's work. But all I saw on the walls at ICP was consistency, and that's where the problem lies. It seems to be hard for curators in this town to accept the fact that artists do different types of work in a lifetime, that they grow and change and shift directions, and that they often explore two or more creative impulses simultaneously. So, more often than not, the curators water down the work until it fits into their neat little categories. By the time it gets to the viewing public, the richness and complexity of the creative experience has been virtually obscured from sight.

These artistic castrations depress me, and I keep hoping that I'll stumble across an exhibition in which diversity is a major concern. So, I was overjoyed when I saw the display of photographs by Barbara Mensch that was on view at P.S. 1[1] last week. Mensch is a young (twenty-seven-year-old) artist who worked primarily as an illustrator until a year and a half ago, when she decided to use the camera as her medium of expression. Mensch's early training outside of the field of photography was evident to me as soon as I saw her imagery. In her working methods and approaches, she is refreshingly free of the prejudices, postures, and constraints that govern most photographers' and curators' vision of the medium. To Mensch, the camera is a tool, a means to an end—and every photograph is simply one expressive aspect of a conceptual project. This attitude has allowed her to be extremely flexible in her use of the medium—and it has also allowed her to be eclectic in her curatorship when she presented her past year's work to the public.

---

1   P.S. 1 is now MoMA PS1. To mark the tenth anniversary of the merger between the former P.S. 1 Contemporary Art Center and MoMA, the museum changed its name to MoMA PS1 in 2010.

The exhibition at P.S. 1 consisted of three installations. Two of them—"Twelve Views of a Pregnancy" and "Twenty-Four Hours Before Death"—were completed projects; one, "Location, Sonoma Grove," was a work in progress. (As Mensch put it: "I wanted to show birth, death, and what happens in between.")

"Twelve Views" is composed of eleven black-and-white contact sheets (presented as eleven single photo series) that document successive stages of the pregnancy of a friend, and one "straight" photograph of the father, and the result: twins. The pregnant woman is shown lying on a white surface and is seen from mid-thigh to the waist. Each frame within the individual photo series was recorded at regular intervals (or "pulses," as Mensch calls them) of one second.

Seen together, the photographs work on several different levels. First and foremost, the images document the body changes that occur during pregnancy (in fact, in some of the later pictures it is possible to discern the child's movement within the womb). But the abstraction of the torso also works to create an undulating formal design that sometimes metamorphoses into a symbolic landscape. And the ebb and flow of the forms and spaces capture the rhythm of pregnancy, allowing the viewer to recreate the photographer's experience of ongoing time.

The pregnancy series was exhibited on the walls of P.S. 1; the spectator participated in the birth as she or he walked past the photographs. The five straight black-and-white, 11" × 14" photographs of Mensch's mother dying in a hospital bed, however, were displayed on a table at the end of the gallery. The time element remained an intrinsic part of the series: Mensch's father entered and left the pictures, the mother's pained expression changed, and then we saw her lifeless in the final, double-exposed print. But the shift in the placement of the images drastically altered the viewer's relationship to the photographs. I was forced to look downward at the prints to view them closely, almost intimately. The proximity of the photographs to my own space, my own body, did not allow me to see the images as distant, detached, "out there." Instead, they became, literally, a part of my own experience and were much more disturbing because of that.

Back to the walls for the third project, "Location: Sonoma Grove," which consisted of seven Cibachrome prints with texts underneath that documented the lifestyles of hippies who banded together in a northern California trailer park community. Mensch's pictures of the people, the trailers, the abandoned cars, and the living spaces of the Sonoma Grove show us a style of life that both clashes and converges with "The American Way." The first image, for instance, depicts a grassy field bordered by mountains and a raised platform furnished with tables, benches, chairs, and flower boxes. A painted plaster stork sits in the middle of this open vista. But the illusion of peace and freedom created by the scene becomes ironic when the viewer reads the underlying quote: "We had a newspaper...we had two anarchists...we fought with our management, Creative Properties, Inc... There's a lot of political struggles in the Grove." The text subverts our romantic notions of alternative lifestyles and allows the colorful reflective surface of the Cibachrome prints to counterpoint the all too familiar sounding aims and statements of the community residents.

Needless to say, Mensch's three projects on view—and I'll reiterate that they were all done within the past year—were very different in structure, mood, and meaning. Yet each installation had its own internal logic, its own artistic integrity, its own individualized consistency; each worked as a self-contained statement, not only about the subject matter, but also about the ways in which imagery can be used in various contexts. The interplay of these diverse modes made the exhibition an exciting as well as a challenging one. Mensch made demands on me: I was not asked to simply look at images; I was forced to experience them—intellectually, spatially, and viscerally—and to constantly grapple with their implications. That was wonderful because it's too easy to get lazy looking at most of the exhibitions displayed on the walls of this city.

Unfortunately, this is the kind of energizing experience that I've come to expect only from alternative exhibition spaces like P.S. 1. It should come as a surprise to no one that Mensch has had difficulties with most of the established curators when she's shown them her work. To them, the diversity of her production signifies artistic indecision. "Come back," they tell her, "When you've found a mature style." Well, I personally find her lack of style most refreshing, and if maturity means monotony, we've got plenty of that already. Institutional curators should begin to take their cues from younger artists like Barbara Mensch who revel in the breadth and flexibility of their creativity. If we had more exhibitions like this one to look at, we would undoubtedly have more open-minded and responsive artists. And we would also be allowing the viewing public to see just how rich and how complex artistic expression can be.

IMAGES OF WOMEN
(November 9, 1978)

ONCE EVERY YEAR or two, I do an advertising census: I buy thirty or forty magazines, tear out the advertisements, and catalog them according to themes. Over the years, I've found that this is the most efficient way to keep in touch with the mass American psyche. It allows me to spot-check cultural changes and to recognize shifting attitudes as they are translated into visual mythologies. I recently finished my latest survey, and the most interesting discoveries I made involved the visualization of sexual stereotypes. Ten years after the women's movement hit the big time, I found some hopeful signs that new, feminist mythologies are beginning to jell. But I also noticed some patterns that are disturbing and that may have serious consequences for the future development of our sexual roles and attitudes.

By far the most interesting changes in advertising had occurred where images of women were concerned. A few years ago, during my last census, I was frustrated when I realized that the traditional stereotypes of the wife/mother/lover were still dominating the visual landscape in women's magazines. But happily, that is no longer the case. It is, of course, still possible to find pictures of women preening for their men, or smiling gleefully over sparkling bathroom bowls, or beaming with delight over the succulence of their husbands' breakfast biscuits. But even in the more conservative women's magazines, like *Redbook* and *Ladies' Home Journal*, these stereotypes coexist now with images that give out very different messages. There's a new emphasis on the active woman, the woman proud of her strength and autonomy, the woman who "has come a long way" (to quote the Virginia Slims cigarette campaign). Ads celebrating women's newfound prowess in jobs (both those involving office management and those involving strenuous physical labor) are abounding; images of female victories in athletic competitions are becoming commonplace. Even ads in which single mothers proclaim their ability to support their families alone, though still rare, are occasionally visible in national magazines. Advertisements are beginning to reflect the range of options, choices, and lifestyles that are open today to the female sex; a more complex, and more respectful, narrative about women is being offered to the mass public.

Since, by definition, ads *follow* trends that have already taken hold in the culture (and thus have found a paying audience), these changes are certainly positive indicators. But there is a catch to all of this good news, and it's a catch that, I'm afraid, makes the feminist victory a provisional one. In spite of the fact that images of women have undergone major transformations in advertising, images of men have scarcely budged in recent years. The Marlboro Men, our perennial cowboys, sportsmen, and rugged macho heroes, are still sharing the spotlight with distinguished-looking business executives as the ideal stereotypes put forth for men. Often these men are seen alone or working with each other to accomplish their goals. But just as often these men are seen with women—and at that point the "new woman" loses her sass.

Traditionally, women have been used in advertising as the accessories of men, the tangible rewards that reflect the measure of their masculine success. That hasn't changed a bit over the past few years, regardless of the major shifts that have occurred in female imagery. We still have the CC (Canadian Club) Man, who arrogantly stares at the camera with glass in hand while his woman clings to him sensually in the background; we still have Camel cigarette ads in which the dude, again directly facing the viewer, admires his smoke while his woman admires him. So, a double message is coming through in today's sexual stereotypes as they are portrayed in advertisements. Women's strength and autonomy are fine as long as they don't threaten the ego needs of American men. To quote Roland Barthes: "Like Don Juan between his two peasant girls, (advertising) says to women 'you are worth just as much as men'; and to men, 'your women will never be anything but women.'"[1]

As long as advertising straddles the sexual fence in this way, feminist advances will be acted out in a cul-de-sac with a very narrow cultural base. As long as the rates of change in our sexual stereotypes remain

---

1 Ibid., pp. 51–2.

imbalanced, the real issues involving adjustments in male/female sexual roles will never successfully be resolved. I've found only two ads that address themselves to the sensitive problems that now plague relationships between men and women, and unfortunately, they only pay lip service to the issues. In both instances, the innovative up-to-datedness of the theme is belied by reliance on, and manipulation of, the most conventional notions of sexual roles.

One of these ads—a poster promoting the new Lark Lights cigarette—is currently riding around on the New York subways. A black-and-white picture of a man and a woman, who stare fondly into each other's eyes as they smoke their cigarettes, is juxtaposed with the following copy: "It's Lark Light Time. A moment ago, women's rights! Male chauvinism! Suddenly...a warming smile. A light time...and a Lark." Needless to say, such an advertisement scarcely deals with the problems it raises. The whole question of women's rights and demands, seen in this context, becomes a "lark," another hysterical female outburst that can be manipulatively dissolved by the warmth of a smile and a cozy cigarette.

The Lark ad is a new one; I've only seen it around for a few months, and there's no telling at this stage whether or not it will be successful with the public. The other advertisement, however, has been published in national magazines for several years, which leads me to believe (and I say this with some disgust) that it has been highly effective in selling the product.

The ad was designed to promote Secret Roll-On Anti-Perspirant. A glossy color photograph of a woman and a man dominates the page. The woman, centered within the frame, stands facing front and smiling at the viewer while the man, seen to the left, looks at her (an obvious role reversal as far as visual stances and positions are concerned). I've seen at least three versions of this ad, with different sets of models (two of the pairs are white and one Black), but the relationship depicted between the man and the woman remains constant. The woman is always dressed in a fancy evening gown and jewelry, while the man is always some kind of blue-collar worker (a hard hat, a cabbie) seen "on the job."

There's a dialogue going on between them (and there are slight variations between the ads). The man asks: "You say Secret antiperspirant is strong enough for a man?" And the woman replies: "You heard right. But it's made for a woman. Sorry, fellah." The copy, seen to the right, reads (again, with some slight variations between ads): "Come on, girls, you know that old feminine weakness myth is nowhere. We need an antiperspirant that's strong. That's why Secret roll-on is so effective... even more effective than the he-man spray...Yet Secret has a soft, delicate fragrance to tell you it's made for a woman. Secret. Strong enough for a man but made just for you."

A feminine victory? Hardly. First of all, the ad builds up feminine strength and assertiveness, only to retreat back into the worn-out stereotypes of the "he-man" and the "delicate woman." But there's another, more heinous way in which this advertisement undercuts the revolution it supposedly supports. The he-man depicted is not an ideal masculine type, a cowboy, executive, or sports pro. He is from the working class. The woman, by contrast, is a fancy lady, clearly a woman of wealth and leisure. So, the interaction between them is not simply a conversation between societal equals in which the woman gets her way. It is a power play between economic classes, in which the woman's assertiveness is seen as a prerogative of her social advantage. Conversely, the man's rejection becomes a degrading reflection of his economic—and, by extension, sexual—inferiority. Notions of sexual power are here merged with paranoia about economic status, and the result is an advertisement that severely undermines, not all men's sexuality, but the potency of our labor force in relation to women.

This is, to me, a horrifying way to begin to explore the ramifications of women's liberation. But until the time when our cultural ideals of male sexuality evolve enough to encompass the newfound strength of women, I'm afraid that this is all that we can reasonably hope for. It would be naïve to expect radical new definitions of masculinity to originate in advertising, which simply reflects the values that have already gained currency in the culture. But the discrepancies in contemporary ads should alert those of us involved in image making of our own—whether written, oral, visual, or whatever—to a problem that desperately needs resolution. It is up to us to create a new, more humane definition of masculinity that can, eventually, have an impact on public consciousness.

I know there have already been some attempts to grapple with this problem in "art" photographic terms. The two books published in 1977, *Women Photograph Men* and *Women See Men*, though problematic both politically and aesthetically, did manage at least to state the problem. And Marcuse Pfeifer's *Male Nude* exhibition last June helped to create an awareness of the taboos that restrict our visual understanding of men. But these few isolated attempts are just a start. We've still got a long way to go, and all I know is that we'd better get there. Because until we succeed in revamping American attitudes toward masculinity, our feminist victories will remain provisional—and, consequently, all our advances will be frighteningly vulnerable to backlash and eventual obliteration.

PHOTOGRAPHY, POWER, AND OPPRESSION (PART 1)
November 23, 1978

CONTEMPORARY "ART" PHOTOGRAPHERS think (and talk) a great deal about the artistic qualities of their medium: its formal properties, its self-expressive possibilities, and, lately, its collectability. Judging from what I've seen, though, they think very little about the functions of photography outside of the art system—and they think even less about the destructive ways in which the medium has been used as an instrument of power and oppression within our society. Interestingly enough, these questions about photography and power, so long ignored by most "straight" photographers, are being addressed in works by artists in other media. Several of these artists are keenly aware that "image making" and "image consumption" are more than purely aesthetic issues and have consequences that reverberate far beyond the sanctity of gallery walls.

Two such artists—Eric Bogosian and Richard Newton—have recently shown some excellent work in New York. Bogosian, the subject of this week's column, wrote and acted in a performance entitled *Garden* that was at Artist's Space on November 2 and 3. Three characters—two of them male and one female—were present in the piece, and their interactions crystallized in dialogues that did not develop narratively or linearly. Instead, short broken phrases, aphorisms, and allusions, which never defined specific situations or events, became indicators of roles and relationships that were reinforced and amplified by body language, tone of voice, pacing, spatial positioning, lighting, and music. So, the dynamics that occurred among the three performers became metaphoric actions, *tableaux* stripped of references to time, place, or specific personalities.

Most of the action took place on a 40-foot ramp set up across the gallery space. In the first "scene," the men climbed onto the ramp and, after surveying the audience, sat down on chairs placed at one end and began to discuss some nebulous project or lesson. During this dialogue (and I use the term loosely), the personas and relationships of the men were clarified. It became evident that one of them was the strong man, the kingpin, the teacher. His statements were cold, rigid, devoid of emotional response. The other man, who obviously had a marked propensity for sadism, was the henchman, the underling, the student. A repartee ensued between them in tones that were menacing in their controlled violence, and the brisk, clipped pace of the discussion was measured by flashing slides of women's smiling faces—slides which the men projected on the wall and scrutinized intently, for no apparent reason.

After a slight verbal clash between the two men, the henchman left the ramp and walked into another room, where he stood in the shadows and watched his teacher through a window. Meanwhile, the woman, who until this point had been seen only when she served drinks to the men, walked across the ramp and seated herself on a chair at the opposite end of the ramp from the remaining man. Then, lit only by a red light and accompanied by music, she spent five minutes painstakingly painting makeup on her face while the man, and the audience, watched.

After this sequence, the music quieted and a dialogue took place between the man and woman. The subject of most of the discussion was, once again, the nebulous project, but the interaction had implicit sexual overtones that were kept carefully under control. Again, the personas and the relationships between the performers were clarified through broken phrases and retorts. He was the dominant party, she the subservient; he was active, she receptive/passive; he was emotionally hard, she soft and at times ingratiating. Yet eventually she, too, displeased him, and he left the ramp—only to return and recite a monologue, which gained in intensity and repressed agitation, that consisted of eighty "lessons to be learned:" "Keep everything under control. Any breach of diligence is a vulnerability. To touch is to destroy. The rules are clear." At the end of this diatribe, however, he walked over to the woman and took her chin in his hand—and the performance ended as the other man rushed from the adjoining room and captured their gestures on film with the flash of a camera.

Garden was, essentially, a performance about "looking"—and about the visual violations and power plays inherent in the voyeuristic impulse. Throughout the piece, Bogosian manipulated the voyeurism implicit in the actor/audience/performance situation. The actors surveyed the audience and turned the viewers into the viewed. The performers watched each other and became the spectators of their own activities. In fact, Bogosian continually emphasized the ways in which the dynamics among the actors were dictated by visual distances, by barriers bridged and reinforced by watchful scrutiny. The kingpin stared at the woman as she painted her face and transformed an intimate action into a public display; later he confessed to watching her and commented on how she looked. All the while the henchman peered from the shadows, a silent spectator seen only by the audience—until, with the flash of a camera, he turned the passive act of "seeing" into an aggressive act of blackmail.

Within this context, Bogosian's references to photographs and the camera became the concrete extensions, indeed the embodiments, of his theme. During the first scene, the men stared intently and judgmentally at the images of women—frozen, plastic pictures of smiling faces—while they discussed violence and death. Who were these women? Why were the men studying their images so intently and so coldly? Were these the photographic records of people who were to become targets for sexual exploitation, political sabotage, or violent assault? Bogosian never said.

Nor did he say why the henchman rushed from the shadows with his camera to capture his superior in the act of committing a transgression. Surely this was an invasion of privacy, a visual assault; surely the power balances so rigidly established between the characters were being violated and, possibly, reversed. But who was being caught, the man or the woman? And how? How was this photograph to be used?

Bogosian never answered these questions; the meanings of all the images remained ambiguous at the conclusion of the performance. Only one thing was clear: with each flash of a slide, each click of a shutter, someone was being exposed—and thus irrevocably condemned. Someone became a victim of visual evidence.

To be continued.

PHOTOGRAPHY, POWER, AND OPPRESSION (PART 2)
November 30, 1978

For the past two weeks, the *Image Making* column has been devoted to artists whose work raises questions about the various ways in which photography is used as an instrument of power and oppression in our society. In the previous column, I discussed Eric Bogosian's performance, *Garden*, which was a metaphoric exploration of the repression and victimization inherent in situations governed by voyeurism and surveillance. In this column, I'll focus on Richard Newton's *I take you to a room in Brawley and we smell onions*, which is a more specific, and on many levels a more personal, examination of the ways in which photographs are used as the vehicles for sexual and emotional exploitation.

I take you to a room in Brawley and we smell onions was originally a performance, with Newton as the primary actor. In its present form, it is a one-of-a-kind book available for viewing at the Franklin Furnace.[1] The performance took place in Los Angeles in 1975, and shortly thereafter Newton decided to create a document based on the event. For this purpose, he asked friends and participants to write statements describing what they saw on the stage. These descriptions were, in part, incorporated into the final book, along with text from the performance, picture postcards of motels and street scenes in Brawley, California, and direct color Xeroxes of memorabilia and props used in the piece. Throughout the book, images and text are counterpointed as "documents" of various places and events, and the narrative voice continually shifts from audience to actor and back again.

The book begins with several reproductions of Brawley motels and with written descriptions (all by onlookers) of the stage set, which simulated a "sleazy motel room." The viewers describe Newton's entry

---

1   Richard Newton, *I take you to a room in Brawley and we smell onions* (San Francisco, California: Blurb, republished 2019).

onto the stage in scene one, and we see pictures of him dressed in a white bridal gown and veil and carrying a candle. The text from the performance begins with a first-person monologue by Newton, "the bride," in which s/he recounts the events of "her" wedding night. This particular segment of the text is absolutely brilliant; I've never read anything written by a man that so completely captures the watchful anxiety and fear experienced by a passive and dependent woman who needs—and does not get—sensitivity and understanding from a man. The bride describes her husband's actions. She watches as he organizes his belongings in their motel room and ignores her; she recoils from his aggressive touch as he "takes" her clothing. The sex act, as s/he describes it, is agony: "It felt as if we were fighting." Throughout the monologue, the contrast between the unstated notion that wedding days are the happiest days of our lives and the reality of the woman's anguish is underlined by the colorful garishness of the Xeroxed pictures—of motel rooms and accessories, of bridal lace and accoutrements, of the bride herself—which are interspersed throughout the text.

The monologue ends, the bride leaves the stage, and the narrative voice shifts to the spectators. Their written texts describe "the hawkers," who emerged from the audience to sell colorful Polaroid prints of the bride taken during her "confession." Like Bogosian, Newton manipulates the audience's voyeuristic impulses by incorporating them into the piece. The dichotomy between the bride's personal and tortured display of vulnerability and the crass commercialism of the salespeople becomes even more pronounced when the hawkers bring out plastic viewers that contain peep shows of Newton in various pornographic states of dress and undress and offer them for sale by dangling them tantalizingly before the audience's noses. (Both the pictures of Newton and the pictures of the hawker selling the pictures of Newton are interspersed throughout the text, which includes direct transcriptions of the sales pitches.) Then onlookers tell us of Newton's reemergence onto the darkened stage, this time dressed in a black leotard, garter belt, stockings, chain bracelets, and red fetish shoes and portraying a whore whose sex remains ambiguous. After s/he aggressively flashes a spotlight on the audience, the text from the performance begins once more.

The second monologue, like the first, is written (and was spoken) in the first person. This time, the whore is the subject and his/her client the object. As the whore, Newton is very much in control in this scene, and s/he is the active party in the events described. S/he attempts to seduce the audience, telling them of "tricks," of sadomasochistic interactions, of fantasies, and of sexual power plays and consummations, and the text is interspersed with pictures of him/her and of bar and street scenes from Brawley. The monologue ends with the words: "I take you in because I like you…because I like sex…cos I need money, I want money," and Newton leaves the stage. The hawkers enter once more, this time pitching their sales even more aggressively, and the spectators' texts describe how the audience, which had been reticent before, was eager this time around to find and buy the "best" Polaroids and peep shows available.

But the black humor of the situation ends abruptly when Newton arrives on stage for the third time, and onlookers describe the chains wrapped around his body. There is no monologue in scene three. There are only pictures and texts which recount how Newton entered the stage area, looked around, and then collapsed in his chains at the foot of the bed, while the hawkers, rallying around him, offered his sexual services for sale to the audience. There were no takers, and the book—like the performance—ends as the hawkers drag the helpless artist off the stage.

Needless to say, *I take you to Brawley and we smell onions* is an extremely disturbing document. On its most superficial level, it functions as a statement about sexual roles and role reversals, and the ambiguity of its sexual references heightens the tensions underlying the situations described. The raw brutality and prurient interest of this subject matter alone is jarring, and it provides the initial shock of the piece. But once this shock passes, layers of meaning begin to emerge from the text, and these meanings interact and merge to create a complex metaphor that transcends (as it encompasses) issues of simple sexuality.

I take you to a room in Brawley and we smell onions is, above all, a statement about exploitation—about power and money, about aggression and passivity, about voyeurism and victimization. On the most general level, it can be seen as a representation of all or many interactions that are dictated by these motives in a capitalistic society. More specifically, it can be seen as a statement about artists—about selling out, about commercialism, about the intimate relationship between imagery and the self. And it can also be seen as a statement about the ways in which photographs can be used to violate the self, to turn the private into the public, and to transform even the deepest human emotions into cheap commodities and sleazy voyeuristic displays.

Richard Newton and Eric Bogosian do not paint pretty pictures of the state of photography. The power plays, manipulations, and violations they describe are bleak but accurate assessments of some of the ways in which images are used in the modern world to degrade, control, or oppress human beings. It is absolutely essential that the seriousness of this situation be communicated to a broad audience because, as both artists know, the relationships that exist between photographers and subjects, or between the makers and consumers of images, in our society directly reflect the relationships that structure our interactions in everyday life.

It seems natural to me that visual artists should be aware of this sordid reality and interested in grappling with its implications in their work. But I find it ironic that performance artists, and others working in media other than straight photography, are the ones who are doing the most to bring this information to public attention. Meanwhile, the people who devote their lives to photography and photographic education (namely the artists, teachers, critics, editors, and curators who comprise the self-proclaimed photographic community) have chosen, for the most part, to remain silent on issues of such overriding importance.

And not only silent—*defensively* silent. Any attempts to raise theoretical questions about the ethics (or lack thereof) underlying the uses of the medium in our society (and here I'm thinking specifically of Susan Sontag's book, *On Photography*) have been greeted by howls of derision and anger by members of the photographic community.[2] Maybe these people feel that ignorance is bliss; maybe their best interests demand that they blithely reject any suggestion that photography may, after all, be more than a purely aesthetic medium. But the rest of us must begin to confront the unpleasant truth about the uses of photography if we are to remain free citizens in what Sontag calls

---

2   Susan Sontag, *On Photography* (New York: Farrar, Straus, Giroux, 1977).

our "image-choked world."[3] And the works of artists like Bogosian and Newton, which open up a Pandora's Box that desperately needs to be explored, can ultimately help us to regulate a situation that is almost out of control, and to create an "ecology of images" that is more humane than the one that currently exists.

---

3   "Image-choked world" is from *Susan Sontag, On Photography*, Picador (Farrar, Straus and Giroux, New York 1977), p. 15.

VISUAL CONSCIOUSNESS: AARON SISKIND AND ANDREA KOVACS
(December 21, 1978)

> I am concerned, in any case, only with the world as *my point of view* orients it; I shall never know any other. The relative subjectivity of my sense of sight serves me precisely to define *my situation* in the world.
> —Alain Robbe-Grillet,"Nature, Humanism, Tragedy"[1]

PHOTOGRAPHY GAINED CREDIBILITY as an art form in the twentieth century when the public began to recognize what photographers have attested at least since the days of P. H. Emerson and Stieglitz: that photographs can be the mirrors of human consciousness, the direct reflections of the "subjectivity" of an artist's "sense of sight." The history of art photography is, therefore, the history of changing visual consciousness; read in a certain way, the evolution of photographic forms becomes the chronicle of evolving "situations in the world." There are times, even within the flux of contemporary experience, when this evolution becomes strikingly evident, as it did for me when I saw two exhibitions currently on view uptown: one by master photographer Aaron Siskind and another by a young artist named Andrea Kovacs.

Siskind's exhibition of recent (1976–1978) work on view at Light Gallery marks an important occasion: the photographer's 75th birthday. Siskind has been an important force on the photographic scene, both as an artist and as a teacher, since the 1930s, when he began documenting architecture and the urban environment. By the 1940s, the photographer had become involved with the painters who were soon to be known as the Abstract Expressionists, and his work since that time has echoed and expanded the vision that crystallized during the "heroic generation" of American painting.

The works currently on view at Light, all of them straight

---

1 Alain Robbe-Grillet, "Nature, Humanism, Tragedy," *New Left Review* 1:31, 1965.

black-and-white prints, reiterate Siskind's fascination with close-up views of familiar forms—walls, peeling posters, eroded rocks—that have been "found" by the artist, isolated from their experiential context, and transformed into abstract designs that seem to float within a shallow pictorial space. Self-contained and classical in the harmony of their formal designs, his images of peeling, paint-smeared, and graffitied walls capture as they freeze the processes of decay and change that mark the passage of time. A single moment frozen by Siskind becomes the embodiment of an eternity—but this is an eternity scarred and pockmarked by the human dramas that have unfolded within it.

For Siskind's universe is, above all, anthropomorphized. Mundane forms found and chosen by the artist transcend their original identities and are transformed into mirrors of the human condition, metaphors deep and rich in human associations, illusions, and allusions. Eroding surfaces become reminders of mortality; abstract forms metamorphose into gestures, relationships, and "conversations" (as Siskind calls them). Contrasts of black and white become dramas, struggles held in tension by forces of light and darkness. The reality Siskind seeks to express in his photographs is the reality of essences, of universal truths hidden beneath the surface and linking all things. For him, the world exists in unity with—indeed as a reflection of—the timeless and often tragic consciousness of humanity.

The recent works of Andrea Kovacs, now on view at Brooks Jackson Gallery Iolas, are also expressions of the unity of human consciousness and the world. But whereas Siskind searches for single images that can embody his perception of timeless truths, Kovacs' commitment to artistic immersion in time has caused her to create mural-sized works pieced together out of countless colored photographic fragments. Where Siskind isolates, and thus aggrandizes, particular forms, Kovacs' cumulative vision subsumes individual objects and figures, dematerializing them in order to transform them into building blocks in a network of colors and shapes that define, as they reflect, emotional response. And where Siskind's straight photographs become metaphors for a universal human condition, Kovacs' multiple images are highly personal records of her subjective mind-states as they evolve through the ongoing process of photographic expression in time and space.

Like the Surrealists, Kovacs describes her working methods as a form of "automatic writing." All of the images were taken in her studio; she always chooses "subjects" that have come into her world and gravitates toward objects, people, and spaces that have emotional meaning for her. She photographs in a continuous series, collecting sequences of 3 ½ × 4 ½ inch Kodacolor images that she sees as the "fractions" in her "equations of experience." As the images accumulate, they begin to suggest "natural formations" to her, personal assemblages (often arranged in the order in which the photographs were taken) that can unite her instantaneous perceptions (as captured by the camera), and her memories of emotional involvement. "Each image provides evidence, the residue of involvement," she has written. "The sequence (display) becomes a product of the activity itself, in itself the performance of photographing." So, the completed pieces, grand in scale as well as in impact, are the arenas in which the fragments and overlays of visual data that provide the raw materials of perception come together to formulate a holistic and multifaceted expression of lived experience.

The assemblages currently on view at Brooks Jackson Gallery Iolas span a period of only two years (1976–1978), but important changes are evident in Kovacs' style. The early works—*Enigmatic Ninety and Nine, Red Eye of Love, Bouillabaisse,* and *Surrogate Love*—are dark in palette. Dominated by deep shades of red, orange, green, and purple, they are densely packed pieces often permeated by implicitly erotic overtones.

Bouillabaisse, for instance, is a rectangular assemblage of images arranged 14 high and 10 wide (and it is one of the smallest pieces in the show). A central rectangle, which contains twenty-four mauve-toned views of a woman's nude body lying in various positions on a sheet, anchors the composition by creating a dense block of local color. The outer rows of imagery move around this stable form, creating a montage of colors and shapes. Pinks, reds, greens, and skin tones blend in patterns, and from these layers of color recognizable forms emerge: a fish head, lace panties, red-stained anatomical fragments, and whole torsos. Kovacs' viewpoints on these forms shifted continuously during the photographic process, and her juxtapositions of images (for instance, a torso might be seen next to several close-ups of various anatomical parts) create a shifting sense of space that becomes cinematic in texture.

Although the cinematic quality of Kovacs' vision is evident in the early works, it becomes far more assertive—and its implications are developed much more fully—as her work evolves. The dense, often formal organizations of her photographic patterns begin to open up, to become more fluid and energized—more reflective of the rapid movements of the eye—in the later work. The ominous eroticism disappears. The colors grow brighter. Areas of white appear, functioning as rhythmic counterpoints to areas of color and form. Patterns of movement become overall instead of local, and the narrative importance of objects and figures diminishes as forms are subsumed more completely into the emotional ambience of the total design.

The Portrait of Andy Warhol, for instance, a tall hourglass-shaped assemblage composed of three stacked polygonal shapes, contains portraits of Warhol and his friends in the Factory. But the faces, dotted throughout the bottom two-thirds of the work, are seen as if by peripheral vision, embedded as they are in a mosaic of telephones, video cameras, hands in motion, shiny reflective surfaces, and wires that move with a taut, serpentine grace. The slick, fast-moving surface is the real subject of the piece, and the individual images become the participants in a dance of energies enacted in fleshing shades of pink, mauve, green, tan, yellow, and orange. In the *Diamond Precept,* Kovacs takes the expressive qualities of design to even greater extremes, as recognizable objects, for the most part, disappear—and the viewer is overwhelmed by a dizzying, wall-sized montage of delicate organic shapes that dissolve and crystallize into elusive diamond patterns in shades of blue, brown, and green.

The works of Aaron Siskind and Andrea Kovacs represent two moments, not only in photography but also in the constantly changing definition of the human "situation in the world." Siskind, whose vision was formed amid the heroism and angst of the 1930s and 1940s, shows us a world that is reflective of human mortality but that reveals forms and shapes embodying an artist's vision of the timeless essence of life. Kovacs, who grew up under the influence of Conceptual Art and Robbe-Grillet, has rejected the notion of essences, as well as the notion that there is one, unchanging human reality. Instead, she sees reality as a kaleidoscope of subjective impressions, a plethora of perceptions that can coalesce into an individual's sense of self in time and space—an individual point of view.

There is no doubt that Siskind's sensibility is the more traditional of the two, or that Kovacs' vision represents innovative new directions for contemporary photography. But I can't bring myself to make qualitative judgments on the basis of that distinction. I just finished reading Janet Malcolm's article on photography in *The New Yorker*, and I must confess that I'm sick and tired of hearing critics pontificate about the criteria for what is "modern" or "avant-garde" (and thus good) and what is "traditional" (and thus bad).[2] Clement Greenberg might have started the artistic counterpart of the Darwinian rat race twenty-five years ago, but by now it's a tedious bore, having long since outlived its usefulness. The coexistence of sensibilities like Siskind's and Kovacs' is what excites me, for it allows me to comprehend the living texture of artistic creation and change. These two artists represent two moments in time, two evolving sensibilities, two deeply felt points of view. So be it.

---

2   Janet Malcolm, "Two Roads," *The New Yorker*, Photography Column, December 4, 1978, p. 225.

BARBARA KRUGER GOES TO THE BATHROOM: SELF AND WORLD
(January 11, 1979)

This article is dedicated to my friend Bea, who was convinced that I had kidney trouble.

I HAVE A HABIT. Or to be more accurate, maybe I should say I have a ritual: I go to the bathroom a lot. I know that sounds strange, since everyone goes to the bathroom all the time. But I'm not talking about biological necessities now, I'm talking about psychological ones. I have a tendency to excuse myself from public functions—dinners, parties, conferences, etc.—and retreat into the privacy of the john. I sit there in my little cubicle for a few minutes, staring at the door, the floor, or my feet, and I let my mind wander wherever it wants to go. I think about the events of the day or the state of the world in general. I let my subconscious take over and carry me to a psychological space far away from the noisy crowds that throng just outside the door of my secret garden of solitude. This ceremonial act works every time. After a short while, I feel rested and refreshed, in touch with myself; my batteries are recharged, and my energy levels are high. At that point, I pull up my pants and walk back into the mainstream of life.

I've always considered this little ritual to be my ultimate private act, my own very personal (and, yes, eccentric) expression of individuality. So you can imagine my surprise when I came across Barbara Kruger's photographic homage to this experience, which is now on view at the Franklin Furnace. Entitled *Public Space/Private Sector,* Kruger's artwork consists of six 16" × 20" Kodacolor photographs taken "on the pot" from the vantage point of a "sitter," who peers downward at her legs, her underpants, her feet, and the floor of a public bathroom. The basic structure of the six large-scale photographs is identical, but the floor patterns, the style and color of the shoes and panties, and the position of the feet change from one picture to the next. And each image is accompanied by a short text that documents the mental musings and meanderings elicited by each particular context, as it is seen from this habitual point of view.

Throughout the series, Kruger contrasts the enclosed physical space of the bathroom (and, by extension, her limited field of vision) with the freewheeling, wide-ranging, and unencumbered ramblings of thought. All of the soliloquies are rooted in some aspect of the sitter's immediate environment. The patterns of the tiles on the floor, the smell of the bathroom, the colors of her shoes against a rug: all are noticed and remarked upon. Yet these mundane details only serve to carry her thoughts beyond her physical surroundings, to link her imagination with the world "out there."

Sometimes she thinks about events in progress: the luncheon engagement from which she excused herself, the basketball game from which she called "time-out," the movie still unwinding in the darkened theater. But sometimes her thoughts roam farther, and she allows concrete objects to act as springboards for philosophical reflections. Her yellow panties become evidence of the sorry state of American consumer products. Floor tiles are transformed into symbols of hypocrisies or reminders of the religious practices of Italians in northern New Jersey. Urine smells become traces of mortality, and menstruation stains—her "biological landmarks"—conjure up visions of injury and intrigue.

Elaborate fantasies begin to blossom as her thoughts unfold—or are they, indeed, just fantasies? Did that man really carve into his finger? Was that veiled woman really watching from a tenement window? Was that café a memory, or a figment of her imagination? It's hard to say—because soon the reader begins to realize that, just as the sitter's context colors her thoughts, her thoughts are coloring her context, both mirroring and shaping her perceptions of the outside world. The boundaries between mind and matter seem vague and amorphous as the shifting levels of consciousness assert themselves and become indistinguishable within the piece. Public and private sectors begin to intermingle during these moments of solitude framed and isolated from the flow of time. A union between the self and the world is being forged within the confines of these bathrooms—and this union will, undoubtedly, be reaffirmed and reenacted with ritual regularity for the rest of the "sitter's" life.

That, essentially, is the meaning of Kruger's piece. *Public Space/ Private Sector* is a celebration of a biological necessity that becomes a connecting thread within the complex fabric of human experience. Contexts and clothing may vary; people, situations, and events may come and go. Thoughts may wander, and moods or emotions may range. But the vantage point of the images remains the same, and the first sentence of each individual text is repeated over and over again. "You pull down your pants..." Some things never change—and the inevitability of this private action, the incessant regularity of this personal ritual, is the one constant that unifies the series, just as it unifies the existence of all living beings. As Kruger writes, "After all is said and done, we are stains and drippings." And, of course, we all end up on the john.

SOLITUDE, PRIVACY, CULTURE: MANUEL ÁLVAREZ BRAVO
(March 22, 1979)

> Man is alone everywhere. But the solitude of the Mexican, under the great stone night of the high plateau that is still inhabited by insatiable gods, is very different from that of the North American, who wanders in an abstract world of machines, fellow citizens, and moral precepts.
> —Octavio Paz, *The Labyrinth of Solitude*[1]

I WALKED INTO the Manuel Álvarez Bravo exhibition at the Center for Inter-American Relations yesterday for the fifth time. To say goodbye to it, I told myself. And that was true, but there was more to my obsession than simple sentimentality. I went again to that exhibition because I felt impotent, because I needed to find out why it was that I could not "know" these pictures.

Critical knowledge—especially of photographs, which are so inextricably entwined with the world "out there"—is a peculiar sort of perception, and its limits are the limits not only of language but also of culture. The limitations of my cultural awareness hit me squarely in the face when I confronted these 182 Mexican photographs, which grew from a space so foreign to me that I could only gape, like a tourist, in their presence. I looked in vain for a way to unravel these (primarily) black-and-white images with words, to find a clue that would reveal the source of their richness, their profundity. I saw the influences in the early works—the experimental forays into European modernism, the convergences with the works of Weston, Modotti, Cartier-Bresson, and Strand, the association with Orozco, Siquieros, and Rivera. But knowing these influences didn't help me much, didn't tell me why I stood, transfixed, unable to grasp the source of this vision. This

---

1 Octavio Paz, *The Labyrinth of Solitude: Life and Thought in Mexico* (New York: Grove Press, 1977), pp. 19–20. Trans. Lysander Kemp.

knowledge didn't tell me why these photographs made me nervous.

* * * * *

Real art has the capacity to make us nervous. By reducing the work of art to its content and then interpreting that, one tames the work of art. Interpretation makes art manageable, comfortable…Interpretation is the revenge of the intellect upon art. Even more. It is the revenge of the intellect upon the world.
Susan Sontag, Against Interpretation[2]

I've read several interpretations of Álvarez Bravo's work: one a symbolic exegesis, one a formal analysis, one a cultural and historical one. All of them were written by North Americans, as far as I know, and all of them, however intelligent, fell flat, unable to reach the emotional core of these images. None of them could penetrate the impassive, immobile faces that stare out of from spaces walled and narrow, pregnant with the gloom of an indecipherable past. None of them could recreate the mysticism that turns objects into symbols at will, without effort, in these photographs, and permeates everything with the smell of death. None of them could tell me who Álvarez Bravo was, is—but more than that, none of them could tell me about Mexico, could make me say with confidence that I understood the roots of this indigenous vision.

* * * * *

There are, I know, many ways of using a camera, many ways in which a photographer can wield a machine and ask it to mediate between him/herself and the world in which he/she moves. Two of these ways are relevant here.

Some photographers use the camera as a means of communicating intimate knowledge, of merging mind and eye with matter that has become a part of the soul. But there are other types of photographers, many more in number, who use their machines to possess experiences that are distant from them, incomprehensible, essentially alien. Who use the camera as a means of incursion, a way of "capturing" on film

---

2   Susan Sontag, *Against Interpretation* (New York: Dell Publishing Co., 1966), p. 14.

what cannot be experienced, truly known, in real life. A soft murder, Sontag called it. A visual rape.[3]

* * * * *

Álvarez Bravo is a photographer of the first type, at least when he looks around at the Mexico which is his home. His intimacy with his culture is so profound, so inviolable, that it becomes almost impossible for an outsider like me to separate the man from the imagery, to ascertain the boundaries between perception and reality.

Privacy—the most extreme sort of solitude, not to be confused with introspection or self-reflection—permeates every inch of these windows onto the world. The silence in these photographs is monumental, the stillness eternal, even when—especially when—people are present. This silence sheds an aura over everything that Bravo envisions, transforming life into death and death into life, condemning both of them to remain entangled and inseparable forever in a crumbling ruin or a furtive, dark-skinned face. There is a mystery here, an ancient one, a secret left by souls long since gone yet kept alive in empty streets and blackened doorways, preserved in dilapidated crucifixes, enshrined in windswept landscapes shrouded in darkness. This is a mystery impenetrable to me, culture bound as I am. I can feel it chilling my bones, but I cannot explain these pictures any more than I could presume to explain their sources. Viewers too can be murderers.

* * * * *

I was both deeply moved and shaken the first time I saw this exhibition, and I was confused. Many North Americans—I not among them—have gone to Mexico. Is this what they saw? I wanted to know. So I wandered into my travel agent's office and picked up a Mexican brochure. "The Real Mexico," it said, brought to you by Eastern Airlines in glorious Technicolor. I saw pictures of blond-haired tourists feasting in quaint restaurants, lounging in crystalline pools overhung with vegetation, shopping in exotic gift shops managed by smiling Mexican mamas. I saw spectators enjoying a sideshow in the Arroyo Restaurant,

---

3   Susan Sontag, *On Photography* (New York: Farrar, Straus and Giroux, 1977), p. 24.

where "you can rent a young bull and practice your veronicas...in a mini bullring. (P.S. The bulls are never killed.)" And I saw a glittering skyline, just like home, spotted with an occasional ruin for scenic effect, and an ancient totem pictured side by side with an ersatz playground, Disney-style. Yes, it's true, I thought. We see what we are, what we look for, what we buy. And even vision can spread over the world like a plague, bridging unbreachable distances of time and place and character by murdering the Other, sacrificing the ineffable in order to make it over into our own image.

* * * * *

But what now? I wondered. What will happen to our preconceptions now that Álvarez Bravo's photographs have come to our country, advertised on buses and in newspapers, seen by an average of ninety people a day in New York alone? Will the stereotypes fall by the wayside? Will people become more sensitive and more humble, more cognizant of the unbridgeable gulfs that forever separate culture from culture, Man from Fellow Man? Will they be able to accept their solitude, and allow it to change their lives?

Maybe, just maybe, some eyes have been opened, some hearts exposed; maybe some peoples' lives have already been changed by this experience. But there are those among us who deal with experience more assertively, who know that there are other methods of possession, methods less subtle than knowledge, than interpretation, than visualization. Ask collector Harry Lunn, who will tell you that there are other ways to deal with photographs, very North American ways. And who will undoubtedly be glad to tell you how, in the shrewdest of economic moves, he walked in and bought the entire show, pleased to know that he saved himself time and money by buying a collection that has a ready-made catalog to go with it.

A. D. COLEMAN: LIGHT READINGS
(April 5, 1979)

WELL, FOLKS, I'M back. This column has been suffering severely under the weight of my other obligations in recent weeks, and I want to apologize to my readers for my absence (and to thank those of you who expressed concern about it). But I'm breaking my month-long silence with good news about a soon-to-be-published book that is an important document in the critical history of photography.

Entitled *Light Readings* (Oxford University Press, 1979), the book is a collection of essays on photography written by A. D. Coleman and published during the years 1968–1978 in such periodicals as *The Village Voice, The New York Times, Artforum,* and *Camera 35.* Various types of articles are included in the book and the range of topics is wide. There are short, journalistic reviews of books and shows by artists as diverse as Paul Strand, Richard Kirstel, Roy DeCarava, Clarence John Laughlin, Bernadette Mayer, Ed Ruscha, Bea Nettles, and Minor White; profiles of individuals active within the photographic community during the late 1960s and early 1970s; and extended essays on aesthetic and social issues. So *Light Readings* is a mixed bag—and even though the book is not intended as an all-inclusive survey of contemporary photography, it is still the most comprehensive journalistic description of the last decade of which I am aware.

Oxford University Press's decision to publish Coleman's essays establishes an important new precedent for photography. Collections of journalistic writings by contemporary art critics have been commonplace in the art world since the early 1960s, when Clement Greenberg published *Art and Culture*.[1] The advantages of such compiled volumes are obvious. They provide the chance to preserve significant articles that originally appeared in transitory journals and make it possible for readers to gain an overview of an individual critic's attitudes, strong

---

1 Clement Greenberg, *Art and Culture* (Boston: Beacon Press, 1961).

points, and shortcomings. But until now, to the best of my knowledge, there was nothing comparable to, say, Lucy Lippard's *Changing,* Max Kozloff's *Renderings,* or Lawrence Alloway's *Topics in American Art Since 1945* in contemporary photographic literature.[2]

So, the publication of *Light Readings* is, I take it, a signal that the publishing industry is finally ready to recognize the importance of photography criticism (and, of course, its salability—the enormous commercial success of Sontag's *On Photography* must have convinced these people, somewhat belatedly, that there's a market for this stuff out there). It's fitting that the man who pioneered in establishing and expanding the field of contemporary photographic criticism should be the author of the first of these books. As far as I'm concerned, there are few, if any, photo critics working today whose writing is as intelligent, as extensive, and as durable as his.

The articles included in *Light Readings* are arranged chronologically and, since Coleman's writing has gone through several permutations, this arrangement allows the reader to follow the course of his developing critical style and ideas. The essays written during the years 1968 and 1974 are primarily newspaper reviews—short, snappy statements that report on, and assess the importance of, publicly accessible photographic exhibitions, books, and events. Chock full of information and observations, these articles serve as an ongoing chronicle of the art, the personalities, and the situations that laid the groundwork for the current photographic scene. I found myself comparing Coleman to Apollinaire when I read these reviews. Both men write almost diaristically, and yet have the ability to make past events, in all their historical complexity, come alive for future readers. Coleman, like Apollinaire, is opinionated (and never hesitates to speak his mind), so the essays have an immediacy and a vitality that makes them a pleasure to read.

As models of photographic discourse, the early reviews are clearly the weakest articles in the book. Considering the circumstances under which they were written, that's certainly understandable. Coleman began writing his *Latent Image* column in *The Village Voice* in 1968, when he had few predecessors to guide him and no previous experience

---

2   Lucy Lippard, *Changing: Essays in Art Criticism* (New York: Dutton, 1971); Max Kozloff, *Renderings: Critical Essays on a Century of Modern Art* (New York: Simon and Schuster, 1968); Lawrence Alloway, *Topics in American Art Since 1945* (New York: Norton, 1975).

to fall back on. He was, at the time, "the only game in town" (to use his phrase) as far as photography criticism was concerned.

The shortcomings of these reviews stem from the deficiencies of Coleman's early critical vocabulary. Concise descriptions of artworks and intelligent visual analyses are often lacking in these essays, so critical judgments seem unsubstantiated, and the reader comes away with little understanding of the works in question. This changes around 1973, when Coleman's critical vocabulary improved noticeably and, while descriptions and analysis have never been (and probably never will be) his strong points as a critic, the essays written during and after 1973 are much richer in their discussions of the physical, emotional, and conceptual nuances of individual photographic works.

His strong points as a critic, however, are evident very early in his writings on photography. Coleman has always been admirably perceptive about the political and social implications of the photographic medium, and acutely aware of the multifaceted relationships between photography and contemporary life. In his earliest reviews, Coleman articulates a vision of photography that remains the central precept of all of the subsequent writings. Throughout his career, he has worked to alleviate the "visual illiteracy" he sees in the culture as a whole by focusing his attention on issues that pertain to the communicative properties and influence of photography. He has thus committed himself to being a critic of social as well as aesthetic affairs, and his greatest strength as a writer lies in his ability to merge these two intertwining roles with integrity and intelligence.

He does this in several ways: by exploring the political implications of artistic images and exhibitions, by examining the nature of the museum and the academy, and by analyzing the various functions of images within our society. Certain themes recur over and over again in his work. The relationship between politics and aesthetics (Coleman's views are, by the way, left of center), the ethical responsibility of imagemakers and consumers, the democratic implications of the photographic medium, the urgent necessity for a "freedom of vision," and the importance of photographic education are only a few of them. Although these issues are put forth in his earliest essays, they are developed most fully in the articles published after 1974, the year he stopped writing reviews and began working on longer critical essays.

The later articles have, by necessity, a different flavor than the earlier newspaper pieces. Thoughtful, refined, and often scholarly in tone, they lose the immediacy of journalism but gain in depth and in breadth. In some of these articles, Coleman explores the work of individual photographers like M. Álvarez Bravo; in others (like "On Plagiarism" and "Lament for the Walking Wounded"), he raises ethical questions about photography; in still others (like "My Camera in the Olive Grove" and "No Future for You?"), he examines the state of photographic education. Unlike the reviews, which are strongest when read serially, these essays stand alone as individual but interrelated statements. A few of them, like "The Directorial Mode: Notes Toward a Definition," are among the finest contemporary writings on photography that I have seen to date.

But the significance of Coleman's book does not lie in the success or failure of individual essays. It lies in Coleman's ability to act as a catalyst, to raise questions that remain unanswered about the role of photography today. Discourse about the medium has been frighteningly narrow in recent years; notions of aesthetic purity dominate the scene, and the very real relationship between photographic imagery and contemporary life is rarely considered. A. D. Coleman offers us an alternative vision of the medium that places photography squarely within the culture from which it grows. Readers can accept or reject Coleman's vision of photography, but it is my sincere hope that they will pay close attention to the issues that he raises because these issues are crucial to our age. It is time for us to acknowledge their urgency and to open up a new round of discussions about their implications.

ALTERED PHOTOGRAPHS
(April 19, 1979)

I ALWAYS FIND IT hard to keep a straight face when I hear members of the New York photographic community congratulating themselves on being the center of vanguard art photography. It is, of course, true that most of the money pumped into photography is channeled through the Big Apple. It is also true that most (though by no means all) of the photographic publications emanate from this town. But in terms of vanguard thinking and commitment to experimentation, I've found New York lagging far behind some other cities in this country.

Part of the problem stems from New Yorkers' fetish for straight, single images, a fetish institutionalized and raised to the level of a moral statute by the Museum of Modern Art's John Szarkowski and his followers. Photographers, curators, and critics in other parts of the country (most notably California) have long since recognized that straight photography is only one alternative and have applauded the amazing diversity of techniques, styles, and formats being utilized by contemporary artists. A few of these people were asked to contribute their talents to *The Altered Photograph* exhibition, which is P.S. 1's attempt to provide New Yorkers with an expanded vision of the photographic medium.

The Altered Photograph is a cast-of-thousands exhibition that occupies eight rooms on the first floor of the P.S. 1 schoolhouse in Long Island City. Included are well over one hundred works by more than seventy artists chosen by twenty-four guest curators from various parts of this country and Canada. The definition of an altered photograph is left wide open in this exhibition, which includes all sorts of images adjusted either prior to or after the printing process. Among other things, there are hand-colored prints or photographs with drawings by artists like Duane Michals, Ellen Carey, Barbra Riley, William Wegman, Judith Golden, Christo, Barbara Kasten, and Biff Henrich;

sequential or multiple images by Eve Sonneman, John Baldessari, Bill Jones, Leandro Katz, Andrea Kovacs, Eileen Berger, Roy Barge, Jan Dibbets, etc.; photographs with text by Anne Turyn, Jack Fulton, Doug Metzler, and others; composite or collaged imagery by artists like Hermine Freed, Lucio Pozzi, Edmund Teske, Raul M. Guerrero, and so on. In addition, there are manipulated Polaroids by Lucas Samaras, telephone transmissions by William Larson, photographs embedded in fabric and Plexiglass boxes by Colette-Justine, a photo-etched stainless-steel coil by Terry McMillan, and even some record jackets, a pop-shot photo card and jigsaw puzzle reproduction of a Jackson Pollock painting submitted by Sam Wagstaff (who wins my award for the most imaginative curating). So, *The Altered Photograph* show is a mixed bag and an ambitious undertaking on the part of P.S. 1.

With such a massive turnout and such a big range of material, it should come as a surprise to no one that the exhibition is a sprawling and uneven affair. There are, no doubt about it, some terrific works in this show. Certain well-established artists (many of them chosen by Weston Naef, who wins my award for the most conservative curating) like Jan Dibbets, Lucas Samaras, and Chuck Close come off looking really good in this context. Photographers like Bill Larson, Andrea Kovacs, Ger Van Elk, Eileen Berger, Ray Metzker, and Ellen Carey also hold their own with panache. There are works by a number of artists—Colette-Justine, Judith Golden, Richard Haas, Gerald Incandela, Edmund Teske, and Leandro Katz among them—who are both interesting and competent. But by and large, these are the exceptions rather than the rule, and their works are almost overshadowed by a large number of mediocre, derivative, or pretentious statements that make viewing a haphazard and often tedious affair.

There's a lot of posturing going on in this show, a lot of self-conscious artiness tempered only by a lot of self-conscious rawness. I saw too many bad single images that artists couldn't salvage with paint or scribble, too much shallow and sloppy conceptual work, too many tongue-in-cheek narratives, and too many second-rate attempts at formalism. As I walked through the galleries, I got madder and madder at what was displayed there, primarily because there is so much fine altered photographic imagery being produced in the United States today. Works by Bea Nettles, Martha Madigan, Joyce Neimanas, Robert

Heinecken, Karen Truax, Wendy Calma, Syl Labrot, Barbara Crane, and Suda House, to name only a few, would have done wonders for this show. But instead, I had to look at pasted heads by Jill Giergerich, pretensions of profundity by Doug Metzler, boring painting images by Swenn Thomas, found photographs with drawn lines by Gary Stephan, cute travel photos with text by Jack Fulton, and much, much more.

I suppose this state of affairs has to be blamed on the curatorial system, and the curators, chosen for this show. Anyone who allows twenty-four pairs of curatorial eyes to run amok, unedited, in a gallery is playing Russian roulette. Since the people selected to put together this exhibition were so wildly divergent in taste, ability to discriminate, and knowledge about photography, the organizers at P.S. 1 lost this round.

Some New York curators like Wagstaff, Naef, Roger Welch, and David Bourdon did competent if uneven jobs (though interestingly enough, between them these men could only think of two women who alter photographs!). Some out-of-town curators like Linda Cathcart (Albright-Knox Gallery, Buffalo), Janet Kardon (Institute of Contemporary Art, Philadelphia), and Melinda Wortz (Fine Arts Gallery, University of California, Irvine) contributed new names and some fine works that have rarely if ever been seen in the New York area. Obviously, though, most of the curators were not as discerning as these, and that's a shame because there are plenty of people working in the photographic field who could have given P.S. 1 a hand in making this an important and pioneering show. But the organizers didn't ask these people, so they're stuck with a hodgepodge that does little to expand anyone's notion of what altered photography is all about. And I, for one, am stuck wondering whether a show like this does more to help or hurt the cause of the non-straight photography in New York City.

THE MALE NUDE
(May 3, 1979)

SOMETIMES REVOLUTIONS HAPPEN quietly, and unbeknownst to many, there's been an important one afoot now for the past year. After a long time in the closet, the masculine image has begun to emerge as a presence in art again. Several events that have taken place since last June have done much to usher this new subject matter into the photography scene: Marcuse Pfeifer's exhibition of *The Male Nude in Photography*, the publication of Margaret Walter's *The Nude Male* and Duane Michals' *Homage to Cavafy*, and Robert Mapplethorpe's economically successful and controversial show at the Robert Miller Gallery, have all played a part in increasing public awareness of masculine imagery.[1] In retrospect, I'm happy to declare this past year The Year of the Male—and I'm even happier to announce that the first New York gallery devoted almost exclusively to the masculine image in art, the Robert Samuel Gallery located at 795 Broadway, has been thriving since November 1978.

I know it might seem surprising for readers who have assumed that male supremacy is a given in our culture to hear me herald the arrival of masculine subject matter onto the gallery scene. But in spite (because?) of the fact that men have been the primary imagemakers, consumers, and distributors in Western culture, male imagery (and especially male nudity) has been, and remains, one of the most overtly censored aspects of the modern visual heritage. Many, many artists—male and female, heterosexual and homosexual, from Thomas Eakins to Lowell Nesbitt to Berenice Abbott to John Button to Imogene Cunningham to Larry Rivers—have created images of nude men that have rarely if ever been seen, that have been barred from exhibitions in galleries and excluded from circulation in the mass media. The fact that this taboo

---

1 Margaret Walter, *The Nude Male: A New Perspective* (London: Paddington, 1978); Duane Michals, *Homage to Cavafy* (New York: Addison House, 1978).

is still operative in our supposedly liberated culture has done much to hinder our understanding of men and masculinity, and as a result, it has undermined the progress of both women's and men's investigations into the nature of sexual stereotypes and roles. So, I'm optimistic about the potential impact of the Robert Samuel Gallery, whose owner and director, Sam Hardison, is committed to the idea of making all kinds of masculine imagery accessible to a broad public.

Since last November, Hardison has shown the work of artists like David Martin, Robert Gable, Paul Cadmus, Joseph Raffael, Jared French, André Derain, and David Hockney in solo and group exhibitions. (To date, the gallery has shown only the work of men, but they have seen the work of a large number of women in recent months. Beginning with the group show in June, women's art will be introduced into the exhibition schedule.) Hardison feels that the strongest concentration of work he's seen on this subject has been in photography, and thus far he's shown imagery by Duane Michals, Irving Penn, Richard Avedon, Robert Mapplethorpe, Lucas Samaras, and Larry Clark.

On the walls right now, in fact, is an exhibition of black-and-white prints by photographer Arthur Tress entitled *Men Between Themselves*. Long known within the photographic community as a directorial imagemaker who explores various psychological states, Jungian archetypes, and the unconscious, Tress in this show has focused his considerable talents and imagination on envisioning the darker side of the male psyche, of sexuality and homosexuality. Tress' subjects (usually nude or clothed men seen alone or in couples) are frozen in sharp focus tableaux as they enact fictional dramas that give visual form to the most extreme, and often the most bizarre, aspects of masculine fantasies. Humiliation, pain, power, loneliness, despair, and violence, often intermingled with (and inextricable from) ecstasy, eroticism, and romance, are present in these images, many of which depict their subjects stranded in the deserted wastelands of the urban environment: in crumbling buildings, graveyards, abandoned alleyways, and on waterfront docks. These silent and often stylized figures express their fantasies by interacting with props—guns, machines, animals, dolls, boots, coins, etc.—that begin to resonate with phallic overtones and disturbing psychological associations.

Androgyny, narcissism, projection, dominance and submission, and the sexual nuances that underlie relationships between young and old, father and son, teacher and student, are recurrent themes in Tress' work. Eroticism is implicit in all these images, but only rarely are men shown in passionate embraces. More often, relationships are expressed at a distance, suggested rather than consummated, embodied in objects, gestures, and spaces that become charged with sexual tensions and desires. The intense psychological isolation of Tress' subjects is echoed in their deserted environments and comes across most forcefully in the images where men are seen alone. Caught in tangled webs of self-love and hatred visualized by wires, ropes, and coils, bent under the weight of statues and of boots, confined by fishnets and plastic bags, his single figures act out private dramas that are transformed into metaphors for a strange and torturous sensuality.

Some of Tress' images are extremely strong; others are not. The weakest prints in the show, which include many of those depicting men in sexual interactions with guns and machinery, are often too predictable, too dependent on clichéd symbols and associations. Even in these images, though, Tress never seems slick and packaged like Mapplethorpe, or effetely chic like Hockney. He is always reaching for something elusive, some shock or recognition that can transform pictorial fiction into the essence of psychological fact, and sometimes he fails. But when he succeeds, he manages to create masculine images that transcend their erotic origins and become archetypal symbols for some of the most basic human fears, emotions, and desires.

Men Between Themselves is a disturbing show, and it is hardly an affirmation of The New Man that, personally, I fantasize about taking tea with in the future. Yet the exhibition is well worth seeing, for it is a powerful if uneven presentation of one man's vision of masculinity today. Naturally, there are other visions, other points of view on this subject, and they all need to be expressed. I'm hoping that we can count on the Robert Samuel Gallery to provide an outlet for their expression, to present the public with an overview of the various facets of masculinity as they are expressed in contemporary art. If it does, the gallery will be doing a great service to all of us, male and female, heterosexual and homosexual, who are attempting to reexamine our notions of what human sexuality is about.

LIVING IN A MEDIATED WORLD: ERVING GOFFMAN AND EILEEN BERGER
(May 17, 1979)

PART OF MY interest in photography stems from my fascination with visual media—ads, magazine and newspaper pictures, billboards, etc.—that have almost replaced nature as the visual landscape for those of us living in the twentieth century. Considering the pervasive presence of these public images, it has always surprised me how little intelligent work, either critical or artistic, has been produced that deals directly (and not obliquely, by reference or incorporation) with the impact of the visual media on our lives. Two such works—a sociology book by Erving Goffman entitled *Gender Advertisements*[1] and a photographic book work by Eileen Berger entitled *Sylvia* (available for viewing at the Franklin Furnace and in the *Altered Photographs* show at P.S. 1)—have recently appeared on the New York scene, and both of them explore, in radically different ways, the influence of the media on, in Goffman's words, "gender behavior."

A noted social scientist whose previous books include *Asylums* and *Relations in Public*, Goffman in *Gender Advertisements* has focused his attention on the imagistic displays that both reflect and shape our contemporary definitions of sexual roles and relationships. In spite of its popular subject matter, the book is actually a scholarly monograph, composed of about one-third text and two-thirds pictures. The introductory text is almost exclusively theoretical, and analyzes gender behavior in "real life," the relationships of photographs to "real life," and methodological uses of images in sociological studies of contemporary behavior. Goffman's commitment to an interdisciplinary approach is admirable, and long overdue as far as the social sciences are concerned. With the exception of scholars like Michael Lesy, there have been few academics adventurous enough to tap the pictorial resources at their

---

1 Erving Goffman, *Gender Advertisement* (Cambridge: Harvard University Press and New York: Harper & Row, 1979).

disposal. But it is unfortunate that the author felt compelled to spend so much time justifying his approach and expounding pedantic (and often hackneyed) theories of image making. Although he makes some good points that provide a framework for the images in the introduction (most notably the observation that in our culture women are envisioned very much like children), on the whole, I found the text tedious and difficult to read.

Once the reader gets to the pictures that comprise most of the book, though, *Gender Advertisements* becomes intriguing and enlightening. Arranged in pre-selected groups, the pictures (all public images chosen from ads, the media, and illustrated books) are accompanied by brief captions in which the author outlines the insights that he's gleaned from popular imagery, especially from images of women. By far the most exciting thing about Goffman's approach is his decision *not* to discuss the most obvious aspects of sexual stereotyping. There are no analyses here of women joyfully scrubbing toilet bowls or engaging in duties or rituals traditionally perceived as feminine. Instead, he focuses on the not-so-obvious gestures and relationships that define, by repetition, the standard ways that women and men *believe* they interact and behave. He notices height differentials ("Function Ranking," as he calls it), spatial alignments, hand positions, facial expressions, and ways of wearing clothing, and describes how these subtle details, when seen together, flesh out a picture of human relationships that is so pervasive as to seem "natural" to us. These observations make *Gender Advertisements* a pioneering, if somewhat specialized, study of pictorial body language and relationships, a study that establishes a methodology which can—and should—be utilized and expanded by students of visual culture interested in both contemporary and historical analysis.

Erving Goffman is a scholar, a man whose stance of academic objectivity allows him to select, arrange, and comment upon the visual images of women in the media from the outside, as if he himself were an impartial observer. Eileen Berger, on the other hand, is an artist, a woman whose black-and-white photo book *Sylvia* attempts to document the role these popular sources play in the interior life of a fictitious female character. Like *Gender Advertisements*, *Sylvia* (or *A Novel in Progress About a Woman Named Sylvia*; only fourteen completed pages out of a projected *grand oeuvre*) is composed of both imagery and text. But Berger integrates the two language systems completely, giving them equal weight in tightly structured graphic configurations that diagram the psychological mindscape of her character. Within these tight structures, fragments of a contemporary woman's visual experience—advertisements, dress patterns, illustrations, anatomical parts, phrases from books and magazines, etc.—appear and reappear, congealing into constantly evolving sequences that recreate the disjointed and often contradictory processes of perception by which a female self-image is forged.

Berger began her career as a straight photographer. As she explains it, she spent years working outside every day with her camera, "compulsively gathering information about the world." In her earlier work, she ordered this visual information into sequences of multiple images. Several years ago, however, she began to realize that "found" information from the media embodied another, even more pervasive, level of primary material—a level that incorporated not only the world but also the culture. She began to obsessively collect words and images from newspapers, magazines, books, etc. "They just come at you every day," she says, "and I have a need to penetrate the personal meanings of these things."

Her found sources are placed in huge piles, and then categorized thematically in large portfolios. When she's ready to begin a new page of the book, she leafs through the portfolios and intuitively chooses words and images that seem to connect in her mind. These originals are then copied on film in a copy camera, placed in goldenrod sheets (sometimes side by side with her own images), and eventually transferred by making contact prints onto large sheets of silver photographic paper.

Sylvia is not a novel in the traditional sense; the narrative is non-linear, and specific situations and events are never described. Instead, Berger compares her work to the writings of literary artists such as Proust, Joyce, Woolf, and Nin, since her piece progresses as the "heroine" passes through certain mental processes and shifts from one state of consciousness to another. The fourteen completed pages document Sylvia's odyssey through her inner life as she confronts her various personas, longs for escape to a Garden, initiates a betrayal, and suffers a Fall and its consequences. Throughout the work, the life of a particular woman (whose mental landscape is shaped by images of contemporary culture) converges with the archetypal patterns of myth, and the merger of these two modes holds the novel in a state of energized tension.

This tension is reflected in the formal structure of *Sylvia* as well. Berger maintains a precarious balance between the tight graphic order of each page and the unpredictable, seemingly chaotic interplay of disparate visual elements. The structure of each page is different, since none of them is preplanned; the artist allows her visual elements to suggest their own orders and relationships based on the associations that they trigger in her. Within these structural patterns, visual fragments connect and disconnect, alter in scale and importance, recontextualize and reorganize from page to page. New elements emerge, and old ones are discarded. Seen together, these shifting fragments formulate a multidimensional vision of reality—of time and space, of emotion and memory, of the unconscious and the conscious mind—as it is filtered through the perceptions of a very twentieth century woman named Sylvia.

Gender Advertisements and *Sylvia* are, to be sure, quite different. Widely divergent in form, function, and intended audience, they nevertheless represent two efforts to describe the visual society in which we live. It is now almost two decades since Marshall McLuhan proclaimed that "the medium is the message," yet most citizens of technological cultures are still frighteningly ignorant of the ways in which mass media images affect their lives. I'm glad to see that certain serious scholars and artists are focusing their attention on this aspect of the modern experience and are attempting to unravel the mysteries of the media that have, in Berger's words, "replaced the world." We still have a long, arduous process of understanding ahead of us, because old tools of analysis and expression are, by and large, unsuited for the new perceptual patterns created by contemporary information systems. But in their own, very different ways, both Goffman and Berger are working to suggest new methodologies, new forms of awareness, and their pioneering efforts will, hopefully, help us begin to come to terms with the media-oriented society in which we live.

ON VIOLENCE IN THE ARTS
(May 31, 1979)

ONE DAY LATE in February 1978, I was standing around, drink in hand, at a cocktail party in Washington when a photo critic from Chicago introduced himself to me. He was interested, he said, in discussing my writing; he had serious reservations about some of the stands that I was taking in print. "You're so *political*," he moaned, "and that's just not charming or fashionable anymore. Haven't you heard? These are the 1970s—and having morals is antiquated."

I think about that comment often now when I make my rounds to galleries and art world parties. I think about it when I come upon artworks full of racist and sexist innuendos; I think about it when I see artists exploiting violence and sensationalism; I think about it when I notice how easily the establishment art world accepts—indeed celebrates—visual statements that are gratuitously sadistic in tone and theme. But I think about it most when I try to discuss the issues that artistic trends raise with many of my colleagues in the art community—and they yawn in my face. "I don't see what you're getting so upset about," they drawl. "After all, it's only art. What difference can a few pictures possibly make?"

A lot of difference, far too much. I write art criticism precisely because I believe that the images we create and display are the building blocks of our psychological environment. And that environment is becoming increasingly hostile and desensitized now, enough so that I feel it is time for me—and others—to speak out.

I am not in favor of censorship; I have nothing whatsoever against artists who use unpleasant subject matter in their work. Some fine works that I've seen and written about this year—Eric Bogosian's performance *Gardens*, Richard Newton's book *I take you to a room in Brawley and we smell onions*, and Arthur Tress' photographic exhibition *Men Between Themselves* are examples—have focused on destructive aspects of American culture. In these three cases, however, the subject matter was transformed for metaphoric or didactic purposes, and the audience was left with a more sensitive understanding of violence, its causes, and its ultimate aims.

It's a far cry from these works to the S&M photographs of Robert Mapplethorpe and Philip Masnick, the slick misogyny of Helmut Newton's prints and Robert Longo's performance *Surrender*, the *Black Box* torture film of Beth B. and Scott B., and the "N-word Drawings" by "Donald"—works that depict or incorporate sensationalist subjects or language for no ostensible purpose except to exploit the notoriety and media hype that inevitably surround them. Works like these are becoming more and more visible, more and more successful on the New York scene recently—and it is their success, not their content, that concerns me here. Because the establishment's promotion of such works—with little regard for artistic merit, metaphoric function, or didactic aims—is creating a decadent standard of chic that is destructive in the extreme, for it glamorizes artists who assume dehumanizing, antisocial and amoral postures, not only toward the culture, but also toward other human beings.

This is no accident. It is clear, as several artists have pointed out to me, that the artworks discussed above are simply aping trends that have long been supported—both psychologically and economically—by a broad segment of the American public. Gratuitous sadism is all the rage in fashion photography, in window displays, in commercial films, and on prime-time television *because it sells*. It's beginning to sell in the art world now too; look, for instance, at the sales figures and publicity the Robert Miller Gallery enjoyed during its recent exhibition of Mapplethorpe's work.

But then again, everyone knows that art dealers traffic in money, not morals—and there are more than a few of them who will gladly promote fascism, sexism, and racism (or anything else for that matter) in art if they're assured of reaping an economic reward. What is alarming to me, however, is how quickly this new trend has been picked up by other facets of the art world, how easily this new chic has been assimilated into the sensibilities of curators in so-called alternative spaces like The Kitchen and Artists' Space, the thinking of critics like Peter von Brandenburg (who in the current issue of *Arts* magazine weaves convoluted historical and mystical arguments in an attempt to establish the revolutionary importance of Donald [Newman]'s "N-word Drawings"), and the work of a bevy of ambitious artists, many of them young, who seem to be so hot for accolades and financial backing that they will blindly conform to any standards the powers-that-be in the art world might set.

When I see work like this, and hear it touted as the new avant-garde, I can't help thinking about that time in the late 60s and early 70s when artists defined their vanguard status in political terms and used their positions as creative individuals to challenge—rather than echo—the destructive value of the culture around them. Those years are gone, of that I am well aware. But their legacy is still with us, for in many ways the New Wave in art can only be perceived as a backlash reaction to the humanistic thinking that dominated the art scene not so very long ago.

This apolitical sophistication is now running rampant through the art world, encouraging people to anesthetize themselves to the most brutal assaults on their spirit, reminding them that the new chic demands that they take it all in without flinching. If you can't beat 'em, as the saying goes, join 'em. But at all costs, don't lose your cool.

Beneath this supra-political cool, of course, is an undercurrent of the most profound self-hatred and defeat. The optimism that goaded people on in the late 1960s is gone; what remains is a mood of resignation grounded in the assumption that individuals cannot affect meaningful change. I don't believe that. And I know I'm not alone in my feelings about this new artistic ambience, since I've stayed up many a late hour discussing this dilemma with several of my colleagues in the art community. These dissenters sit in bars and lofts and discuss their alienation and dismay; they moan to each other, or to me. But no one says anything to anyone else, no one dares to get up and take a public stand. The atmosphere of fear, retribution, and repression is already so intense that artists are forfeiting their right to speak out.

So I'm asking members of the New York art community to speak out now, to write letters to the Editor, c/o *Soho Weekly News*, in response to the issues I've raised.

In *Scoundrel Time*, Lillian Hellman wrote: "We are a people who do not want to keep much of the past in our heads."[1] She exposes the

---

1   Lillian Hellman, *Scoundrel Time* (New York: Bantam Books, 1977), p. 150.

failure of the artists and intellectuals of the McCarthy era to speak out and describe the manner in which they sold each other down the river during that time. Let us not follow in their footsteps.

Author's Note: I was assisted in the writing of this article by several of my colleagues in the arts community who wish to remain unnamed. My thanks to them for their help.

* * * * *

On Sex, Race, Violence…and Art

Two weeks ago, in her Image Making *column, Shelley Rice wrote that artworks incorporating racist, sexist, or violent images are more and more being shown—and praised—on the New York art scene. She argues, among other things, that the "New Wave in art can only be perceived as a backlash to the humanistic thinking that dominated the art scene not so very long ago."*

The column elicited so many responses that we decided to run a selection of them below.

ED.

Dear SWN:

Since I seem to be one of Shelley Rice's prime targets, and she has asked members of the New York art community to speak out now, I would like to suggest that Ms. Rice take some time off to reexamine herself. What she is calling for is indeed censorship.

There is without a doubt in my mind artistic merit in what I do. Unfortunately, critics like Shelley Rice cannot see beyond their middle-class morality.

Perhaps it is necessary at this point in time for artists, as Ms. Rice, puts it, to "build a few hostile and de-sensitized blocks." Perhaps we must examine these aspects in ourselves before we can grow.

ROBERT MAPPLETHORPE

Dear SWN:

Shelley Rice's article was one of the most exciting I've read in the last five years. It's good to remember that artists of all mediums used their talent to help to show how the world might be if it were more perfect. The "gratuitous sadism" that a lot of people are putting out now is garbage. The artist is simply confused by the audience's and critics' and art administrator's applause. Being fashionable and "exploiting violence and sensationalism" does not solve the problem of making strong art and music...

BETH ANDERSON

Dear SWN:

Shelley Rice's article was a welcome voice of protest to the sadistic themes seen in some of the current "art" work. I saw Robert Mapplethorpe's show, as well as Helmut Newton's, and walked out disgusted that this kind of slick, sick trash was being passed off as art.

What happened to art's function in challenging and recreating the values of our society? Work exploiting violence is only a mirror for the sad condition of a culture always looking for a new thrill...

STEPHANIE VAIL

Dear SWN:

I would like to respond to Ms. Rice's statements about the "violence and sensationalism" exploited by elements of the "New Wave" attitude...

A lot of times it is difficult to define and identify what's going on; nevertheless, clearly some lines are being drawn. There is a DC current flowing that some people are picking up on, others are not. In times of oil tensions, everyday corruptions, acts of international terrorism, repression and a gut-feeling that we all might be proceeding to economic as well as nuclear suicide, some artists will not furnish the Corporate State with status objects, or will choose to make (and make we must) art expressions too hot to handle. The fact that some artists are choosing to use or celebrate the destructive elements of the culture, may indeed be a reaction to the tokenism of the '60s to activate change...

The legacy we, as artists, choose to accept need not be the recent past.

The late (great?) 1960s and early '70s (the art-boom in this country) seems in hindsight to have been dominated mainly by artists (highly formalistic) whose development was independent and directed by persuasive critical theory. This theory was mainly found in the printed word. The main body of work from this period seems determinately abstract and disconnected from all but the "educated elite."

No wonder artists of the period chose to make spoken political stands—it certainly wasn't in their artworks. Some of what is generally interpreted as "New Wave" are the growing undercurrents of change. Perhaps these changes do not fit your own dialectical view of art, Ms. Rice, but if historical roots are called for a suggestion might be to reexamine The Futurists and late '50s Pop Art. The spirit of those attitudes enabled some social and politically aware artists to produce statements which celebrated and reveled in the absurdity and destructiveness of the culture around them. This inverted sense of moral/social/political concerns, then as well as now, might be an attempt to create an atmosphere so hostile and desensitized that some awareness may happen on some level. Surprisingly, in the end it may be a gesture of humanism by focusing on the part to heal the whole. To dismiss these efforts at the beginning as trendy and decadent chic, might let you out on some of the eminent changes happening in the world as well as its reflection in art...

Douglas Hessler

SUCCESS, RIGOR MORTIS, EXPERIMENTATION
(June 14, 1979)

I SPENT A LOT of time walking around town looking at photographs the other day, and what I saw on the walls got me thinking about success and failure, risk and growth. I'm rapidly coming to the conclusion that there is something about the photo art scene that is killing off photographers like flies. In the five years I've been involved with the medium, I've watched far too many vital photographers turn stale and begin, to quote my colleague Andy Grundberg, "circling the same point in an ever-shrinking gyre." The pattern is, in fact, becoming so prevalent now that I'm beginning to wonder about the future of art photography, and I think we'd better discuss the issues it raises before we have too many creative casualties.

Given the structure of the present art world, I see a lot of reasons why photographers would begin to burn out after a few good years. The first is, of course, the pressure to produce. Photographers who "make it" are constantly under pressure to exhibit, publish, and lecture about their work. While this is, supposedly, an admirable situation to be in, it doesn't give the photographer much time (or incentive) to create challenging new work—and more than that, it doesn't leave him or her much "head space" to consider growing with his or her art. Growing—as an artist, as a person—seems, in fact, to be a word that has little place in the current artistic hierarchies. In an art scene where people are recognized by their personal style (as it has, of course, been packaged by the folks in museums, galleries, and the media, who like their viewing pleasures predictable), changes in that style are often greeted with head-shaking pronouncements of the artist's demise. Small wonder that experimentation seems to be out these days—it's a risky proposition for an established artist who has everything to lose but his/her integrity.

And so, in far too many cases, Ossification of the Eye sets in, and this impending academicism even seems to be plaguing some of the more talented members of our community in recent years. Note, for example, the work by Eva Rubinstein that is now on view at Neikrug Gallery. The prints on display reiterate the themes that made Rubinstein a well-respected figure in photography during the early 1970s: there are portraits, nude studies, interior views, and landscapes depicted on Neikrug's walls. But where Rubinstein's earlier works had a dark, emotional edge imbued with an intense and poignant mortality, these prints from 1975 to 1979 are flat and lifeless. The photographer seems to be looking at her old motifs—unmade beds, mirrors on walls, staircases, and religious icons—out of habit rather than commitment, and although there are a few fine photos on the walls (most of them portraits), many of the works look as if Rubinstein were simply imitating her former self. The resulting exhibition satisfies the demands of competency while side-stepping all of the emotional risks that once made Eva a unique and sensitive artist.

This is very discouraging to me, and I keep on wondering what we in the photographic community can do to retrieve the creative impulses of those artists who seem to be sinking into artwork *rigor mortis*. One important thing would, of course, be to create an ambience that encourages photographers who attempt to grow and change—even if the results at first blush are not entirely successful.

An interesting example of such an artist is Mark Feldstein, whose works were recently on view at Castelli Graphics. Feldstein's previous show in that gallery, which took place two years ago, consisted primarily of black-and-white single images of the urban environment (minus people) that emphasized the formal and spatial relationships of light and shadow. The show was competent, highly resolved, and boring—and I remember thinking at the time that Feldstein was backing himself into an excruciatingly narrow corner. But he backed himself right out in his recent show, which consisted of large triptychs that abandoned cool precision in favor of a bizarre, and almost surrealistic, suggestiveness.

Each of the works on view at Castelli contained three black-and-white photographs, usually urban street scenes (this time with people) flanking a still life, often seen close-up. At first glance, the individual photographs seemed innocuous enough, if a bit dark in tone. But once the images were seen together, bizarre associations started to emerge. Gestures that might have seemed mundane became fraught with tension; relationships between people and their environment began to seem menacing and mysterious; everyday objects like ice cream cones started to resonate with peculiarly haunted overtones. There was no specific narration evident in these triptychs. There was only the surrealistic suggestion in the strongest works that these ordinary moments, chopped out of time and reassembled, could somehow reveal the sinister and often violent secrets that provide the undercurrent of contemporary city life.

There were only a few triptychs in this show that were entirely successful, that merged form and content in such a way that the works spoke directly and effectively to the viewer. But the show nevertheless seemed to me to be an important one for this photographer. Feldstein couldn't lose on his earlier cityscapes; he could have gone on doing competent formal studies forever. But he saw the limitations of his earlier work and turned away from those images, choosing instead to work in a way that's much riskier, much more complex, full of potential for development, and, most importantly, much closer to his emotional base. In the process, he left himself open to the "failures" that inevitably accompany transitional work.

I don't see enough of these failures; I'd like to see many more, because more often than not they signal the fact that a photographer is trying to go somewhere new and challenging. I can rest assured, for a while at least, that this artist will not soon be joining the legions of burned-out imagemakers whose ranks have been swelling lately at an increasingly alarming rate.

TWO WAYS OF PICTURING DEATH
(June 1979)

People who've been keeping their eyes open in this town must have noticed that photographic depictions of violence and tragedy in the newspapers have become much more explicit, and much more sensational, since Rupert Murdoch arrived on the New York scene. Susan Sontag was right: people do become anesthetized to horror after being exposed to it regularly, and this past year has seen a series of news stories accompanied by photographs that never would have been tolerated by the public just five years ago. The Jonestown mass suicide took us to new heights of grossness; the "severed hand" on the subway tracks followed closely on its heels. And, last month, we were all witnesses to the murder of Carmine Galante, whose picture was plastered all over the front pages of our three major dailies the day after the Godfather's death.

The photographs that primarily concern me here are those that were printed in the *Post* and the *Daily News*. Unlike *The New York Times*, which in a more conservative fashion pictured Galante's sprawled body at some distance from the viewer, the *Post* and the *Daily News* swooped in for close-ups of the blood-spattered form, the blown-out right eye, the contorted limbs still dangling in what the *News* called "macabre gestures," and the lit cigar that continued to burn even after Galante's life had been extinguished. Indeed, one could practically see the flies swarming over the still-warm corpse in these pictures. They would have done a gangster movie proud.

I mention gangster movies, of course, because the photographs of Carmine Galante have to be understood in this context. Since much of the public's knowledge of the life (and death) styles of the Mafia stems from film and literature, the boundaries between fiction and fact became amorphous here. An individual's death was transformed into an archetypal gangland murder because it had to live up to already established notions of the underworld "rub-out" if it was to satisfy its audience. More importantly, this archetypal death took place in the context of a narrative script that had already been written in the popular imagination. The public needed a climax here, a *denouement* as bloody and cruel as the life that preceded it. They needed to see a bad guy get his, so the moral imperatives of the good guys could be vindicated. The *Daily News* and the *Post* gave the public just what it needed, expressed primarily in pictorial form.

Let us not underestimate the power, or the covert meaning, of these images. Galante was pictured in a manner so ignominious, so degrading, so lacking in human dignity that the photographs themselves became an indictment more damning—and more pernicious—than any jury could have pronounced. Death, as we all know, is the great equalizer, and in this case, death transformed an extremely powerful man into a totally impotent and ravaged corpse. When Galante, for so long immune to many of the legal and moral strictures that govern the rest of us, suddenly was trapped in a position where he could no longer fight back, he became mere prey—first to a hail of gunfire, then to an aggressive "shot" by a photographer, and finally to the eyes of us all.

I've never seen a situation in which the violations inherent in picture-taking (and viewing) were so mercilessly exploited as this one. These images were, in essence, a cowardly form of social vengeance, a thumbs-up-the-ass gesture leveled at a corpse—a "soft murder," to quote Sontag, that was the visual continuation of the violence initiated by the ski-masked gunman.

Ironically, these photographs appeared on the newsstands here the same week that Nikon House mounted an exhibition of one of the most sensitive and compassionate photo-essays about death that I've seen: a series of award-winning pictures taken by photojournalist George Wedding for the *West Palm Beach Post-Times*, chronicling an eight-year-old girl's losing battle with cancer. The sixteen pictures document Margarita Bertram's illness, hospitalization, and ultimate death. The first picture in the series is a photograph of a photograph— Margarita well and smiling. Seen against a landscape vista, the child seems like the epitome of youthful promise. This photograph appears and reappears throughout the series like a sad refrain, hanging even over the girl's deathbed. As the viewer witnesses the child's physical deterioration, this unchanging image acts as a constantly effective reminder of human mortality.

Like the murder of a gangster, the death of a little girl elicits a stock public response; Wedding's subject is a natural tear-jerker. But unlike his colleagues at the *Post* and the *News,* this photojournalist refused to exploit the facile and stereotypic associations provoked by his subject matter. He avoided heavy-handed sentimentality and instead gave us a straightforward documentary record of Margarita's last days that is sensitive, low-key, almost quiet in tone and focus. We see the child getting treatments in the hospital, but we also see her, in a wheelchair, looking at pictures in a museum. We see her scars and her frail body, but also the love and support she gained from family and friends. In fact, though Wedding's primary subject is Margarita, it can be said that his major emphasis is on the world that rose up around her, sustained her during her illness, and finally was left to cope with her absence after her death. The people in this child's life, like the photographer himself, were on her side—and the photo-essay that results from this viewpoint gives us a picture of human dignity and courage that is deeply moving.

It was strange for me to see in one week two such different interpretations of death—and stranger still for me to realize that both are equally fictitious, myths built on a foundation of visual fragments that tell only partial and simplified truths. I now wonder whether still photography can ever capture and communicate the complexities inherent in our relationship to death, whether a medium that isolates moments from the flow of time could ever give us a reading of human mortality as multifaceted and enlightening as the vision expressed, for instance, in Nancy Holt's 70-minute videotape *Revolve.* I'm not sure, but I do know that I'm more comfortable with the attitudes toward life and death expressed by Wedding than with those put forth by the *Post* and the *News.*

POSTSCRIPT: PART 1

THE FLIP SIDE OF GLITTER—POLITICAL PHOTOGRAPHY
(*Afterimage*, January 1981)

THERE'S A NEW trend emerging in New York galleries this year: all of a sudden, everyone's into "political art."[1] It's hard to say what exactly started this ball rolling; there seem to be a number of factors in operation. First of all, since this is an election year, it's only natural that political subject matter would be of interest to artists and their patrons. Second, the outcry against Donald's "N-word Drawings," which were shown at Artists' Space in the spring of 1979, caused a number of artists and critics to organize in support of political activism in art. But third, and probably most important, is the fact that the recent Joseph Beuys show at the Guggenheim threw institutional weight—and critical acclaim—behind an overtly political artist. Beuys made it into the establishment by being antiestablishment and thus made it clear to art world *aficionados* that revolution and naughtiness too have their rewards within the system.

Since the Beuys show, political art—art which focuses on social or political issues, most often from the liberal point of view—has gained more and more visibility within the New York art world. Occasionally exhibitions of such work have been held in nonart community spaces: the Times Square Show and the Internationalist Art exhibition at ABC No Rio (on New York's Lower East Side) attempted to take political statements out of the art ghettos and into the neighborhoods. More often, though, this work has been seen in alternative spaces like Franklin Furnace, the Kitchen, Printed Matter, and Artists' Space; the

---

1 *Photo Politic*, at P.S. 1, Long Island City, NYC, September 28–November 9, 1980
Originally published in *Afterimage*, Vol. 8, #6, pp. 6–7, January 1981.

New Museum is also planning a political art show to be held in 1982. But art with political content is even surfacing in commercial galleries like Elise Meyer and Stefanotti and is being discussed regularly in *Artforum*. To the casual observer, it might seem as if the conservative trends now manifesting themselves in the culture at large are giving rise to a burst of liberal conscience on the part of artists, critics, and curators.

I have only one comment to make about that: conscience is cheap. There are, of course, some people involved in the arts-politics movement who are sincerely committed to social change, but they are in the minority. For the most part, the powers-that-be in the art market seem to be perceiving the new wave of "concerned" art as a trend like any other. Their promotion of such work costs them very little and indeed gives them (and their audience/collectors) the illusion that they're working to promote social and political equality. This is, very definitely, an illusion—for the fact that the art world can assimilate, even celebrate, works challenging the social structures that allow it to exist is simply one more assertion of the system's ability to adopt, and thus defuse, all attempts at reform and revolution.

Both John Berger (in *Ways of Seeing*) and Susan Sontag (in *On Photography*) have described the ways in which a capitalistic society uses changes in imagery as a surrogate for actual social change and equates the freedom to choose from a number of images with freedom itself.[2] The art world, especially in recent years, has become quite adept at similar imagistic sleights of hand. By allowing the coexistence of different points of view in the galleries, the system gives the impression that artists do indeed have freedom of expression. Yet this so-called freedom is ultimately meaningless—because it leads nowhere. Whereas Jacob Riis and Lewis Hine, in the early twentieth century, could use photographs as goads to action toward real social change, contemporary imagemakers following in their footsteps are given grants and exhibitions.[3] The buck stops there. Everyone concerned feels that they've done what they can to assuage their liberal guilt, and life goes on as before.

---

2 John Berger, *Ways of Seeing* (New York: Penguin, 1972); Sontag, *On Photography*..
3 See Jacob Riis, *How the Other Half Lives: Studies Among the Tenements of New York* (New York: Charles Scribner's, 1890); Lewis Hine, *Men at Work* (New York: Dover reprint, original 1932).

Just to reinforce my statements, I will point out that one other trend surfaced in the art world this year at around the same time political art came to the fore: a lot of New York artists have gone "glitter." Ever since Frank Stella unveiled his latest decorative *tour de force,* a number of artists and curators have committed themselves to transforming gallery spaces into miniature versions of Disneyland. Holly Solomon and Kathryn Markel are only two of the dealers who have been promoting colorful, playful, often childlike paintings and constructions that are covered with the sparkle of glitter and that are prime illustrations of Matisse's maxim that art should be a "mental soother."

At first glance, it might appear as if glitter and political art were antithetical trends. But these apparent polar opposites at times coexist within the same gallery spaces. The Alternative Museum, for instance, showed a very fine and very political installation work by Terry Berkowitz concurrently with a glittery exhibition entitled "New Imagists." The art context itself is a leveling force powerful enough to negate any conflicts between these disparate works, which become flip sides of the same coin. The International Center of Photography, after all, effortlessly moved from showing "concerned" photography to concentrating on images of media stars; the art world, moving in reverse, is now tired of *haute couture* and is amusing itself with political liberalism. We're not talking about deep-seated moral convictions here: when it comes right down to it, we're talking about fashionable style. It's extremely hard to *épater les bourgeois* when they've rendered such a posture chic, and indeed adopt it themselves as if they were donning a new set of clothes.

It would be unfair to blame all of this on the wheelers and dealers who set economic and social policies in the art world; artists themselves have done much to dilute the meaning of political art. Too many imagemakers, eager to jump on the latest bandwagon, are using political rhetoric as a trendy posture. More often than not, these so-called political artists fail to think through any of the issues that are the ostensible subjects of their art, and use Marxist, socialist, or revolutionary slogans aggressively and self-righteously in their work in an attempt to conceal the fact that they have very little to say about the current state of human affairs.

It has become commonplace, for instance, to walk into a gallery and to be assaulted by an enormous blowup of a news photograph accompanied by a caption describing a terrorist act or a revolution. Since it's often hard to tell exactly how the artist feels about these issues, these works provide viewers with no more insight into terrorism or revolution than the original newspaper clipping would have. I also see a lot of haphazard collage works with political subjects around town and will often enter a gallery space only to be confronted by a political slogan which has been scrawled on the walls in a drippy mess that has none of the energy or *raison d'être* of graffiti. These artists are borrowing the language of revolution without understanding its impulses and are thus transforming once-vital visual symbols into lifeless and empty forms. Empty forms, of course, are very easy for the art world to co-opt.

There were plenty of empty forms in the *Photo Politic* exhibition at P.S. 1, which was on view in the first-floor galleries, and which consisted of eight visions of politics and photography put forth by ten different curators. Bonnie Benrubi and Lori Gross surveyed images of war from 1855 to 1945; Alana Heiss chose photographs by Richard Kalvar and Gilles Peress, taken at the Republican and Democratic conventions in 1976 and 1980. Slawomir Magala selected images focusing on social conditions in Poland, and Carole Naggar contributed works documenting the plight of various minorities. Alvise Passigli and Uliano Lucas chose photographs describing a number of political events in Italy over the past twelve years; John Stringer displayed images taken by Susan Meiselas and Alon Reininger that focused on revolutions and reforms in Nicaragua and El Salvador. Seth Tillet selected photographs, clippings, and advertisements concerned with various events in Europe, and Sam Wagstaff showed a *pot pourri* of imagery on political themes culled from both artistic and popular sources.

As should be obvious, this was a something-for-everyone exhibition: the people at P.S. 1 decided not to focus on a single issue or aspect of politics but instead tried to cover all the liberal bases. Such an overextended reach automatically made the exhibition a superficial survey of an enormously complex subject, and the show's ambitious size didn't make up for its lack of depth. There were hundreds of pictures on the walls. Though most of them were black-and-white prints, there were some color photographs, some collages, some color Xeroxes, and a few clippings or tear sheets taken directly from the popular press. Throughout the exhibition, artifice was played down. Most of the images were straightforward photo-documents and were displayed with detailed captions that emphasized their connections to life (and photojournalism) rather than to art. The seamy side of politics was played up: pictures of war and battles, bomb explosions and revolutions, poor people, terrorists, demonstrations and rallies, tyrannical rulers, and—last but certainly not least—an abundance of dead bodies. These subjects, in fact, comprised the major themes in the show. They were repeated, over and over and over again, throughout the eight galleries.

These thematic emphases were apparently meant to be seen as the curators' statements of their political position. John Stringer attempted to clarify his understanding of the political uses of photography in P.S. 1's catalog. He wrote: "Political photography in its most debased form takes the guise of premeditated propaganda with the intention to mislead and falsify. But on a more optimistic level, in the hands of responsible photojournalists, such photography has flourished in our time as a means to publicly expose injustice and exploitation." Obviously, the curators equate the exposure of "injustice and exploitation" with photographic realism and truth—a loaded assumption, and an astoundingly simplistic assessment of politics and political relations. Small wonder that the show seemed so one-dimensional, so lacking in any kind of human complexity and emotional depth.

If we were to believe our eyes as we viewed the pictures and read the captions on display at P.S. 1, we would have had to concede that politics is a pretty predictable business. The same things seem to occur all the time: the rich always exploit the poor, those in power always oppress those without it, people on different sides of the political fence always kill each other, the masses are always right and always make revolutions that are for the good of humanity, etc. After a while, the predictability and thematic repetitiousness of the imagery in *Photo Politic* started to alter the viewer's perception of the individual pictures. The photographs began to bleed together. Political leaders started to lose their identities and to become transformed into mythic Heroes and Villains, while specific events morphed into archetypical situations: Variations on the Theme of Oppression. This was to be the irony inherent in the exhibition. Though it purported to be a documentary chronicle of specific moments in modern political history, the show ended up negating the autonomy of those particular events. In the context of *Photo Politic*, individual incidents became mere building blocks in a totally ahistorical description of the human condition.

In this regard, this exhibition can be compared to *The Family of Man*. Whereas Steichen's MOMA exhibition of 1955 used photography to prove that all human beings are alike and therefore comprise a brotherhood (sic),[4] *Photo Politic* used photography as evidence that all people are adversaries, polarized by their political positions, who do nothing but exploit, oppress, murder, and revolt against each other. The earlier show was upbeat and naïve, and the current show is cynical and naïve, but both were based on equally shallow and simplistic generalizations—and both refused to acknowledge the complexity and diversity of human lives, human societies, and human histories.

As might be expected, the simple-minded vision of human affairs around which *Photo Politic* was organized severely misleads and falsifies the viewer's understanding of many of the pictures. All differences in the content of the pictures were negated when photographs became grist for the Liberal mill. No consideration was given to historical, racial, or cultural circumstances that might have overly complicated the issues and thus have made it impossible for the curators to maintain their illusions about the clear-cut nature of Good and Evil.

For example: there was an image, dated 1905, in Sam Wagstaff's section of the show that depicts Congolese Belgian subjects whose hands have been cut off as punishment for infringements ("sometimes rather minor," the caption read) of the law. No anthropological context or background was given for this photograph, no explanation of the penal codes that governed this society, and no discussion of the ways in which these peoples' concept of justice might differ from that of the Belgians. But the viewer was not supposed to look further. Since this photograph was seen in the midst of hundreds of pictures of bloody murders and popular revolts, it is clear we were being asked to see this picture as just one more bit of evidence that "the people" are always oppressed by the rulers. A similar distortion occurred when an anonymous photograph (taken in 1980 and selected by Benrubi and Gross) of South African natives fighting it out with shields and

---

[4] See Edward Steichen, *Family of Man* (New York: Simon and Schuster, 1955).

sticks was viewed in the context of the show. The combat positions of the men, who are dressed sparsely in native outfits and beads, seem extremely ritualized; it seems as if this might be a posed portrait, yet the circumstances surrounding the taking of the picture were never clarified. Nor were the differences between this type of face-to-face, hand-to-hand combat and the mechanized warfare depicted in most of the photographs—differences which describe not only divergent levels of technological advancement but markedly different attitudes toward human relationships, life, and survival—even hinted at. The natives' ritualized battle, surrounded as it was by fifty-three other battle scenes, became just one more stanza in the Ode to War, just one more bit of proof that Men Always Fight.

Unfortunately, most of the pictures on view in Photo *Politic* were not strong enough to resist this sort of manipulation. By far the majority of the images were straightforward photo-documents taken by working photojournalists; presumably, to sustain the illusion of the objectivity and authenticity of the show, the curators chose few pictures that embodied strong personal statements or points of view. So most of the photographs were easily malleable, very open to verbal interpretation—and the curators took advantage of this in their captions and statements, often going overboard to ascribe politically suitable meanings to pictures that might not have much intrinsic meaning at all. The most amusing example of this occurred in the Polish section of the show, where four extremely boring and empty photographs of "The Polish Situation" by Lopienski were accompanied by a lengthy statement that provided a symbolic exegesis of their "prophetic" iconography. Clearly, curator Magala saw what he wanted to see in these images—not necessarily what was there. Isn't this one way to "mislead" viewers and "falsify" photos?

Is it possible that the curators didn't realize that pictures so easily manipulatable by the Left could just as easily be manipulated to suit the purposes of the Right? Many of the images in *Photo Politic* could easily function within a conservative exhibition or newspaper, accompanied by different captions (of course). The only major difference between this exhibition and a mass media tabloid (besides the captions), in fact, is one of emphasis: there were more pictures of revolutions and minorities in the show than might be acceptable to the ordinary picture editor. But generally, the subject matter of these photographs was pretty standard journalistic fare, and even the picture editor at a major conservative newspaper wouldn't quibble with P.S. 1's definition of what constitutes a political event.

In short, for all of their subversive pretensions, the curators of *Photo Politic* didn't bother to rethink the definition of politics given to us by mainstream culture. They simply interpreted the same old stuff differently, but not that differently. The experience of looking at the pictures in this show was not dissimilar to the experience of looking at the pictures in the *New York Post*: the emphasis on violence as the most important (i.e., the most pronounced) aspect of human political relations is identical. Walking through these galleries, the spectator became immersed in a blood bath of which Rupert Murdoch would heartily approve; even the movie *Jaws* doesn't have so many gruesome climaxes. Liberals can tell me that the ends justify the means until the cows come home, but I still know that violence is violence—and all the dead bodies plastered on the walls at P.S. 1 didn't give me the sense that I would be any happier in a world of their making. For all its moralistic rhetoric, the *Photo Politic* show was infused with a disregard, indeed a contempt, for human life no different from that found in the *Post*, or in the policies of repressive governments.

Ironically, many of the artworks that have proposed the most sweeping changes in our definition of politics, and in our understanding of its relationship to human life, have never been labeled "political art" at all. Perhaps not surprisingly, much of this work has been done by women who have been working to expand the notion of politics to include all aspects of daily life. Many feminist artists—for instance, Jo Anne Leonard, Mierle Ukeles, Jackie Livingston, and Judy Chicago—have described the political nature of subject matter (like housework and child-rearing) until recently dismissed as apolitical, and therefore trivial. What these women are proposing is nothing less than a reassessment of the hierarchy of values in our society. Laurie Anderson, Suzanne Lacy, Jacki Apple, and Mimi Smith have done multimedia works that focus on the ways in which the sociopolitical environment affects personal behavior and emotional interactions. Their complex descriptions of the connections between our self-images, our lifestyles, and our political ideals make it very clear that attitudinal changes must precede changes in the social order. People like these are not interested in slogans or rhetoric. They are interested, instead, in bringing abstract ideas home to roost by developing a more inclusive and human vision of human interactions. These artists know that deep-seated moral, psychological, and intellectual changes are the only firm foundations for revolution.

PART 2: IMAGE MAKING IN THE EXPANDED FIELD
ONLINE MAGAZINE, JEU DE PAUME MUSEUM, PARIS (2012)

PREFACE
ABOUT ME AND MY INTENTIONS
Blog: lemagazine.jeudepaume.org

Proposed Categories:
News and Updates
Reviews
Commentaries
Interviews
Social Networks

I AM WRITING THIS now because of Director Marta Gili's invitation, her request that I serve as the Jeu de Paume's *Bloggiste* for the next six months. It has been a while since I beat the pavements of Soho, but suddenly I am once again engaged in the dynamic world of journalism, though with a very different spin. Still living and working in Lower Manhattan, I am older of course, and the world has changed. Issues I fought for in my youth—photography's acceptance as an art form, for instance—are old news, now that the medium has pride of place in galleries and museums all over the world. Civil Rights and identity politics have taken different forms; diversity has a more international flavor now, and class divisions define the art world more sharply than before. Most important for this blog, perhaps, is the fact that the whole process of human interaction has been redefined in technologically developed parts of our digitized world.

Our so-called social networks both unite us and alienate us from the habits of sociability taken for granted in my youth. Face-to-face Time takes a back seat now that people build virtual communities across continents and political movements across classes and cultures. People still read, but in fits and starts, checking posts and tweets from myriad information streams; news sources are as dispersed as the people they serve, always on the move. This blog will be published in Paris while being based in New York, but it will cast its net wide—to Canada, Switzerland, China, and beyond—thereby reflecting the realities of an increasingly global art scene. Interactivity and reader response will no longer involve a shout-out in the streets of my neighborhood. Instead, comments will be posted online, traveling in seconds from Portugal or Ghana or Brazil. I am thrilled to have the chance to "meet" these new, far-flung readers, and to update my journalistic experience by learning to navigate within this brave new world of communication and media. How easy it is to publish photos online, to embed video, to enliven text with color images moving and still! Local experiences and expressions have been enhanced by interfaces that are increasingly global, multicultural, and virtual.

Art historians are complemented by others studying photographs from different perspectives, and images are often hard to distinguish from information. Thanks to changing technologies and international circuits, pictures move literally and digitally from context to context, changing both material support and message as they beam from one continent or century to another, bouncing between audiences and interpretations with kaleidoscopic rapidity. These continual shifts in context, the movements in time, space, and meaning that define the rough parameters of what critic Terry Smith calls *contemporaneity*, will be the focus of this blog over the next six months.[1] Which media, which messages are colonizing our brains today, and how? Highlighting specific images, issues, and case studies, my invited colleagues and I will explore (and hopefully suggest new perspectives on) the possibilities and permutations of photography in what Lawrence Alloway called "the great holding pattern" of the present.[2] Linking the Then of my life with the Now, I am hoping to highlight not only my own changing responses but also the evolving nature of the interfaces that bind us to each other as well as to the increasingly complex network of our visual expressions.

---

1 Terry Smith, "Contemporary Art and Contemporaneity," Critical Inquiry, 32:4 (2006), pp. 681–707.
2 Alloway, "The Complex Present," p. 241.

REFLECTIONS ON THE WIND
(March 20, 2012)

Today I woke up with the wind on my mind.

It might have been the storms that whipped through Manhattan overnight. Loud and boisterous, the winds made it hard to sleep. But it might also have been my preoccupation with an article I read before bed: Suzy Hansen's "The Istanbul Art-Boom Bubble," in *The New York Times Magazine* dated February 10, 2012. With lots of photos, the article discussed the transformation of this Turkish town, from what writer Orhan Pamuk called a "pale, poor, second-class imitation of a Western city" in the twentieth century to a booming cultural center in the twenty-first century. I lived in Istanbul off and on during the late 1990s, teaching at Bosphorus University; I was there when Vasif Kortun (now director of the SALT Art Center) arrived back from a stint as director of Bard College's Museum of the Center for Curatorial Studies in New York and decided to create a contemporary art hub in this extraordinary metropolis. I experienced the contempt for the arts that were holdovers from military rule at that time; I saw the tensions growing between the religious majorities and the worldly minorities of the privileged class; I worried over the lack of cultural infrastructure that made it necessary for talented artists to leave. I have heard over the last few years that things have changed, that this town is bustling with art spaces, collectors, and activities, and I am trying to update my memories by replacing them with this new and shining image. Even for a native New Yorker, who has experienced many vagaries of art and life in the Big Apple, this is not an easy task.

Interestingly enough, I seem to be on the same wavelength as many Turks, who are enjoying their moment in the sun while being aware of the fragile dynamics of their recent success—in exhibitions, in the marketplace, and within the international art scene. Yasemin Nur, a thirty-five-year-old artist who is a member of AtilKunst, an all-female art collective, was quoted as saying that "We're like girls and boys playing…Now Istanbul has become the hip city and is chosen as a hip city. The system needs the hip city, and next it will be Beirut, and next somewhere else. This is our time. We will be sad, but the wind will go."

I think that Nur's wind was the one on my mind this morning. The breeze in question seems to be a temporal marker, like the arrival of Mary Poppins and her umbrella, pointing the finger of the *zeitgeist*. Hansen's article highlights young hipsters who used to live in London or New York and who have chosen to blow in on this latest wave. Mari Spirito, a longtime director of 303 Gallery in New York, recently moved to Turkey. "In New York it feels like the best years are behind us," she said. "In Istanbul it feels like the best years are yet to come." Everyone in Manhattan knows what she means, of course; more and more we feel like a *passage* rather than a place, a conduit for economic exchange rather than a center of creation. Artists and writers (when not talking about real estate) whisper about how boring a city with nothing but rich people must inevitably be; foreign artists who once flocked here in droves are blocked either by prohibitive costs or by visa restrictions imposed since 9/11; neighborhood shops, family businesses, and artisans, even our downtown hospital, have fallen by the wayside, replaced by Starbucks, McDonald's, huge drug store chains, and infinite numbers of insanely expensive condos being purchased by millionaires from everywhere. An exhibition like the one currently at Pace Gallery on 25th Street, a wonderful show of photographs (by Robert McElroy, Fred McDarragh, Robert Frank, and others), artworks, videos, and audiotapes chronicling the early days of Happenings in the 1960s, seems to describe a place more distant than Johannesburg. Young artists as well as the rest of us gaze in disbelief at black-and-white documents recording the antics of Allan Kaprow, Red Grooms, Carolee Schneemann, Claes Oldenburg, Simon Forti, and others, marveling at the energy, playfulness, spontaneity, and community that were hallmarks of a moment when life in the Big Apple was not quite so Darwinian. It is no coincidence that shows like this one, and the *Fluxus and the Essential Questions of Life* exhibition shown at the Grey Art Gallery last fall, are being mounted now in the city. Retro is the new local; looking back, we inhabit a temporal utopia instead of a spatial one.

What intrigues me in all this is the complexity of life on earth in 2012. Being an artist or critic means becoming a meteorologist, figuring out where the winds will be blowing next and grabbing the next train headed in that direction. As Nur said about Vasif Kortun, "he seems to be able to predict where art institutions will go." The crystal ball no longer reflects the environment of birth or habitation; space is malleable and changeable, and we are all on our own in negotiating the shifting relationships between personal experience, national loyalties, and the global marketplace. The irony, however, is that the "incredible lightness of being" (to quote Milan Kundera's words) brought on by this condition puts a lot of pressure on artists to hunker down and figure out who they are.[1] Hansen writes: "Even as Istanbul artists are merging with the international community, they are also looking backward to discover themselves." History, psychology, sociology, whatever: one of the conditions of international stature is that artists are required to cultivate an authentic local voice to communicate with the global audience. And in countries whose histories are riddled with violence, dictatorship, repression, or colonialism, the nature of such a voice is not self-evident.

Hansen's article catalogs the usual demands that Turkish art be Turkish and not Orientalist, whether or not the artists in question were taught to imitate Western modernism in school. Creative people and gallerists are often stumped about what "real Turkish" art would look like, or what percentage of Western education and expectations they would have to shed to be considered authentic. The same week that Hansen's article was published in *The New York Times,* Chika Okeke-Agulu came to lecture in the Art History Department at New York University about the painter "Ibrahim El Salahi's Postcolonial Modernism," and about his impossible struggles in the 1950s and 1960s to accommodate critics who expected him to reject his European education—and his interest in communicating with his international peers—in order to create an authentic Sudanese art. It is easy to see that there's a pattern here. But in a world where "everything is central and everything is the periphery," as Sylvia Kouvali (the Greek owner of a hot Turkish Gallery) said, we should stop putting so much irrelevant

---

1   Milan Kundera, *The Unbearable Lightness of Being* (New York: Harper and Row, 1984).

pressure on artists whose privilege has been to work in the international art world. We should perhaps see ourselves, and the artists who share our experiences, as the messengers who can use the global language of art to describe local experiences, understanding that their authenticity in 2012 might be within the temporal and spatial *bouillabaisse* of what historian Terry Smith has called "contemporaneity." Young artists from Istanbul, a privileged few who might have more in common with art students in New York than with the compatriots my friends often referred to as "the locals," might want to say something about this rather than about their Ottoman past or their essential "Turkishness."

Probably the most moving commentary in Hansen's piece came from the artist Kutlug Ataman, who has been negotiating the delicate relationship between his local roots and his international experiences for some time now. He left Turkey after the 1980 military coup and returned to Istanbul ten years ago. Hansen says that Ataman doesn't think Turkish artists have confronted the real source of their material. He described a recent incident when a mob of Turkish men attacked gallerygoers sipping alcohol on the street in their fashionable clothes. In the center of Istanbul, Turkey's two worlds came face to face, and Ataman considers this the "real" Turkey. "When I look at artists' practice in Europe, I am not inspired," he is quoted as saying, "If the artists here can engage with Turkey, they will be ahead of the rest of the world. Because the world is this. This desert."

And this, of course, is the point of my essay. I am writing because "the world is this," and "this" is New York too. I spent the day walking around Chelsea, looking at art in various galleries. There's a lot of bad or just plain silly stuff out there as usual, but this has been a pretty interesting season. And that's because Ataman's "desert" has permeated our town and has invaded the slick expanses of new condos and juice bars and fancy gyms. Some American artists may not be acknowledging the new landscape any more than some Turkish artists, but other voices are speaking loud and clear. Adel Abdessemed, an Algerian who studied in Paris, has a terrifying exhibition of sculptures and drawings entitled *Who's Afraid of the Big Bad Wolf?* at David Zwirner Gallery. Freehanded sketches of various animals with explosives strapped to their backs are juxtaposed with, among other things, a capsized boat filled with ominously stuffed black garbage bags. *First Look*, a group show at

Yossi Milo that brings together works by artists whose first New York exhibitions were presented at the gallery, is a powerful assemblage of photographs by South African Pieter Hugo, Norwegian Simen Johan, Chinese Liu Zheng, German Loretta Lux, Japanese Kohei Yoshiyuki, and American Alessandra Sanguinetti, among others. These are often grotesque images, filled with explicit and implicit violence against persons, animals, and the environment, and together they create a powerful statement about life on earth in the twenty-first century. The desert winds have, indeed, come home. We may no longer be the "hip city," but we are still a place where urgent voices can be heard—and sold.

SHORT TAKES: REVIEWS
(MARCH 20, 2012)

THE RADICAL CAMERA: NEW YORK'S PHOTO LEAGUE, 1936-1951
The Jewish Museum, November 4, 2011–March 25, 2012

Curated by Mason Klein of the Jewish Museum and Catherine Evans of the Columbus Museum of Art, this important exhibition draws on two museum collections with rich holdings on the history of New York's Photo League. Begun during the Depression, the brainchild of photographer and teacher Sid Grossman, this organization—which encompassed darkrooms and meeting rooms, lecture series and photography classes, exhibition spaces, and a newsletter called *Photo Notes*—was seminal to the formation of New York's late twentieth century photography community. But despite its considerable influence, little has been known about this chapter in the city's cultural history, in large part because the League and its founder were blacklisted by the government during the Communist Scare of the 1950s. This is the first museum exhibition in three decades to comprehensively explore its contributions in order to correct what Klein calls "a historical myopia," and it is a terrific show well worthy of its complex subject.

Founded to provide instruction and meeting places for photographers and artists who were often the children of immigrants, The League has been known primarily for its Socialist-oriented, left-wing politics and its rejection of the artsy and elitist salon style of the Pictorialists. Faced with the diversity and the dilemmas of urban life during the Depression, idealistic young people like Walter Rosenblum, Aaron Siskind, Max Yavno, Helen Levitt, and Morris Engel chose photography and aimed to follow in the footsteps of supporters like Lewis Hine and Paul Strand. Famous artists and critics—Lisette Model, Berenice Abbott, Weegee, Edward Weston, Ansel Adams, and

Elizabeth McCausland for example—counted themselves among its contributors, and photographers as far-flung as Edouard Boubat, Henri Cartier-Bresson, and Álvarez Bravo were invited speakers. In other words, in spite of its urban emphasis and its general leftist tendencies, the League was a lively, open-ended, and global center of photography open (and economically accessible) to everyone.

This is significant, and it is also a central tenet of both the exhibition and the excellent book that accompanies it. Most discussions of the League in the past two decades have emphasized either its political ideologies or its "camera club" aspects, and neither of these points of view tell the full story. While many of its members were deeply engaged in documenting the social and political complexities of their surroundings, Grossman's emphasis was always on the evolution of the photographer in relation to his or her subject—the formation, in other words, of a personal photographic vision that allowed the artist to perceive him/herself within the environment described. The demands of this vision changed over time, as the Depression gave way to World War II and then the unexpected prosperity and political hysteria of the postwar years. *The Radical Camera's* greatest triumph is in its ability to trace not only the historical shifts but also the evolving definitions of photography that characterized members of this talented group. The relationship between the objective world and subjective vision, between documentation and art, was constantly being negotiated within the organization. Klein emphasizes that personal interpretation came to the fore in the later years of the League, in a poetic documentary style that was further developed in the works of the more solipsistic New York School artists—Robert Frank and Louis Faurer among them—who came to represent American photography during the 1950s. The complexity of this shifting ideology and aesthetic, the range of expressions set forth within its theoretical and pedagogical arena, are palpable on the walls of the Jewish Museum, embodied in wonderful pictures that continually interrogate the relationship between the world and the imagemaker's eye. It has taken a long time, but these remarkable men and women have finally vanquished the blind spot created by the League's prejudicial past and taken their rightful place within the histories of both photography and the city of New York.

JUAN DOWNEY: THE INVISIBLE ARCHITECT
Bronx Museum, February 9–May 20, 2012

Juan Downey: The Invisible Architect is a dense and highly conceptual exhibition, one that at first hardly seems at home on the Grand Concourse in the Bronx. A lively and active figure in the New York art world from the time he arrived in 1969 until his death in 1993, Downey was born in Santiago, Chile, in 1940. He finished a degree in architecture before moving to Paris to study printmaking. By the time he arrived in New York, therefore, this young man had roots in Europe as well as in North and South America. These diverse cultural threads, and his lingering attachments to (and critiques of) them all, are the subjects of the first US survey of his work, which includes video, drawings, paintings, photographs, and installation works as well as the artist's notebooks. His deep connections to Latin America link him to the Bronx Museum, where he exhibited during his lifetime, and to the multicultural neighborhood outside the gallery walls.

Curated by Valerie Smith, Curator and Head of the Visual Arts, Film and Media at Haus der Kulturen der Welt in Berlin, the exhibition was organized by the MIT List Visual Arts Center as well as the Bronx Museum. Best known as a video artist for works like the two-part *The Thinking Eye* (on Diego Velásquez's painting *Las Meninas* and the idea of reflections in Western art), Downey was engaged in cutting-edge conceptual and technical experiments during the 1970s and 1980s. Obsessed with the idea of invisible energies and architectures, he shifted away from material objects and toward performative and interactive works like *Plato Now* and *Fresh Air* (with Gordon Matta-Clark). But the eye-openers in this show are his stunning large-scale drawings, many of them engaged with mapping and the idea of shifting geographic boundaries and cultural identities. Much of Downey's work, especially his series *Video Trans Americas* (footage of Indigenous people observed and encountered throughout his travels in North and South America), is almost contemporary in its search for the self within overlapping cultural, national, and political arenas. The slippages and the power plays of nations; the ties that bind races, places, and traditions; the transcultural usages, hierarchies, and vagaries of symbols: these were his themes, and this beautifully organized exhibition allows Downey's multifaceted and still timely *œuvre* to shine in all its complexity.

DOUG WHEELER, SA MI 75 DZ NY 12
David Zwirner Gallery, January 17–February 25

One of the hottest shows in New York this month—if you judge "hotness" by the crowds of people waiting to get in—was the large-scale installation work of Doug Wheeler. Raised in the desert of Arizona, Wheeler began his career as a painting student in Los Angeles and soon became a pioneer of the "Light and Space" movement in California during the 1960s and 1970s. This is the first time one of his large-scale "infinity environment" is being presented in New York, and its minimal calm was such a contrast to the dense urban fabric outside that people were willing to stand in line for hours on end to experience it. And the experience of this piece was the point: while exploring the materiality of light, SA MI 75 DZ NY 12 was first and foremost about the viewer's physical and perceptual interaction with boundless space, marked only by changes in light that simulated dawn, day, and dusk in a thirty-two-minute cycle.

The viewer walked into the brilliant white void of the installation unable to perceive its boundaries; dematerialized, the space of the gallery disappeared. (Those who are familiar with the *Tibetan Book of the Dead* will surely reference the Great White Light allegedly encountered by the newly deceased in this and other spiritual traditions.) Disoriented, most viewers spent the first few minutes lost, often trying to locate borders or limits before they finally gave in to the shining emptiness. The first thing I noticed was the texture of the bright light, which seemed almost palpable, like a cloud. Wheeler himself called it "a cloud of light in constant flux, a molecular mist. It comes out of my way of seeing from living in Arizona, and the constant awareness of the landscape and the clouds."

That heightened awareness made the experience extraordinary, and surprisingly complex. Other viewers wandering in this unmarked arena seemed like dark spots on eternity, existential symbols of themselves unmoored from physical space but beautiful and reassuring in their isolation. After a while most of us settled into a corner (so to speak, since there were none) and just stared into the void, surrendering to the warmth of the light's embrace. Closing my eyes at a certain point, I panicked and almost lost my balance when I opened them onto the unremitting emptiness. I stayed for a long time and felt (more than saw) the light fade, disappear, and reappear. Both my body and my mind found the subtlety of the experience intense, a meditation accessing levels of consciousness not readily available in the Big Apple. Some art allows us to experience another culture; Doug Wheeler's installation expedited an extraordinary journey through the porous boundaries between physical space and the landscape of perception.

OBSERVED: MILAGROS DE LA TORRE
Americas Society, 2012

For me, the most unnerving thing about the Milagros de la Torre exhibition at the Americas Society, with almost forty photographic works produced since the 1990s, is its proximity.[1] A constant feature of the work selected for this artist's first monographic show in New York is that either the artist or the viewer must get close, too close. An example: *Fears,* a series made in 2004, is based on a survey carried out among residents of Mexico City during a period of six months. De la Torre asked people to describe their deepest fear. No camera was involved in this work; the framed rectangular prints are monochromatic tones of dark or reddish brown. Puzzling over the seeming lack of content, the observer must move closer in order to finally notice small, barely perceptible, texts written in Spanish at the bottom of the picture plane. The texts are one sentence long. Squinting to read them, the viewer inevitably confounds his/her own reflected image with the fears confessed by the urban dwellers. These citizens are terrified of kidnapping, beating, and rape—and so are we, because our face is mirrored in the frame and our breath is clouding its glass surface. Who is the observer, and who the observed; who is the confessor, and who has confessed? These distinctions are suddenly unclear.

This transmutation—from viewer to subject—is the power of Milagros de la Torre' work, and though it operates in different ways it

---

1   Curated by Edward J. Sullivan, *Americas Society,* February 8–April 14, 2012 (organized with the Museo de Arte of Lima, Peru).

finishes by drawing everyone very close into the circle of the human condition. That condition, in her world, is often violent. Lines and relations between people are in question, and images dissimulate identities *Under the Black Sun* of the photographer's gaze. The most familiar objects become the agents of heinous crimes; beautiful abstract designs, once perceived correctly, are shown to be contusions on the artist's skin. De la Torre grew up in Lima, Peru, when terrorism and crime were rampant, and as the daughter of the Chief of the city's antidrug military police force, she lived with the constant uncertainty about when violence would erupt into her family's domestic life. Educated in Peru and London, living in Paris, Mexico, and New York, and working in Spain, she has seen enough to understand that this violence is everywhere, has been everywhere, and probably will be everywhere. Though many of her works are based on archival research in specific venues—like The University of Salamanca Library, The Palace of Justice, and the Larco Herrera Psychiatric Institution in Lima—their tales of murder, of crime, of insanity, censorship, and discrimination multiply and resonate beyond and between countries, continents, and historical époques.

There's a series called *Bulletproof*, large prints documenting clothing, specifically men's jackets, on hangers. Seen life size, the garments are high end, fancy, or everyday, full of color and decorative patterns. Once again, the viewer is seduced into moving close, this time by the texture of the image; de la Torre chose a cotton paper that is soft and tactile, making one want to reach out and touch (or acquire) this item. But all of these warm and fuzzy fashions are bulletproof, worn by people armoring themselves against a violence foretold. The empty garments hover between expectation and mourning—just as the common personal objects documented in *The Lost Steps*, familiar things like belts and skirts, wallets and shirts, are ripped from their place within the fabric of everyday life when we realize that they were submitted as evidence in the trials of felons. There is no safe place in Milagros de la Torre's universe, and all of us are implicated under the black sun.

WHITNEY BIENNIAL (MARCH 1–MAY 27, 2012)
by Shelley Rice and Rob Perrée
(March 29, 2012)

I invited my friend Rob Perrée, in New York for this month's exhibitions and fairs, to write his assessments of the Whitney Biennial for this blog.[1] Though he saw some good works and some positive aspects of the exhibition, in general, Perrée feels that the incorporation of time-based arts—performance, film, video—into the fabric of the show weakens the curators' statement. This opinion is not shared by our colleague Roberta Smith, whose review in The New York Times Weekend Arts section on Friday, March 2 found this aspect of the exhibition challenging and exciting. My own feelings, I must admit, are closer to Smith's than Perrée's; but I'm delighted that they both highlighted certain stand-out works—Werner Herzog's, Forrest Bess,' and Wu Tsang's—that particularly struck a chord with me. And, perhaps not surprisingly, both critics noticed that one of the strengths of this year's exhibition is that it is not top heavy with famous, "blue chip," (most often male) artists, who have tended to steal the spotlight from younger, lesser-known participants in some recent shows. Instead, famous artists are there, but discretely, integrated into the installation with no special fanfare. Marsden Hartley has a few lesser-known paintings scattered throughout the show, and Warhol has a terrific but very low-key photomontage of a bicyclist tucked away on a side wall. This allows the exhibition to be less of a circus and more of a learning experience, offering

---

1 Invited Blogger: Rob Perrée, (ed.), *Kunstbeeld Magazine*, Amsterdam. Review of the 76th Whitney Biennial, The Whitney Museum of American Art, March 1 through May 27, 2012. Organized by Elisabeth Sussman and Jay Sanders, with Thomas Beard and Ed Halter.

invaluable information about the intergenerational nature of artistic creation in the United States. When Garry Winogrand shares the space with a young talent like LaToya Ruby Frazier, who contributed a documentary project about economic crises in New Jersey, we learn not only about "stars" but also about those who follow in (or resist) their footsteps.

A Good Concept Works Out Badly
by Rob Perrée

THE CURATORS OF the 76th Whitney Biennial have set themselves a very challenging task, to organize an exhibition based on an inspiring concept. They want to redefine what an artist can be at this moment, and they do this in two key ways within the show. In the first place, they emphasize the connecting points between the visual arts, performance, dance, music, and film. Secondly, they highlight the resonances between artists. Not only did they invite a few artists to curate parts of the biennial, but they also included a number of people who use, or who quote the work of, other artists within their own expressions.

This second part of the exhibition concept works out well. Robert Gober, among others, curated an interesting small show of the rather unknown Texas artist Forrest Bess (1911–1971). His visionary abstract paintings are based on the theory that male and female can be united in one body, and the display includes notebooks, sketches, and photos from his personal surgeries. Richard Hawkins uses fragments of reproductions of the work of other artists in his collages. Nicole Eisenman quotes many colleagues in her forty-five expressionistic portraits on view—among them Marsden Hartley, present elsewhere in the show with a beautiful portrait from 1940.

With the exception of a stunning film installation by Werner Herzog, which combines landscape images by the seventeenth century Dutch artist Hercules Seghers and the music of contemporary composer Ernst Reijseger, in such a way that sound and image become one, the first part of the concept fails completely. This is due to highly underestimated practical circumstances. Film, performance, dance, and music are time-based disciplines. They need to be presented at certain times and in certain locations. To make that happen, the curators earmarked the 4th floor as a theatrical setting for the various dancers and performers taking part in the show, and they organized a film/video program in a separate room. The consequence is that the 4th floor is an empty, useless space (at least as far as the more traditional, static visual arts are concerned) for 80% of the exhibition time. The film program, in itself very diverse and interesting, relates in many different ways to the artworks on view and has, for that reason, a comparable problem. The objects in the exhibition can be seen every day, but the viewer can only watch that special, related film or video one month later. However wonderful the program connections may seem on paper, the average visitor will never experience many of them.

There is another side effect. Because all the works are so connected, and need each other in a way, the exhibition itself is not strong enough to "live" on its own. There are good visual images and objects presented, but also weaker ones. They depend on their relationship with the time-based works within the context of the show. When the viewer cannot see them on the same day, they lose ground. And the overall exhibition loses quality.

To end on a more positive note, it is refreshing that the curators of this year's Whitney Biennial did not go overboard for big names and big works. Young, old, known, unknown, deceased, or alive, there is no difference in the way the participants are presented or treated in the show. That is a relief. The overblown Jeff Koonses and Anish Kapoors are already everywhere to be seen.

ON AGING, ABSENCE, AND ANGELS: CINDY SHERMAN AND FRANCESCA WOODMAN
(April 3, 2012)

I WAS AT THE Press Preview for the Francesca Woodman exhibition at the Guggenheim Museum last week, and I was watching her videos with Richard Armstrong, the Museum's Director.[1] We started talking—reminiscing, really. I explained that I knew Francesca Woodman—long ago, when she was alive, making art. We talked about her friends, who were often my friends; we talked about the scene then, in the late 1970s, and the influences so evident in her work as well as mine. At a certain point, Armstrong looked at me with a bemused expression on his face. "It must be strange," he said, "to see your life flash before your eyes like this." Yes, I said. Yes.

This has been a particularly odd moment, when art and life seem to be doubling back on me. It is obvious from reading some recent criticism or listening to hushed conversations in the galleries at MOMA, that I am not alone in my current perplexed relationship to Time. Eva Respini's Cindy Sherman exhibition is a real *tour de force*; it upends Sherman's work, removing it from the chronological context of her life and career and going instead for thematic juxtapositions and visual drama. This shock unmoors the images from space and time, and forces viewers to see the work—and its principal sitter—in surprising and unexpected ways. But in spite of its cuts and curlicues, and its refusal to adhere to a master narrative of artistic evolution, the exhibition cannot hide the salient fact that Cindy—like her recent subjects, rich society matrons—has aged in front of our eyes.

When I say this, I am not speaking offhandedly, noticing wrinkles

---

1   Cindy Sherman, *Museum of Modern Art*, New York City, February 26–June 11, 2012, curated by Eva Respini. Francesca Woodman, *Guggenheim Museum*, New York City, March 15–June 13, 2012, organized by Corey Keller, *San Francisco Museum of Modern Art*.

or bulges or other signs of middle age in pictures that are, of course, so heavily shaped by special effects and make-up. I am speaking instead about a life process: Cindy Sherman is, ultimately, a performance artist, and her self-images move through time as she does. They are connected to her like Peter Pan's shadow was to him, in a way that, let's say, Julian Schnabel's paintings or John Chamberlain's sculptures are not connected to them. Those rich women of a certain age, holding on to their money and their youth with every ounce of will they have, break my heart. This has nothing to do with feelings of empathy or cruelty that others might attribute to the artist, reactions discussed at length in Johanna Burton's provocative catalog essay. Those matrons remind me of the passage of time, and so they remind me that Cindy and I have made it to this point—and that Francesca has not.

Very girly of me to think this way, isn't it? This blog post is obviously not a high-level theoretical discussion, or an objective art historical commentary, eh? No. One of the things that has to happen when we allow works like Sherman's, Woodman's, Martha Wilson's, and Sanja Ivekovic's into the mainstream of international art is that we have to adjust the terms of its reception. And we are at the moment facing such a readjustment, now that the first waves of feminist artists lucky enough to make it to their Golden Years are beginning to express their reaction to the ravages and rewards of longevity, maturity, and decay. Whether or not these are Cindy's (or her curator's) intentions, her retrospective has forced me to see myself in time and to ask questions about temporality, duration, and absence—and what these have to do with, in this case, women's art.

Let's start with Francesca, since she had so little time. Born in 1958, the daughter of well-known and well-connected Manhattan artists, Woodman committed suicide in 1981, when she was twenty-two years old. What we have, in other words, are photographs she produced before, during, and right after she was in college. She had very little time to go beyond that, though the scale of her exhibition makes clear that she worked obsessively and with focus during her passage on the planet. The hoopla surrounding this body of work, the canonization of this young woman as a great and tragic photographic artist, has always been deeply problematic for me—a conundrum not at all dispelled by Keller's well-organized and informative exhibition. Francesca was very gifted, and beautiful. It's evident in the pictures that she absorbed lessons from everywhere: from Surrealist artists, from the performance artists and feminists who were her teachers, mentors, and friends, from Duane Michals, Deborah Turbeville, and Aaron Siskind (whose wonderful show, *Spaces*, organized at the Rhode Island School of Design around the time when Woodman was a student there, was obviously an influence on her as it has been on me). Looking at her work, frozen in time as it is, I see the urgency and excitement that marked this particular moment when American art met American photography. And I also see a young woman trying very hard to disappear into eternity.

Woodman, like Sherman, specialized in self-portraits, but hers illuminated the modernist moment right before postmodernism came on the scene, so the comparison is instructive. Romantic, black-and-white, often blurry, Woodman's images describe a subjectivity that never stopped wiggling—and that could never, somehow, see itself without a mirror or camera's lens. Jumping, climbing, tracing its outline on the ground, Woodman's beautiful and usually naked body—with breasts sometimes visualized as angel wings—is hard to grasp, since it is most often disappearing into a blur, a fireplace, a decaying wall, or an armoire. There was an article in *The New York Times Magazine* on March 25, 2012 by a young writer named Elisabeth Donnelly, describing her eagerness to purchase a dress from the *Mad Men* fashion collection at her local Banana Republic store. Obsessed with the popular television show about office and boudoir politics in the 1960s, she is excited to "try on" the accoutrements of femininity that visually defined its historical moment. Donnelly is perplexed by her mother's pained refusal to perceive these dresses as simple fashion; the older woman sees them as signifiers of her difficult youth, and she refuses to treat stories about the abuse and cruelty suffered by women during this era before the Feminist Movement as entertainment. Francesca Woodman was younger than Donnelly's mom, but she was alive during the years of transition between these two generations. These were years when it was hard to pin down what exactly was expected of us, and her art is of that moment. In one of her videos, she writes her name on a large sheet of paper draped between the camera and her nude body. She then proceeds to tear the letters and finally, the paper, walking through its constraints and out of the picture altogether. Looking at Woodman's photographs, seeing that nubile torso and its discontents, I think about Deborah Turbeville's book *Wallflowers* and Joan Didion's novel *Play It as It Lays*, created around the same time.[2] Awash in a sea of liberated bodies and endless possibilities, all of these women made art about being lost in space.

It is important to understand that a number of Woodman's photographs, especially those created in Providence, Rhode Island, were initially art school assignments. There is evidence, in late work with which I was unfamiliar, that she might have gotten tired of such self-absorption if she had lived, might have one day ceased to focus on the wiggly subjectivity hidden beneath the curves of her youth. Just the very act of photographing obsessively, of transforming movement into stasis, hot flesh into cool two-dimensional silver, was this young woman's bid to leave the world's disorder and inhabit the looking glass realm of art. Her later, large-scale works moved further in this direction; they began transforming her body into stone. In these she became a caryatid, large and forceful, her youthful limbs no longer personal, translucent, and weak. Merging with the Ancients, she left the flesh behind and passed into the immortality of Classical Greece.

Premonition of death? I doubt it. But this transformation from individual to icon does in fact curiously lead us to Woodman's artistic afterlife, and to Cindy Sherman. Francesca died in 1981. Five years later, Ann Gabhart, then director of Wellesley Art Museum, organized an exhibition that traveled to Hunter College and other university museums in the United States and asked Rosalind Krauss and Abigail Solomon-Godeau to write essays for the slim catalog. Thus began the transmutation of Woodman from a vibrant, social, and engaged young woman, recently deceased, into a canonized female artist, self-made loner, and tragic practitioner whose sole creative forebears were male Surrealists. Conveniently dead, unable to either evolve or talk back, Woodman was transformed into an empty stone caryatid, in this case upholding the pantheon of groundbreaking women artists. Lolita, in a high art context.

The advantage of Corey Keller's exhibition is that it begins to breathe life back into Woodman's *œuvre,* to reconnect time and evolution and sociability into her brief and productive time on earth. But I remain

---

2 Deborah Turbeville, *Wallflowers* (New York: Congreve Company, 1978); Joan Didion, "Play It as It Lays," in Joan Didion (ed.), *The 1960s and 70s* (New York: Library of America, 2019).

fascinated by Woodman's interest in classicism at the end of her life, and her move to create large-scale works in which her body transcends rather than expresses subjective concerns. Caryatids were aspects of public art, not private expression. She was, in other words, moving (four years after the *Pictures* exhibition, around the time Sherman was making the *Centerfolds* commissioned by *Artforum*) in the same direction as the postmodernists.

Cindy's early work, those wonderful film stills presently on view at MOMA, were shocking at the time of their creation precisely because they completely suppressed the personal uncertainties and internal dialogues that were the currency of art in those days. They were not about Sherman's emotions but about her desire to transform herself into the icons in our public domain. Stereotypes of women—vulnerable, anxious, frightened, threatened—from the films of our youth, proclaim that we are not what's inside us but *what we behold*. Sherman, of course, grew up in suburban America during the early days of television, the time when mass media images breached the walls of our homes. Moving into the living room and the bedroom, they muddied the boundaries between the public and the private, the here and there, the outside and inside—in the process rewiring, perhaps replacing, those anguished internal dialogues. We are molded into the world of *Mad Men*, these pictures seem to say, one photo, one television show, one movie at a time.

The film stills show Cindy creating and then walking into stage sets of cities, of bars, of domestic environments. A housewife, a nurse, a student, a hitchhiker: she tried on roles that were already there, already recognizable. Through about the year 2000, in fact, Sherman most often embodied iconic figures, male and female, omnipresent in the visual *bouillabaisse* of our media culture: sorcerers, fashion plates, monsters, Art History paintings, Mrs. Santa Claus. As she moved into her 50s, though, with the photographs of Los Angeles types, this focus on icons began to erode. Sherman left the silver screen and stepped down into the far murkier landscapes of living beings, where those that you behold are not archetypes but your friends and neighbors. Which of course brought both her, and now me, back into Time.

I became aware of this while viewing the exhibition. I was staring at one of her earliest color works, where she, posing as a young urban ingénue, was smilingly lifting a glass to an unseen entourage at a bar. In those days (c. 1980), of course, Sherman worked alone in the studio; no one was there, and the environment was often a slide projected behind her on the wall. But what struck me, in fact, was her joyful youth, and the ease with which she fit into this role. This scenario was familiar and welcoming; like Elisabeth Donnelly, she embraced the narrative of her fantasy alter ego with grace and confidence. It was, after all, only play-acting, and even the most anxious, vulnerable, heartbroken, or lonely ladies were part of the dream of womanhood in those days.

That ease, that grace is gone from the latest works, which is one of the reasons that they are so hard to bear. Often made in Photoshop with digitized or painted backdrops, they create visages and environments for the sitters (usually, of course, Sherman herself) that are, quite simply, out of joint. Holding on desperately to their youthful faces and bodies, the only positive archetypes our youth-oriented society offers them, these life-sized women are most often seen against backgrounds that also look toward the past: cloisters, walled gardens and courtyards, ornate salons. This temporal orientation marks a very important difference between Sherman's early and later works. Her early ingénues (like Elisabeth Donnelly) were propelling themselves into a future, inhabiting their fantasies without thinking much about the consequences. The visual models embodied by the society matrons, on the other hand, do not flow forward in life and time; retro here means more than an attraction to 50s fashion. Like Donnelly's mom, Sherman's subjects cannot don styles that function as empty signifiers, ready to be filled with dreams. The choices available to them are engorged with memories, echoes of an *ancien régime* of flesh and spirit and culture inhabited not with grace but reluctantly, with strain. The strange disjunctions between figure and ground in these photographs make it seem as if each of these living women is in the process of ossifying, metamorphosing from a living being into a monument—a caryatid, perhaps? Like their classical forebears, these matrons are large, full-bodied, and strong; they dominate the picture plane with their intense psychological presence. But most important, and ultimately more to the point: however poignant or complacent, desperate or arrogant they may appear, these mature women—like Cindy and me—are still here.

DIGITAL IMAGES: THE SHORT AND THE LONG VIEW
by Verna Curtis
(April 11, 2012)

I asked my friend Verna Curtis, Senior Curator of Photography at the Library of Congress in Washington, D.C., to write about her experience at the "South by Southwest" Conference in Austin, Texas, in early March. A cutting-edge gathering, the conference posed important questions for the future of our digital media, and the Library of Congress is obviously taking a proactive position on the archiving and preservation of our information networks.

WAS A FIRST timer at the quarter-century-old spring conference/festival in Austin, Texas, known familiarly by young people as "South by Southwest" (run by the company SXSW) which started as a music festival. Today more than 30,000 people attend three festivals: music, media, and film rolled into one. The media or "Interactive" portion, which took place from March 9 to 13, 2012, was a smorgasbord of panels, interviews, solo presentations, group discussions, book readings, mentoring, and training workshops.

Kristen Joy Watts, a contributor to *Lens* (the photography blog at *The New York Times*) and a content strategist working for the New York agency R/GA, invited me, as the senior photography curator at the Library of Congress in Washington, D.C., to be on her interactive panel, "Is Our Photo Mania Creating Magic or Mediocrity?" The Library's involvement in collecting materials "born digital" goes back at least a dozen years to its pilot project in acquiring websites. Since then, websites on such topics as the US national elections, the Iraq War, and the events of September 11th have been archived. In Spring 2010, Twitter gave the Library all of its tweets since March 2006 from which the Library will post selective content. Watts' panel included Kevin

Systrom, cofounder of the new and wildly popular Instagram app, and Richard Koci Hernandez, an avid Instagram user who teaches about media in the School of Journalism, University of California, Berkeley.

At 9:30 A.M. on that Sunday, after a night of partying on a wet Saturday night, we were surprised to look out at an overflowing crowd of more than 250 people, which was standing room only. The panel's back and forth was lively. Questions we pondered were:

Is the mass adoption of digital photography ushering in an era of greater creativity?

Are we missing out on experiences because we are too busy taking and sharing our photos?

Are features like the "like" button limiting our emotional responses to photographs?

What are the implications for photojournalists of pictorial newsgathering by cell phone users?

Taking center stage was Instagram, which is less than two years old but which caught on quickly; it reached 100,000 users in its first week of existence. A social media network for photo sharing that interfaces with a variety of networking services, the site now archives hundreds of millions of photographs in the cloud. As immensely gratifying as it might be for today's hip photo enthusiasts to filter their daily observations with Instagram's digital options and then share them with friends, can this justify the long-term existence of their images? If there are 380 billion digital images that exist today, what will their future be? I pointed out that since the introduction of the Kodak camera in the 1880s, the problem of sorting through too many photographs has already existed. Editing or choosing those photos—by camera users, artists, curators, and archivists—has been and will be our watchwords.

I was at SXSW unofficially, but Bill LeFurgy represented the Library of Congress as digital initiatives manager for the National Digital Information Infrastructure and Preservation Program (NDIPP). Congress mandated this program to build "a national strategy to collect, preserve and make available significant digital content." The panel in which Bill took part addressed a provocative topic indeed: "Digital Immortals: Preserving Life Beyond Death." Acknowledging that it is not possible for institutions to come close to saving all the visual material (or should I say, immaterial) being generated, he called for new approaches. The public will need to preserve their own digital files and the world of libraries will need to advise them how to do so. LeFurgy's presentation made it clear that the Library of Congress has already begun the task for the United States.

INVISIBLE BORDERS: TRANS-AFRICAN PHOTOGRAPHY PROJECT
by Shelley Rice, Jennifer Bajorek, and Erin Haney
New Museum
(April 18, 2012)

On view at the New Museum in Manhattan this spring is the 2012 Triennial, billed as the only recurring exhibition in the United States devoted to presenting young artists from around the globe.[1] Curated by Eungie Joo, the show features thirty-four artists, artist groups, and temporary collectives. Entitled "The Ungovernables," the exhibition highlights artists born between the mid-1970s and the mid-1980s in countries as widespread as India, Brazil, Lebanon, China, Thailand, Mexico, Egypt, and Korea as well as North America; many of the fifty participants have never before exhibited in the United States. The curator wanted to emphasize the resiliency and hopefulness of a generation marked by local and global political, economic, religious, and military crises, and signal the museum's interest in cultural production outside of the usual Western centers. There's a big range of work, some of it good and some of it bad, in this show; "The Ungovernables" is a sprawling and, yes, unruly affair. Rather than cover the entire exhibit, I asked my friends Jennifer Bajorek and Erin Haney, scholars of African photography and archives, to focus on a particular collective they first encountered in Mali in 2009; the group is represented by photographs, videos, and a blog on the first floor of the museum. Centering, as the wall text announces, on annual road trips taken by ten to twelve photographers and writers traveling by land across the "invisible" barriers that separate nationals and people on the continent, this trans-African project is "an attempt to disrupt the randomness

---
1 At the 2012 New Museum Triennial, "The Ungovernables," February 15, 2012– April 22, 2012.

of the borders as they exist and acquire a more realistic sense of the similarities and differences between peoples suggested by cultural and geographic divides."

Invisible Borders Collective
(Founded 2009, Lagos)

Nike Adesuyi-Ojeikere, Kemi Akin-Nibosun, Lucy Azubuike, Unoma Giese, Emmanuel Iduma, Uche James-Iroha, Ala Khier, Chidinma Nnorom, Nana Oforiatta-Ayim, Amaize Ojeikere, Charles Okereke, Emeka Okereke, Ray-Daniels Okeugo, Uche Okpa-Iroha, Tom Saater, and Jumoke Sanwo
By Jennifer Bajorek and Erin Haney

W<small>E MET UP</small> with the group of Nigerian photographers at the Bla-Bla in Bamako in November 2009. Exhausted from the Rencontres, they faced a long journey back to Lagos on public transport the next day. Lucy (Azubuike) and Unoma (Giese) recounted outrageous bits of their trip from Lagos; Emeka (Okereke) filled us in as the stars came out overhead.

The inconveniences and indignities presented at each national frontier were the main theme, and performance, of *Invisible Borders* at Bamako that year. A broken-down van, Accra's car parts markets (unfortunately closed by 3 A.M.), endless bribes paid, language barriers, all needled the Lagosians, known for their can-do attitude. They were anticipating some discord, not to mention more expenditures, come morning.

They were, of course, going to be snapping pictures the whole time.

The idea behind that first journey had been simple—an experiment. Instead of taking the Air France tickets offered by the *Rencontres*' organizers, which would have limited Nigerian participation to a handful of exhibiting photographers, the group decided to pool their money and travel overland, making it possible for a much larger group of photographers to attend. The initiative's original target—the unimaginative nature of the biennial's travel protocols, for an exhibition that had been elaborated on the theme of "Borders" that year!—was soon eclipsed by a changed experience of African geography and a desire to chronicle it.

Fast forward three years: the roving band of photographers has already transformed itself several times. Their project—now funded by an impressive array of backers—has grown to encompass at least one new overland itinerary every year, always to a photography festival in Africa. No longer exclusively Nigerian, the group is challenging itself to reflect on the borders crossed in a kaleidoscope of new ways. The trip across Sudan, and the addition of Sudanese photographer Ala Kheir, opened unprecedented vistas on subjects as diverse as Darfur and Internet connectivity. Who knew Khartoum had the best wi-fi access of the cities toured in 2011?

The strengths of the project lie in its multi-perspectival qualities: the artists work on their own independent projects as they go. Equally important are conversations with a growing network of photographers. Advice from more established artists and professional-level training are in demand and at a premium. This explains why young collectives crop up in African cities with few institutions and still fewer opportunities for critical exchange with working artists. *Invisible Borders* follows in a long line of trans-African activism seeking to expand this dialogue. Harder to sustain are works that evoke the variegation and depth of those conversations. Longer stays in Khartoum or Addis Ababa might afford more provocative images. Their blog traces their movements for audiences for whom connections are no big deal; only a few African cities and territories afford such connections. Renegade exhibitions, impromptu programs, *plein-air* projections: all could entail more fruitful *in situ* exchanges. At the New Museum in February, Emeka answered a question about disparities in connectivity in trans-African contexts and consequences for creative projects optimistically: "It will come."

SHORT TAKES: REVIEWS
(SPRING 2012)
MEN ON THE EDGE (AND VIBHA GALHOTRA)

Rotimi Fani-Kayode: Nothing to Lose,
The Walther Collection Project Space

Alec Soth: *Broken Manual,* Sean Kelly Gallery

Vibha Galhotra: The Utopia of Difference,
Jack Shainman Gallery

I'M FEELING LIKE men are in need of equal time on this blog. They have, as usual, had more than equal time on the walls of New York galleries and museums this month. But I am less interested in numbers than in a confluence I've noticed recently: two of the exhibitions by accomplished photographers in Chelsea galleries this spring, one an American and one an African, one living and one dead, use male subjects to embody an edginess, a nihilism even, that tilts the idea of patriarchy wildly off center. Exploring the works of Alec Soth and Rotimi Fani-Kayode together is not a self-evident choice, but I think that the juxtaposition may yield some insights into the farther reaches of the male psyche during these early years of the twenty-first century.

Rotimi Fani-Kayode, in fact, never made it to this new century: he died of AIDS in England in 1989 at the age of 34. Born in Nigeria to a prominent Yoruba family who fled to the United Kingdom as political refugees in 1966, he studied in the United States (a BA from Georgetown University in D.C. and an MFA from Pratt Institute in Brooklyn) and then returned to Britain to live and work. Active in both the Association of Black Photographers and the lively queer culture in England, he saw his photography as both a public and a political act—a surprising perspective, considering that his work consists mainly of male nudes in both black and white and color. "We aim to produce spiritual antibodies to HIV," he wrote with his partner Alex Hirst. Transforming symbolic gestures into public acts bearing witness for a generation decimated by disease, he responded to imminent death by asserting the power of beauty.

While there are black-and-white works in this exhibition that can hold their own with Robert Mapplethorpe's, the large color prints in the *Nothing to Lose* and *Every Moment Counts* series express his vision at its greatest intensity. Undressed (or occasionally dressed in African or Biblical robes) and adorned with feathers, fruits, leaves, masks, or paints, Black men adopt highly ritualized postures and gestures—though, as Kobena Mercer has pointed out, these actions only deepen the enigma of what the ritual might actually be.[1] Christian, Yoruba (the artist's family members, in their native country, were the keepers of the shrine for Yoruba deities), and other religious icons meet and meld in these works. Mercer calls Fani-Kayode Afro-Modern in his emphasis on the generative possibilities of cross-cultural exchanges and encounters. But the stylized language of the body is what makes these pictures so extraordinary. This is a Dance of Death, a dance to the death, a defiance of shame, fear, or anger. Independent of nationality, race, religion, or ideology, born of the artist's displacement (he called himself an outsider in matters of sexuality as well as geographical and cultural dislocation), this ecstatic theatricality shatters the chains of culture to illuminate more profound and ambiguous aspects of the human condition.

Fani-Kayode, in other words, uses the expressive powers of the Black male body to assert the transcendent force of the finite, the transient, the mortal. This push beyond the confines of particular civilizations is a leap of faith, an affirmation of the primacy of life beyond bounds. His sitters bite into apples, sprout feathers, and cover themselves with plants and berries, uniting their flesh with nature in both its concrete and its metaphorical manifestations. Men also bedeck themselves with flora in the latest works by Alec Soth, but the meaning of the gesture in his photographs is completely different. While Fani-Kayode's subjects

---

1 See Kobena Mercer, "Mortal Coil: Eros and Diaspora in the Photographs of Rotimi Fani-Kayode," in *Travel & See: Black Diaspora Art Practices Since the 1980s* (Durham, NC: Duke University Press, 2016).

are adorned with leaves, affirmation turns to negation when Soth's are practically (and willfully) obliterated by them.

The *Broken Manual* exhibition at Sean Kelly Gallery this spring was a curious and hybrid affair, comprising a number of photographs (black and white and color, most taken between 2006 and 2010), a documentary film, and a site-specific installation showcasing the book of the same title. Ostensibly written by Soth's alter ego, Lester B. Morrison, the book is a how-to survival manual designed to aid others (men, of course) anxious to withdraw from society and build a life in some remote part of the American terrain. The adjective American here is very important. Even though Soth emphasizes that he first became fascinated by hermits when he began studying the life of Trappist monk Thomas Merton, he was moved to begin this project by the story of the 1996 Olympic Park bomber Eric Rudolph, who spent years evading police by hiding in the Appalachian Mountains. Alex Soth is, from my point of view, one of the great American storytellers, with an extraordinary sensitivity to the strength and the strangeness of this young and mysterious land and its motley collection of citizens. The *Broken Manual* exhibition is one of the chapters in his ongoing story, the chapter about a breed of men who never quite emerged from the Wild West into what we so blithely call twenty-first century life.

Whereas Fani-Kayode's men will themselves beyond specific civilizations and belief systems in order to reaffirm both the ecstatic nature of life and the archetypal rituals that sustain it, Soth's reject human society and collectivity outright. As the press release says: "These photographs reflect (the artist's) increasing interest in the mounting anger and frustration that some specifically male Americans feel with societal constraints and their subsequent desire to remove themselves from civilization." "Primitive" in these pictures does not refer to traditional tribal ancestors; it means shedding the trappings of culture altogether and living in the woods with (and like) the animals. In this moral universe, one covers oneself with leaves or branches in order to hunt or evade the authorities; one declares one's allegiance to nature as a way of turning one's back on the alternative. Soth's photographs sometimes show the men, and sometimes their living environments—in caves, on or inside mountains, in trucks or dilapidated sheds. It is a testament to Soth's extraordinary sensitivity that he was granted access to these guarded men, who maintain both a psychic and a physical distance from his camera but who are, nevertheless, in clear contact with both him and us. Constantly lurking just beneath the surface of these images is the latent violence that sustains the hermits' withdrawal, their "escape." This is, in other words, not Thoreau's America; and the *Broken Manual*, teaching lonely men how to survive on the lam, makes manifest a dark side of American life that keeps threatening to erupt into the national consciousness—and political process.

* * * * *

Edgy men also make their appearance in *The Utopia of Difference*, the first American exhibition by Vibha Galhotra, a young Indian woman living in Delhi. But the edginess in this artist's work is urban rather than natural. Whereas Soth's hermits disappear into the camouflage of trees, Galhotra's sculptural figures wear army-style *Neo-Camouflage* imprinted with the image of the city dominating the wall behind them. Impossible to visually extricate from the overcrowded geometries of their environment, the mannequins morph into cyborgs whose organic flesh lives to reflect the architectural chaos of their surroundings. Escape from society, in this case, seems impossible. Unlike the empty wilderness that still covers much of the United States, whose existence is essential for the tales Soth tells, the urban jungles of India depicted in Galhotra's work seem to go on forever. No exit, as Sartre would say.

This photographic project set the stage for the exhibition, but much of the work consists of sculptures and textural wall pieces sewn together with metals and other materials. A hammock threads the image of the world in crystals; a beehive grows and juts out beneath the dark and varnished wood of an old European table. Galhotra is an extremely versatile and inventive artist, practiced at using the media, symbols, and metaphors of our newly globalized world in ways that disrupt their accustomed usages and meanings. Organic and inorganic, urban and natural, male and female: these are the parameters continually being tested in her visual expressions. The shimmering brass or copper metal surface that is a hallmark of her work, for instance, when viewed up close, is constructed of many *ghungroos*—the ankle bells worn by

Indian women as a musical accompaniment for traditional dance. Once these tiny beads are sewn together, *en masse*, they are capable of morphing not only into hives and ropes or words and cityscapes drawn on fabric but also into large and monstrous animal forms that are like a cross between a Lynda Benglis and a Claes Oldenburg soft sculpture. Part dinosaur with claws, part wheeled vehicle with a crane for a neck, these "monsters" are the artist's variations on what Gayatri Sinha calls "a collapsed and somehow humanized earth mover."

I stared at the *Dead Monster* for a long time today, noting the folds of its "skin" flopping over the architectonic body beneath. I then walked home by way of the High Line Park and stopped to stare down at a construction pit on Gansevoort Street in the West Village (that would soon, miraculously, turn into the new Whitney Museum of American Art). A big, bright yellow CAT earth mover was perched precariously on a huge mound of brown dirt; its "scoop" reached into the earth at odd angles, digging and clutching and swaying with a rhythm that was as mesmerizing as it was disturbing. I knew as I watched that I was, indeed, experiencing Galhotra's Beast—the one familiar to all of us who have chosen not to escape from the global cities of the twenty-first century.

EIGHTY YEARS YOUNG: DUANE MICHALS—THE MAN WHO INVENTED HIMSELF
by Duane Michals, Shelley Rice, Véronique Bernard, Anne Morien,
and France Saint Léger
(April 26, 2012)

> "Do not awaken from your dreams, it's too soon."
> —Duane Michals

I met Duane Michals when I was twenty-four years old. Throughout the years, he has been what I call my "spiritual advisor," my role model in living life to the fullest. I was pleased to learn that the French producers (Terra Luna Films' Anne Morien and France Saint Léger) of a new documentary about Michals' life and work were delighted with my plan to interview both Duane and New York coproducer Véronique Bernard. Morien and Saint Léger wrote a wonderful essay about the work in progress which was originally published in French for "La Lettre de la Photographie" (the Naudet brothers' blog); Bernard has translated the text and I have edited it for an English-speaking audience. Director Camille Guichard had a particular concept in mind while making this ninety-minute documentary. He wanted the film to bring forth emotions rather than historical facts. Instead of a predetermined biographical chronology, the work explores what he calls a "kaleidoscope of photographic sequences." And then, finally, as the pièce de resistance: I've posted a short interview with Michals himself, who discusses what he has learned and what he has attempted to express in this latest creative endeavor.

Lettre de la Photographie—Duane Michals 2012
By Anne Morien and France Saint Léger
(translation by Véronique Bernard)

It was 2009 and we were headed to the South of France for the Rencontres d'Arles. A large Duane Michals retrospective was planned that year, and we were curious to rediscover his work that spanned half a century.

The exhibition was held at the Archevêché. The quality of the photographs selected for the show was clear, but there was a peculiar ambiance in the halls. The public was simply enraptured by Michals' stories, his series, his words, his thoughts. Viewers of all ages were transfixed by the photographer's poetic world. And we followed the wave of people, fascinated, amused, touched. Never has an exhibition caused so many laughs and mischievous looks. The visit concluded with Duane Michals himself moonwalking for the spectators. That night, at the ancient theater, the house was packed and the day's infatuation lingered. It wasn't clear who was having more fun, Duane Michals or his audience. One thing was certain: we would have to make a film about him.

Right from the beginning, we wanted to make a film about Duane Michals' inner world. We didn't want just a portrait of the artist but something steeped in his stories that would allow people to discover him as a contemporary, talking Buster Keaton. His energy was incredible. He was always ready to explore new ideas, to take us into a world where humor and seriousness mingled effortlessly. To bring together all these different elements and to harness this amazing energy, we chose director Camille Guichard, whose sensibility, sense of humor, and sensitivity seemed in tune with Duane Michals' work.

The scouting trips to Pittsburgh and New York confirmed that. Duane and Camille immediately hit it off. Duane understood that the film was open to his imagination, and that they would create it together. Once the locations were agreed on and Camille went back to Paris, the two of them were so excited about the project that they were on the phone constantly. Sequences were being dreamed up from one continent to the other. Duane kept offering ideas without worrying about the structure of the film. Camille embraced this way of working. It was up to him to make sense of the multitude of images Duane was proposing.

The first shoot in Pittsburgh was very emotional. Duane retraced the steps of his childhood, his relationship with his mother and with his father, a steelworker. There was no love lost between the couple. These were painful memories, but there were happy ones too. Months later, we were scouting again in New York City and Cambridge, Vermont, where Duane owns a magnificent country house. This is where the film would explore the other themes close to Duane's heart: sex, desire, time, death, and homosexuality. The scenes started to take shape and other characters, friends of Duane, began to emerge. But it was important to stay within the film's own reality, to keep it as a story, a game, a "mise-en-scène." The film was beginning to have its own dreamlike quality, where documentary and fiction merged.

New York became the place where all these new encounters would take place. The invented scenes took shape, changing on Duane's whim and Camille's ideas. One day Duane's shirt was wrong. No problem, Duane swapped shirts with the cameraman in the middle of the street. The next day, he did the same thing with Camille. There they were, bare-chested and laughing their heads off in the middle of Soho. And it worked. The new shirt turned Duane into the character invented for the scene. On another occasion, as the crew was shooting on a rooftop where Duane had photographed Joe d'Allesandro, Duane climbed up a ladder facing the Empire State Building to call out to New Yorkers. Suddenly he stopped. He needed angel wings like in the sequence of *Fallen Angel*. He knew a store nearby. Camille agreed and off he went. As the crew waited for his return, the light was fading. They needed to hurry. Finally, Duane arrived and climbed to the top of the ladder with the wings on his back. He put his hands around his mouth and started shouting, "Wake up New York!" It became the poster for the film.

Other anecdotes followed day after day. Then it was off to Cambridge, four hours north of New York City. The crew had a hard time keeping up with Duane who was driving so fast, as if he was in a hurry to get to the next part of the film. In the country, Camille spent time filming nature, Duane, and his partner Fred. He wanted this part of the film to be in a different reality. He filmed Duane's Garden, flowers, the countryside around the house, trees, and stone walls. Duane suggested a scene where he talked with a stuffed duck. It would be his way of talking about the influence of painting on his photographic work.

Then Duane wanted to take photos for an exhibition dedicated to animals, another sequence with a man plucking a star, and a scene about desire in an abandoned hotel. Duane resembled Méliès shooting in his studio. Duane's ideas come and go like butterflies. You have to catch them. But if the butterfly gets away you have to let it go.[1]

Duane Michals: The Interview
with Véronique Bernard

Shelley: So Duane, why did you want to do this film? Tell me the whole back story.

Duane: I hadn't been in Arles for twenty-five years. They invited me to go and do a retrospective and a big presentation in 2009. It was a really wonderful evening, and the exhibit was very successful. But I started my presentation—in the center there is a spotlight, and someone introduces you. Well, I moonwalked backward onto the stage, and it brought down the house. I just let fly, as you know I can do, and it got a huge response. You get such an international audience there. I had interviews from Finland, from Greece, from everywhere. The next day I ran into Anne and France and they asked me if I would like to do a movie, and I said sure. I never look a gift horse in the mouth. As you know, I've always taken advantage of every opportunity that came my way—otherwise I would still be sitting in dear old McKeesport!

Off the cuff, we had a lot of fun with this film, it was a nice feeling. I worked on another documentary about my life that was a scripted film, a serious chronology of dates and facts. This was more playful, we just made it up as we went along. One thing really got to me, though: after shooting and seeing myself on television for thirteen days, I saw my strangeness. There's a way we view ourselves. Before this, I didn't really know how I sounded, I didn't know my gestures. I couldn't see my body language. I never saw THAT GUY—the ME that others see, and he's strange. In making this film I came into my first recognition of my physical self as it might be viewed by somebody else. That moment

---

1 *Duane Michals: The Man Who Invented Himself*, a film directed by Camille Guichard, produced by Anne Morien and France Saint Léger–Terra Luna Films, in association with Véronique Bernard–Illiad Entertainment.

when you recognize that other self, who may be the self that is more real than you are, it's a little bit startling. So that was interesting, to see all that. That, for me, was big.

The other interesting thing: The big danger for me, in making this film, was that we structured it starting from my childhood in McKeesport, Pennsylvania. Because I'm a narrative person, I saw the whole film as a story, a picturesque tale: Duane leaves McKeesport and his old house with a little suitcase and has a lot of adventures. I go to Pittsburgh, visit Russia, move to New York…and then in the end I literally die. My danger is that I had composed the film in my mind. But: it's not my film.

Véronique: You learned that in filmmaking you don't shoot in a logical order. It had a trajectory, but it was a different logic. The shooting was done using film logic, which is not the same as Duane's. And since this is not a film with interviews, with people talking about Duane's life and work, a lot of the story came together in the editing.

Shelley: Having starred in one of Duane's sequences shot in Paris twenty years ago, I know what a tyrant he is when he works. So, starring in someone else's dream must have been a real shock for him!

Duane: In Camille's version, editing was more like slice and dice, you take the pieces and arrange them and make a stew. My way would be…

Shelley:…to make a sequence!

Duane:…of no (con)sequence! (laughter) So understanding the structure of the movie was a big deal for me, and there were things I thought were important that didn't make it in, since it's not my film. BUT I want everyone to know that we did not use a body double. In all those nude scenes: that's my real ass you see up there in all those pictures on screen. (laughter)

Véronique: The interesting thing for me, since I came into this later than the others, is to work with two creative people like Camille the director and Duane. They get along very well but they are different people, with different minds. All those non sequiturs that are part of the film, they are thematic instead of chronological. The film is told not like a logical narrative, but more like the way Duane *thinks*.

Duane: Well, I can't avoid my process, I've spent eighty years honing it! The film has its own life and its own logic: Camille's logic is wedded to me as source material.

Véronique: You were more than source material! You created material specifically for the film.

Duane: It was exciting. And also, being eighty, being on the cusp of oblivion, that's where I am and so that's what the film is about. First, my huge nostalgia for McKeesport, which I don't really understand, is there. I still have the urge to go back, it's like walking into a dream where all these places are still familiar but they don't look the same, they are all falling down. It's a bit like Miss Havisham, decorating McKeesport now. In one scene in the garden, I said that she lived next door, and invented neighbors like Madame Bovary, who we called Emma and who hit on my dad… though the best part was telling how I saw the Eiffel Tower from a lighthouse tower. There's a lot of whimsy in the film that's not documentary at all. We told a lot of stories.

Véronique: But there is a sort of melancholy to the film, much talk about death and mortality and longing. There's a lot of fun but an underlying seriousness.

Duane: I'm not a serious person but I am very serious; the serious trivia is underneath the other trivia.

Véronique: Deep down you are very superficial! (laughter) That's an Ava Gardner quote, by the way.

Duane: The one overriding personal thing I learned from making this film, as I mentioned before, was the awareness of how I function as a physical object, as a creature in the real world in a way we never see. I find this knowledge rather startling, and upsetting, because it adds to my not knowing, not only my image of myself, or this conversation or this room, but the whole universe. We live in this bad joke; the universe is playing a bad joke on us by giving us consciousness and then letting us know that we're going to die. At this point, I'm beginning to face the fact that we spend our lives distracting ourselves from our own demise. Now I'm really facing the enigma and almost feel a little bit overwhelmed by it. Because there's no help, and no exit. The only reference might be Buddhism; I might have to get back to sitting. It's a very strange place to be. During these last years, where's my attention, what do I do about it?

Véronique: But you do have the work you've created. How do you feel about your body of work?

Duane: Oh, I love my body of work, it's really "built," it's got a great waist. (laughter) I am very happy with my body of work. I've done so much, I'm very prolific, and I've done so many different things: a book on Egypt, a children's book, books on Walt Whitman and Cavafy, on quantum physics, about being gay in the military, my childhood home, etc. I have a huge body of work: it's out there, I've done thirty-two books.

Véronique: And here you are now, making a film. That's why the title is "The Man Who Invented Himself." You do keep reinventing yourself all the time, that's very apt.

Duane: *The Man Who Invented Himself.* "All things that he experienced in this lifetime were his invention. He invented the moon and the trees and all things visible and invisible. At this moment he is inventing me writing this and you reading this. Yes, you too are his invention. But if you told him this he would not understand, he would deny it, even though all things he thought possible became possible, and all things he thought impossible were. And in the end he would even invent his own death. And he would never know that he had invented it all."

To me, that says everything. This possibility of invention doesn't apply just to your writing or creative work but to the whole act of your life and the choices that you make. I think it's a very interesting premise. That's why I'm glad we used it in this film, and for the title.

HERE IS THE WORLD: THE NEW (OLD) ART PHOTOGRAPHY (PAUL GRAHAM AND MITCH EPSTEIN)
by Shelley Rice and Rob Slifkin
(May 3, 2012)

Paul Graham, The Present (Pace Gallery and Pace/MacGill, February 24–April 21, 2012)
By Shelley Rice

FROM MY PERSPECTIVE, April 2012 was a momentous photo moment, in a quietly profound sort of way. On 22nd Street in Chelsea last month, there were two exhibitions—one at Pace Gallery by Paul Graham and one at Sikkema Jenkins & Co. by Mitch Epstein—that announced the opening of what Graham (recent winner of the 2012 Hasselblad Foundation International Award in Photography) has called "a space for photography to work in the world." He obviously doesn't mean this literally, since millions of amateurs walk the streets of the twenty-first century snapping pictures and photographs have all but dominated the art world in recent years. What he means is more subtle, and as I recall I first heard him talk about it at a MOMA Forum a few years ago. These MOMA Forums, first convened by Roxana Marcoci and her colleagues in the Photography Department in February 2010, are a valuable addition to the New York scene. Bringing together a lot of different kinds of people from the community about three times a year, the soirées encourage discussion and debate between artists old and young, curators and critics from the United States and abroad, educators and academics. The viewpoints that swirl around during the two-hour forum (and the informal receptions before and after) pinpoint the differences, similarities, goals, and pet peeves of an increasingly diverse and global crowd. One division, however, has been especially clear, mainly because it was so deftly articulated during the early séances by Graham himself: the divergent approaches to the medium that define the practices of those whose formation was strictly photographic as opposed to those who came into the field through conceptual art, performance, or postmodernist strategies.

There were, naturally, arguments about this division: younger curators especially seemed to think that such a divide was no longer relevant, while those of us who've been in the field for a while (and that does include me) are loathe to simply turn our backs on the classic history of photography in our rush to embrace more contemporary ways of working. But Graham, as I recall, was particularly eloquent that evening in his defense of tradition: the extraordinary power of what Edward Weston called "photographic seeing," the expressive means invented and honed to perfection by imagemakers like Robert Frank, Harry Callahan, Garry Winogrand, and Lee Friedlander. An old-fashioned artist, Paul Graham studies the work of his forebears with obvious reverence, understanding the skill and vision that underlie what might seem like a simple image. His latest exhibition, *The Present*, was his homage to those who have climbed what he calls the "Himalayan range" of New York street photography.

Born in the United Kingdom, Graham now lives in the Big Apple—making him one of the latest in a procession of New York photographers—Frank, Lisette Model, André Kertész, Sylvia Plachy, among them—who use the camera to describe their adopted rather than their native environment. In a thought-provoking interview with Arthur Ou published in *Artforum* in March, the artist described the challenge he faced trying to pay tribute to the legacy of the street photographers from the 1960s and 1970s while moving their genre into a more contemporary place.[1] Graham's "present" is perceived in dialogue with the past captured and preserved by predecessors like Winogrand and Friedlander. With every picture he takes, of course, Graham's "now" slips into that past, to await the gaze of the future. This inevitable temporal flow defines what Graham describes as "the unique qualities of the medium, and its struggle to deal with time and life. I think those are our materials. Not film, not paper."

For a critic who sat on stoops with street photographers during the 1970s, such talk sounds familiar. I recognize the grappling with time

---

1   Arthur Ou, "Paul Graham Discusses his Exhibition at the Pace Gallery," *Artforum*, March 3, 2012.

and form and technique, with the metaphoric possibilities of momentary arrest in defining the ebb and flow of the city. Such engagement is not the same as a postmodernist strategy; immersed in time and space, an imagemaker like Graham speaks with a different mode of address than a Philip-Lorca diCorcia, a Gregory Crewdson, or a Jeff Wall, artists who set up situations or create directorial tableaux and who dominated the scene during the 1990s. Responsive, reactive, a classic street photographer attempts, as Graham describes it, to "dance with the Brownian motion of life," and in the process to visualize "the world as it is."

"I go out and try to find answers to the question 'How is the world?'" he explained in an article in *The Financial Times*. The world described in his exhibition at Pace Gallery consisted of sixteen diptychs and two triptych photographic works taken on New York City streets within the past few years. Twin images separated only by the briefest fraction of time, the "sibling photographs," as the press release calls them, allowed us to see "life and its *doppelganger* arrive and depart." The power and meaning of these large-scale color works (the diptychs measure twelve feet wide and the triptychs more than eighteen) were reinforced by the installation. Hung a few inches off the floor, the pictures gave the startling impression of a panorama unfolding right in front of and beside the viewer, at his/her height and in his/her continuous physical space.

Drawn into the action in this way, the spectator morphs into a pictorial subject—in the same way, of course, that all *flâneurs* are simultaneously *voyeurs* and participants in the spectacle of the city. Graham emphasizes that this is not ordinary black-and-white, 35-mm street photography. Not only are the pictures in color, but they are deliberately made with shallow focus, which he sees as truer to the way we actually see. So the viewer focuses on one pedestrian or sign or gesture, and then passes on to the next detail—or the adjacent picture, where suddenly time and change rearrange and reveal alternate readings or new events. People move out of the picture and disappear, while others remain immobile; sometimes they fall, or fall behind. Policemen appear to investigate legs protruding from behind a pole; trucks change position and in the process reveal formerly invisible city streets. Graham said that instead of "ossifying" the world into a singular moment, he sought to "invite time into the work, making it a quality you feel and experience." He is not the first photographer to use "sibling" images a frame or two apart. Around 1980, Eve Sonneman produced smaller color diptychs, with a range of subjects including still lives, that were shown at Castelli Graphics. But Sonneman's work grew out of conceptual art; her slight shifts in time focused on formal affinities and the enigma of photographic stop-time. Graham's duos, on the other hand, are about perception, about interiority, about the experience of being enveloped by the multiplicity of events in constant motion on city streets. They reanimate the freeze frames of Winogrand, allowing pedestrian traffic to flow like Stieglitz's clouds, never congealing into narrative form. Graham put it this way: In these pictures, he wrote, "you see how events unfold, not only externally but also internally, from the consciousness-flow as we go about our lives."

It's probably obvious that I am bowled over not only by Graham's images but also by his words, by the intelligence with which he enacts and then describes a creative process that quite literally updates the classic definitions of street photography—in the process allowing this hallowed form of expression to take its place with dignity among the large-scale prints that have dominated museum exhibitions in the past two decades. *The Present* was a love song to photography, but it was also an announcement that the practitioners of this medium can now dialogue, in full awareness, with artists who use the camera in other ways. As Graham says, he has taken his knowledge of recent photographic practice and "brought it into play with life-as-it-is, and this closes the circle." Bravo to him, and to his colleague Mitch Epstein, whose exhibition across the street (to be discussed by my colleague Rob Slifkin, an assistant professor at NYU's Institute of Fine Arts) added to my conviction that in fact classic photography is being born anew, right now in front of our eyes, once again.

Mitch Epstein, Great Trees
(Sikkema Jenkins and Co., March 16–April 14)
by Rob Slifkin

One of the most captivating capacities of a photograph is its facility in preserving a discrete moment in time. Paradoxically, this instantaneous historization becomes increasingly fascinating the further we are separated from the moment the picture was taken, the passage of time accentuating the differences between those frozen images and the continued existence of what they depict in the ever-changing world, turning every photograph, as Roland Barthes famously remarked, into a premonition of death. While I have likely walked past the towering English Elm that has grown in the northwest corner of Washington Square for over three centuries hundreds of times, and even stopped on occasion to admire its astonishingly wide trunk and wide-ranging canopy, I initially didn't recognize its portrayal when I saw it from across the gallery in Mitch Epstein's recent show of large black-and-white photographs of monumental trees in New York at Sikkema Jenkins & Co. in New York. No doubt much of this has to do with Epstein's brilliant lens work, which is able to broaden its view to capture an isolated portrait of the tree that no human eye immersed within the typically busting public park could even discern. Like almost all of the trees captured by Epstein's camera, the elm dominates the large print, its extensive and leafless branches determining where the photographer cropped his shot. Confined within one of the world's most imposing and congested environments, the trees of New York are unfortunately all too often forgotten or ignored. Epstein's meticulous portraits, in which the shallow patterns of recessed bark and the subtle tonal variations of different leaves are all rendered with a precise but never cold intensity, present these colossal beings as both fragile and awe-inspiring, and worth being concerned about.

Inspired by a list of 100 great trees assembled by the New York Parks Department, Epstein traveled throughout the five boroughs, the botanical landmarks taking him to neighborhoods and urban territories that are frequently forgotten and rarely represented. Potent symbols of both the endurance of nature and the frequent human folly that attempts to compete with it, Epstein's trees extend the photographer's longstanding interest in mankind's disruption of our environment. This theme was perhaps most clearly addressed in the justly celebrated series of photographs Epstein took between 2003 and 2007 collected in his book *American Power*, which documented the way in which the energy industry has affected the landscape of rural and suburban areas throughout the United States with a body of photographs whose resplendent, colorful detail and compositional wit encourage sustained viewing and contemplation. As in the *American Power* photographs, Epstein in his new work typically addresses this theme of human engagement with nature without recourse to the inclusion of actual people. Instead, it is the way the human environment clumsily perches itself upon and amidst the natural world that defines Epstein's approach to landscape. In the new series, the human artifactual impositions move to the margins, letting nature take center stage. (That said, these photographs, in their human-scale proportions and discrete subjects, are closer to portraits than landscapes, an aspect enhanced by the often anthropomorphic rendering of the trees, presenting some of them empathetically leaning to one side or focusing on their contorted, flesh-like bark and knobby protuberances.) Often Epstein's subjects, many of which ended up in the city as diplomatic gifts, are portrayed as stoic and noble prisoners, as in a White Oak in the Bronx. A complex tangle of its branches emerges out of a scrubby copse of trees whose own less brawny intertwinings find a geometrical resolution in the windows of an apartment building residing in the distance. Epstein's uncharacteristic use of black and white further urbanizes his subjects, giving them a tone corresponding to the cement and glass that surrounds them, while at that same time diminishing the clangorous palette of the city so that the trees might be equal if not superior to their environs.

While the tree portraits might appear as a drastic change from Epstein's previous output, trading in an ostensibly more overt engagement with social issues for an almost romantic appreciation of natural beauty, the social-environmental subject matter that motivated the *American Power* series is also present in these new works. As battered urban survivors, Epstein's trees become monuments to the ways in which human history and natural history converge. Most of the trees Epstein chose to depict are over one hundred years old and their survival within the rough and tumble environs of the five boroughs has left its traces on them in myriad ways: gnarled and stunted branches, constricted roots buckling under the stress of pavement, and most disturbing, the scars left by the incisions of countless lovers and vandals. Epstein has noted in a recent interview that traveling abroad has sensitized him to the relatively brief history of the United States. By focusing on trees planted in what has been one of the most artificial environments in the United States, many of his subjects can be seen as witnesses to the entire history of European occupation of the New World. One thinks of all the passersby who have crossed under the tree's shadow in Washington Square (which is, in fact, known as "The Hanging Tree"); or perhaps what the now suburban neighborhood in Staten Island looked like when the giant Eastern Cottonwood tree, which stands over the white clapboard condominiums like Diane Arbus's Jewish giant over his meek parents, was planted (a question whose historical intrigue is emphasized in the hazy light in which Epstein presents the towering behemoth). Epstein's new body of work, full of technical mastery and visual intelligence, exemplifies the sort of art being produced today by photographers like Rineke Dijkstra, Thomas Struth, and Jeff Wall that, while grounded in a fundamental respect and understanding of the medium, stands alongside any other form of artistic production. If Epstein's work represents this broader apotheosis of photography within the art world, these new photographs suggest an eerie premonition of a time when the medium's hard-won acceptance into the realms of high art might be complicated by the medium's still-vital documentary capacity. Despite their undeniable beauty and complexity (or perhaps because these qualities seem tinged with a degree of melancholy), I couldn't help but wonder if there may come a time when these photographs might appear in natural history museums or botanical archives as documents of now extinct species. Photography, it seems, can never wholly escape its vernacular and utilitarian purposes and the best photographs, like those of Epstein, make this burden into a virtue.

DAK'ART NEEDS A NEW FACE!
by Rob Perrée
(May 21, 2012)

Once again, my friend and colleague Rob Perrée, editor of *Kunstbeeld* in Amsterdam, has stepped up to the plate. He's been on the road recently, and he's sending us blog postcards to report on what he has seen: in this case, *Dak'Art 2012: Biennale de l'Art Africain Contemporain* in Dakar, Senegal.

AFTER FOUR DAYS of *Dak'Art* I can't deny it any longer: in its present form, the African Biennale is outdated. It has outlived its usefulness, it lacks urgency, and it needs a thorough revision—the sooner the better.

Dak'Art began in 1990 as a literary event. Four years later, it was changed into a meeting place for contemporary African artists and other professionals like critics, curators, theorists, etc. The participants—only African artists, living and working on the continent or abroad—were selected out of the hundreds of applications by the so-called commissioners. There was no artistic director who was responsible for the quality of the selected works and for the way they were installed and presented to the public. *Dak'Art* was not independent, it was a state event. Clerks at the Ministry of Culture had more influence than anybody else.

At that time contemporary African art was hardly visible and was just beginning its emergence into the global art scene. There was not much theory about it. African art critics and other art professionals were rare. Therefore, it is understandable that this ambivalent and controversial concept was chosen. You have to start somewhere, somehow.

Especially after the year 2000, contemporary African art made its way around the world through biennials and a few big exhibitions (such as *Africa Remix* at the Centre Pompidou in Paris). Its visibility grew fast. Perhaps there are still people—viewers and professionals—who have trouble accepting the importance of African expression, but not many. By now there is broad recognition of the quality and significance of contemporary art from this continent. Many articles and books are published about it. Several museums have hired African curators, including the Tate Modern in London. Especially through the professionalized infrastructure of South Africa, many artists "made it" internationally: among them William Kentridge, Guy Tillem, Veleko, Malick Sidibé, Samuel Fosso, Tracey Rose, Youssef Nabil, and Zwelethu Mthethwa.

Dak'Art seems to be blind to all this. The concept and organization of the Biennale are still the same. The government is using the same script as twenty years ago. The result is a rather small, poor, loveless exhibition installed in a building that has seen far better days. Of course, there were some nice touches: an extra invitational show dedicated to three known artists (Peter Clarke, Goddy Leye, and Berni Searle) and an exhibit highlighting the work of female architects (though only in two-dimensional, photographic version), a photographer and sculptor added some interest. But these extras hardly changed my opinion about *Dak'Art* as a whole.

I reserved at least part of every viewing day to the OFF program. At more than a hundred locations, solo shows, group shows, performances, and other events were organized. They were both good and bad, predictable and surprising. Sometimes the location was more interesting than the show. Outright amazing was the exhibition curated by the Institut Français. Le Manège was taken over by an installation of Serge Alain Nitegeka entitled *Obstacle 1*. Black painted planks barricaded the whole space and made it into a kind of claustrophobic prison. On the other hand, the structure looked far from solid, it seemed even vulnerable. Escape seemed possible. In the garden, on the walls of an artificial photo studio, hung a selection of Antoine Tempé's portraits of more or less known people from the world of art and culture. Glamorous, decadent, and personal, the pictures were sometimes moving.

Africa: See You, See Me: L'Influence Africaine sur la Photographie Contemporaine was to be seen at The Goethe Institute. Although the space was too small, most works survived that problem easily.

Absolutely stunning were the portraits of Patrizia Maïmouna Guerresi. Technically perfect, they blended irony with a refined mixture of tradition and modernity.

The next *Dak'Art* needs to be accessible to Africans and non-Africans. Confrontation is necessary for a healthy development. There has to be an artistic director who makes aesthetic quality their priority and who fights outdated nationalism and regionalism. And, very important, *Dak'Art* needs to be independent from the government. The new Minister of Culture, the singer Youssou N'Dour, knows how successful it can be to run your own business independently.

LORRAINE O'GRADY: NEW WORLDS
Alexander Gray Associates April 11–May 25, 2012
(May 24, 2012)

Lorraine O'Grady has been around for a long time. An active and avid feminist, a conceptual artist, photographer, writer, performer, and video artist, she has been at the forefront of discussions about African Americans and their relationships to the multiple pasts of our complex postcolonial society. I first came across her art in New York around 1980, when she pioneered ideas that would resonate with the groundbreaking works of women like Adrian Piper and, later, Carrie Mae Weems, Deb Willis, and Lorna Simpson. Juxtaposing two black-and-white images, the faces of contemporary African American acquaintances next to reproductions of sculptural portraits carved in ancient Egypt, she put forth the evidence of genealogy. Like writer Martin Bernal, the author of the book *Black Athena,* O'Grady claimed the African heritage of that shining civilization, a pedigree written into the genetic traces of her race and made visible centuries later by the medium of photography.

This was startling work thirty years ago, and though her latest Chelsea gallery show is quite different, it is still deeply rooted in the experience of the Black female body. The *Body/Ground* series of photomontages, conceived in 1991 and reformatted for this exhibition in 2012, uses that body to describe, confront, and interrogate the condition of the Western landscape. Born in Boston to Jamaican parents, O'Grady was one of the first artists, along with Ana Mendieta, to articulate the complicated conditions of cultural stability, hybridity, and displacement experienced by those who take root in a land not their own. The colonized body, for instance, is the "ground" out of which *The Fir-Palm* tree (an odd cross between a New England fir and Caribbean palm tree) grows upward against a cloudy sky. "My attitude about hybridity," the artist has said, "is that it is essential to understanding what is happening here. People's reluctance to acknowledge it is part of the problem...I'm really advocating for the kind of miscegenated *thinking* that's needed to deal with what we've already created here." The landscape which all of us inhabit today is, from her point of view, the amalgamation of the colonized body and the soil to which it has been transplanted.

Landscape (Western Hemisphere) is, in fact, the title of her most recent work, an eighteen-minute video that once again weaves nature and culture, Africa and the West, into an inextricable web. It is a web, of course, grown from the Black body but inscribed and circumscribed, exoticized and eroticized, by the Others. The dark video resembles a dense forest, a thick underbrush blowing in the wind, accompanied by the chirping of birds and jungle sounds. The luxurious, curvaceous foliage fills the screen, blocking our vision. For almost twenty minutes the camera doesn't move, the viewpoint is stationery and immobilized, and action is described only through the vagaries of sound. The rustle of the winds might turn into a howl; the chatter of the forest grows louder or softer, excited or serene as one stares into what seems like mysterious and impermeable darkness. It takes a long time to realize that the dense undergrowth bending and waving in the wind is, in fact, the artist's own curly hair.

The preoccupation with kinky hair is, of course, well known in African American circles, and has been a fertile theme for contemporary artists as diverse as Betty Saar and the comedian Chris Rock. Straight or curly? For artists concerned with identity politics, the question is hardly naïve. It has instead become the nexus point, indeed the battleground, for opposing definitions of physical beauty: the choice is between "going natural" or succumbing to the standards set by the genetic endowments of white Americans. But of course this is not simply a question of style, since the "natural" Black woman's hair—like her body—was constructed by colonialists as the site of the primal, the untamed, the erotic energies of the race. For Baudelaire, for instance, his mulatto mistress's hair was "the oasis where I dream, the gourd/from which I gulp the wine of memory," a memory as wild as it was exotic:

> For torpid Asia, torrid Africa
> —the wilderness I thought a world away—

survive at the heart of this dark continent...
As other souls set sail to music, mine,
O my love! Embarks on your redolent hair.
—Charles Baudelaire, *The Head of Hair*, from *The Flowers of Evil*
 in Baudelaire (New York: Everyman's Library, Alfred A. Knopf,
1993), p. 45 (trans. Richard Howard)

Under these circumstances, of course, O'Grady's identification of her own head, not only with the "dark continent" described by Baudelaire as "a world away" but also with the landscapes of the West, becomes charged with both ironies and deep-seated cultural truths that implicate all of us living in the postcolonial environment. As Baudelaire discovered, intimacy and distance have become inseparable. For three decades, the most personal details have morphed to embody and embrace the most political realities in Lorraine O'Grady's art. She has carved out her own hybrid territory in this Western hemisphere inhabited by strangers who have become neighbors and who together need to recognize "what we've already created here."

THE 2012 PEN WORLD VOICES FESTIVAL: "GOOD LITERATURE IS LIBERATING"
(May 31, 2012)

THIS YEAR MARKED the eighth annual World Voices Festival of International Literature, sponsored by PEN America. The festival was held in venues all around New York City—in libraries, universities, galleries, museums, cafes, poetry clubs, bookstores, and concert halls—from April 30 to May 6. I've been a member of PEN for at least twenty years, and the organization is one of my favorites; I am proud to be part of this community. Obviously, sharing membership with famous writers like Paul Auster, E. L. Doctorow, and Joan Didion is good for the ego, but that's not really the point. Founded ninety years ago, PEN has branches in 101 different countries, and it takes its mission very seriously. This is precisely why I wanted to devote some space on this blog to the issues that are always raised at PEN meetings, conferences, or events where American writers debate, passionately and continuously, the relationship between art and life.

Susan Sontag, who was President of PEN/America, served for years as the public face of the national organization's commitment to political as well as literary issues. PEN is a watchdog for freedom of expression and assumes responsibility for the welfare of writers at home and abroad. The organization intervenes globally in cases where authors are imprisoned or suppressed; it has been active in promoting controversial figures for international prizes and gaining recognition for people writing under conditions of hardship and censorship. Recently, in the New York branch, there has been outreach toward local communities where reading and writing skills are disadvantaged; published authors work with children and adults to promote the telling of tales coming from diverse cultural points of view. The multifaceted relationships between aesthetics and ideology are always hotly debated topics at PEN gatherings, but they've been especially pertinent since the attacks of September 11, 2001. The destruction of the World Trade

Center forced writers in the United States to re-examine their political responsibilities, and it also pushed PEN to redefine its understanding of the functions of literature. The PEN World Voices Festival was one of the first and most important responses to our collective trauma.

It became clear to everyone, after that day, that American writers had been living in a bubble of isolation, and by 2003 we were becoming increasingly cut off from artists in other parts of the world because of new political realities. The World Voices Festival was established, first and foremost, to reverse this situation by inviting authors from many countries to New York City, showcasing their work, and asking them to interact not only with their American colleagues but also with a large public. Every year there are invited writers who are denied visas, either by their home country or by the United States government; every year the organization attempts to diplomatically work out some kind of an arrangement that will make outreach possible. In a similar vein, about ten years ago PEN decided to place more emphasis on its translation program. It scouts books from all over the world and gives translation grants that make possible the publication of writings—essays, novels, poems, short stories, or nonfiction books—coming from countries like Tibet and Iraq as well as national groups like Native Americans. These translations, and the issues surrounding them, play a major role in the World Voices Festival too.

All of this is intended as backdrop to my main point: that the American chapter of PEN has managed to use literature as a way to bring people together and to ensure that diverse voices—national or international—are heard. Most importantly, this outreach in itself is perceived as a political act, regardless of the content of the book or poem. Left wing or right wing, politically correct, incorrect, or apolitical, writers have a right to be heard and all people must be free to "speak." The diverse languages and literary traditions that make writing so much less portable than art—visual imagery can of course be more universally understood as it moves from festival to fair, from book to blog, from temporary exhibition to museum than a book written in an unintelligible tongue—have forced writers to think deeply about their social obligations to communicate. Rather than simply critique institutions for their myopia and their closed canons, PEN has decided to open up the floodgates and let the party begin. "In the course of our eighty-year history, we hope that our mission has become clear: we seek to present the best of national and international literature and by so doing we adamantly focus on reinforcing the importance of the premise that freedom of expression is the foundation of meaningful existence and the essence of brave and great art," wrote Laszlo Jakab Orsos (Director of the Festival), Salman Rushdie (Chair), and Peter Godwin (President of PEN).

I must admit that this is my kind of politics. Though beautiful in principle, of course, the real question is: how does this utopian idea play out in the context of the festival, which ultimately is a bouillabaisse of meetings, readings, panels, dialogues, concerts, and events aimed at expanding knowledge of international literature in the public sphere. Herta Müller, Nobel Prize-winning Romanian novelist, was one of the main speakers, reiterating the address she gave in Stockholm upon accepting her award. Salman Rushdie gave the "Arthur Miller Freedom to Write" Lecture; Russian writer Ludmila Ulitskaya, Egyptian-born journalist Mona Eltahaway, Irish poet Hugo Hamilton, Swiss writer Noelle Revaz, and Japanese author Masatsugu Ono as well as writers from Harlem and the Black Arts Movement gave presentations. Former French Resistance fighter and renowned scholar Edgar Morin was scheduled to speak (but couldn't make it at the last minute). The "Dialogue" series included long and excellent interviews with novelists Margaret Atwood and Jennifer Egan as well as playwright Tony Kushner, who was also a featured speaker at the oddest event of the festival: the opening night at the Metropolitan Museum, which paired a concert by the Kronos Quartet with the words of Kushner, Iranian graphic novelist and filmmaker Marjane Satrapi, and Palestinian journalist Rula Jebreal. Intended to explore the relationships between music and words (there was, in fact, an entire day devoted to John Cage during the Festival too), the strange evening—during the course of which Jebreal complained about Mitt Romney's politics, Satrapi rejected language and preferred to groove on the peak experience of being seated between an American Jew and a Palestinian in New York City, and only Tony Kushner created and read an amazing poem about loss and absence in time with the music—instead proved how trivial words (no matter how politically diverse and correct the speakers) seemed next to the brilliant "universal" language of the Kronos Quartet.

All this being said, the Festival was interesting as it always is. The audience learned about Occupy Wall Street, life in the Panopticon, the impact of the digital world on storytelling, the Arab Spring, and always, especially, the creative process of writing: whatever kind the writer might do. One thing that is particularly intriguing to me about PEN is that it does not discriminate for or against various kinds of writing. Playwrights, poets, journalists, graphic novelists, storytellers, translators, critics, essayists, and nonfiction specialists (in the humanities as well as science and sports) are all part of the mix. While Salman Rushdie might fill bigger auditoriums because of his novels, most writers do a number of different things, and while fiction might be a privileged medium within the organization there are still no divisions between "high" and "low" culture like those that exist in the art world (primarily, of course, because of elite venues and commodity prices). Because these categories were on my mind that week, the experience of the Festival colored my response to the beautiful photographs by Tim Hetherington on view at Yossi Milo Gallery in Chelsea at the same time.

Hetherington, of course, was a photojournalist, born in Liverpool, who worked mostly in West Africa and the Middle East. He partnered with writers and filmmakers throughout his professional life, which ended tragically last year in Libya. The exhibition highlighted works from Liberia taken during the civil war in 2005 and others focusing on the American troops stationed in eastern Afghanistan's Korengal Valley from 2007 to 2008. Intensely focused on human beings in situations of extreme stress, the pictures capture a range of responses to grief, loss, love, and betrayal. All of the photographs were originally made within a photojournalistic context, and Hetherington's archive in fact became part of the Magnum collection after his death. But of course, in the White Box of an art gallery, the digital files he created (because, as he said, "with witnessing comes responsibility") morph into large, beautiful C prints: the current gold standard of the art world. Transmuted in this way, the images captured by Hetherington—and shown here posthumously in the first major exhibition of Hetherington's work in the United States—take their place within the "universal" language of art fairs, auctions, festivals, and museums. The mobility of photography—its ability to rend both space and time portable—is here expanded by the malleability of the medium's language, from a journalistic statement into an artistic one, even after the imagemaker's own death.

Certainly, this is not the first time this transmutation has happened—in fact, such morphing between popular and high art is becoming a trend, as celebrated pictures by French photographer Luc Delahaye can attest. But of course, the separation between these modes of communication—between journalistic and aesthetic expression—is something that was promoted by Alfred Stieglitz while establishing modern art in America at the turn of the last century. Intended as a means to separate populist art and mass communication from the elite expressions of his peers, the wall Stieglitz built was never acknowledged or emulated by Europeans. André Kertész worked for magazines and showed the same images in galleries; so did Henri Cartier-Bresson, Germaine Krull, and others. We in the photo world in the United States might just now be catching up to them and to the writers of PEN.

The amazing Tony Kushner, who writes plays, screenplays, essays, and poems, insisted during his "Dialogue" at the New School University that he doesn't confuse art and politics, though he is active in both. Political activism, essay writing, and theater are different methods, he asserted. "My power as an artist is an indirect power," he stated, "The ideas in an artwork are riddles that must have a corollary in the human. Theater and democracy both give the gift of empathy, and because of that they both build community." By virtue of precisely that gift of empathy, the strength of the "human" so deeply perceived in Liberians and American soldiers alike, Tim Hetherington's photographs, whatever their origins, have earned their place in the Yossi Milo Gallery and wherever else they may travel in the world of art.

PHOTOGRAPHY AT THE ARAB CROSSROADS: POSTCARD FROM ABU DHABI
(June 5, 2012)

O N THE 13TH of May, a group of about twenty photography curators, critics, artists, and historians from the Middle East, the United States, and Europe met in Abu Dhabi at the Intercontinental Hotel for the first "Photography at the Arab Crossroads" colloquium. Sponsored by New York University's Abu Dhabi campus and the Arab Image Foundation (AIF) based in Beirut, the conference was convened by Shamoon Zamir (NYU Abu Dhabi) and Issam Nassar (Illinois State University). In the introduction circulated to participants, Zamir and Nassar wrote that the "colloquium is conceived as the first of what we hope will become a series of colloquia or workshops focused on the histories and forms of photography from the Arab world. While the primary focus will be on photography produced within the Arab world, the region is also conceived broadly and fluidly and is imagined as a cultural crossroads…The broad goal of the workshops is to establish a network of scholars and institutional partnerships that will enable the development of an ongoing plan of research and publication aimed at addressing both historical and theoretical gaps in our understanding of photography from and about the Arab world."

Toward this end, Zamir and Nassar, and Zeina Arida (Director of the Arab Image Foundation) invited a series of speakers and guests that included historians like Stephen Sheehi, editors and archivists Karen Davis and Jean-Gabriel Leturcq, artists like Yasser Alwan and Tarek Al Ghoussein, curators Catherine David and Martha Weiss and NYU Faculty like me, Fred Ritchin, and filmmaker/photographer Joanne Savio. Two solid days were spent in conversation; there was only a little time to see Saadiyat Island (future home of the Abu Dhabi Louvre and Guggenheim Museums as well as the NYU Abu Dhabi campus), the Emirates Palace Hotel (where one can buy gold from a vending machine), and of course the Sheikh Zayed Grand Mosque (which holds up to 40,000 people). Zamir ran a tight ship and insisted that the event present an overview of the issues facing those of us involved in this increasingly important subject. Nassar and Sheehi gave papers on the history and theory of photography in the region, while Arida, Mark Westmoreland, and others described various aspects of the AIF and MEPPI (the Middle East Photography Preservation Institute). The background from the first day set the stage for artist presentations by Alwan, Susan Meiselas, and Nadia Benchallal on the second day, as well as curatorial explanations of upcoming exhibitions (Weiss, from the Victoria and Albert Museum in London) and general issues involved in researching, writing about and exhibiting this material and all "off center modernities." (David) Between presentations, there was much lively dialogue and dissension, which was fascinating due to the varied backgrounds, situations, and professions of the participants.

I think everyone present agreed that the high point was precisely this conviviality and debate. All of us were grateful for the chance to meet (or reencounter) so many knowledgeable people from so many different countries and to analyze these timely concerns from such varied points of view—either during the open forums or later among ourselves over coffee or meals. The politically correct, the essentialist, the isolationist, and the cosmopolitan: all of these types of remarks surfaced during the lively discussions, and once on the table they could be examined, rejected, accepted, or morphed into premises and possibilities more agreeable to everyone. The most heated debates, of course, were over the definition of an "Arab" photographer in the twenty-first century: is this someone who was born and remains within the region, or is such a definition too restrictive? (We noticed, of course, that if we upheld this restriction none of the artists—in fact almost none of the speakers—who had presented work at the conference could be invited back to speak or to publish their work in any resulting books!) Does the idea of a cultural crossroads mandate an open attitude toward those born in the Middle East who left for long or short periods of time (like Yasser Alwan or Walid Raad, as well as Issam Nassar himself), those from other countries or cultures who've done significant work in the region (like Susan Meiselas) or those born elsewhere because their parents emigrated, but whose work is about retracing their heritage within the Arab world (Nadia Benchallal, born of Algerian parents in

France)? Evidently, this first colloquium was convened with an open attitude toward the mobility of twenty-first century life, and after much-heated discussion, the group voted to leave the initial definition in place for the next workshop.

Similarly, Zamir posed questions about the organization of subsequent colloquia and books. How does one choose categories for contemporary research that are not based on previous Orientalist or Western-centered attitudes? This was perhaps the most critically delicate issue, since of course "Calls for Papers" have a way of pushing research or artistic expression in certain predetermined directions. The decision was made to leave the categories very general—Art Photography, Documentary, Vernacular Imagery, and Collections—in the hope that these very wide fields can be filled up with many different points of view, types of research, art, and curatorial projects that provide multifaceted regional perspectives on these essentially universal aspects of the photographic medium. After two days, we did leave—exhausted, but with a plan—feeling like something important had occurred in Abu Dhabi, and knowing that all of us were grateful to have taken part in laying the foundations of a project that will change the visual landscape of the globe yet again.

INTENSE PROXIMITY: AN ARCHAEOLOGY OF SPACE AND TIME
Palais de Tokyo, Paris
(June 15, 2012)

THIS IS WHAT I wrote in my notebook upon leaving *La Triennale 2012: Intense Proximity*, curated by Okwui Enwezor (Artistic Director) with Mélancie Bouteloup, Abdellah Karroum, Émile Renard, and Claire Staebler, at the Palais de Tokyo in Paris: *This exhibition is the future, and at the same time, it is the end of the world.*

This impression was certainly sparked by the first artwork I saw on entering the newly renovated Palais: Peter Buggenhout's *The Blind Leading the Blind.* An enormous, heavy, and dark sculpture made out of metal, rubber, canvas, wood, and fabrics, coated with blood, resin, and dust and hanging from the ceiling, the piece is described in the wall label as a "monumental disaster." This hyperbolic description is, in fact, perfect: I felt like I was standing under an airborne shipwreck. I am not entirely sure that Buggenhout's piece is actually meant to be part of the show, but it set a tone that resonated with the powerful and altogether disconcerting renovation of the Palais (by Anne Lacaton and Jean-Philippe Vassal). By the time I had "descended" into the lower levels of the exhibition, I was sure I had somehow crossed over and was traversing the scenography for the movie *Blade Runner.*

I begin my postcard this way because I want to emphasize that the Triennale is not simply an art exhibition. It is, rather, an *experience* of art, lots of art, in a context that feels like an archaeological expedition through space and time. A stage set filled with high drama, the show does not aim to set off discrete objects or highlight artists, trends, or movements. Rather, as Enwezor wrote in his introduction, it aspires to be "a zone of encounter… in which contemporary realities become immanent, visible, present…(as) a field of contending discourses."[1]

---

1 Okwui Enwezor, *Intense Proximity : An Anthology of the Near and the Far* (Paris: Centre national des arts plastiques, 2012).

Moving down and through the complex labyrinths of the building, with its unfinished walls and its stripped surfaces that boldly display their historical layers, the viewer sails through time as well as space. The flashy and extravagant convergences of sculptures and paintings, installations and media, sound works and films glowing in the dark are experienced as kaleidoscopic in nature. Expanding outward into global space and moving both forward and backward in time, filled with works by artists living and dead, young and old, from many continents and traditions, the exhibition EMBODIES rather than explains the notion of "intense proximity."

Okwui calls this the "politics of anti-difference:" the collapse of the distance between the Self and Other, the recognition that now we live with disjunction, in "the thickness of ethnocentric and identity-based processes." The exhibition begins with works by Marcel Griaule, Claude Lévi-Strauss, Jean Rouch, and Pierre Verger: classic ethnographers who traveled through space to bring news of cultural differences to their neighbors back home. For Enwezor, ethnographic fieldwork and curatorship have much in common. But with the collapse of spatial and temporal distances taken for granted by earlier generations, the contemporary curator becomes an ethnographer by definition—and fieldwork begins at home, with the study of the stranger who, through migration, slavery, colonialism, and tourism, has now become a neighbor. The exhibition, essentially, stages this collapse.

Everything is in motion in the galleries of the Palais de Tokyo. This is an exhibition, and a world picture, with no center or still point, only continually shifting parameters and peripheries bound together by fences ("frontiers") designed by Daniel Buren. Time, space, and generations are seen as contexts as well as potentialities; and all of us are tourists in someone else's reality when we cross boundaries defined by geography, race, class, or culture. African American women like Lorraine O'Grady and Carrie Mae Weems relate their experiences, respectively, to ancient Egypt and nineteenth century American slavery. Timothy Asch's film from South America, showing an *Ax Fight* among Yanomami Indians, is juxtaposed with Helen Levitt's record of children bashing each other in play on the streets of New York in the late 1940s. The German Lothar Baumgarten lived for a while in Brazil, and Michael Buthe (also from Germany) learned from the

North Africans and American Terry Atkins from the Inuit Eskimos of Alaska. Turkish-born Koken Ergun's video installation documents the subcultures and ceremonies of Philipino workers in Tel Aviv, while Israeli writer Ariella Azoulay describes, through drawings and texts, the marginalization and effacement of Palestinian history in the national archives.

Thomas Struth and Guy Tillim take ironic looks at the exoticism of tropical paradises in their large color photographs, while Luc Delahaye finds a *nature morte* of war and death in Libya. Antonio Muntadas, Thomas Hirschhorn, and Alfredo Jaar interrogate the ways in which translation and media deflect and disable our ability to empathize and communicate while magnifying our terror of the unknown and each other. *Fear Eats the Soul,* in fact, is transcribed on one of the T-shirts pressed in the silkscreen printing workshop space of Rirkrit Tirivanija; and T-shirts, along with every other form of quotidian object, fill the ephemeral installation space of Georges Adéagbo. Born in Benin, Meschac Gaba married his blond Dutch girlfriend, and in his *Marriage Room* documents the experience in detail and shows us the cross-pollination of objects and people such a union makes possible. The young Polish artist Aneta Grzeszykowska's terrific video—called *Headache*—was only one of a few fine feminist contributions from Eastern Europe; the older pioneer Ewa Partum also stood out in this context. Two of my favorite artists—El Anatsui and Nick Hlobo, born in Ghana and South Africa, respectively—have works in the show, as do Chris Ofili and Huma Bhabha, Annette Messager, Wangechi Mutu, and Yto Barrada, Hassan Khan and Trinh T. Minh-ha.

The list might seem endless, but this is just the beginning. There are, in fact, 109 projects in the 5,000 square meters of exhibition space available in the renovated Palais de Tokyo. All told, I think I spent roughly seven hours in the building, and the Triennale continues in other Parisian venues like Bétonsalon—Centre d'art et de recherché and Centre d'art contemporain d'Ivry-le Crédac. Overwhelming? Chaotic? A bit, yes, but ultimately that is in fact the point. There are no neat edges or tidy *-isms* in this show. There are only endless artists and images rubbing shoulders and trying to coexist in a space—real and conceptual—whose delineations are not, and may never be, clear. All in all, the 2012 Triennale is both a cornucopia of plenty and a deeply unnerving vision of dissonance, and I remain committed to my first impression: for me, it represents, simultaneously, the future and the end of the world. As I see it, Enwezor's ability to envision and shape such a complex and irresolvable experience is, indeed, a major achievement.

DOCUMENTA 13: WALID RAAD, ARABIAN NIGHTS, AND THE PITFALLS OF PILGRIMAGES
(June 22, 2012)

ALONG WITH THOUSANDS of others, I made the pilgrimage to Kassel, Germany, this year, to attend the opening festivities of Documenta 13. There were, of course, obvious reasons to go—first and foremost the chance to see Carolyn Christov-Bakargiev's impressive show. Sprawling all over Kassel and beyond (e.g., Kabul), the show includes work by over 200 artists (living and dead) and collectives from fifty countries and aims to reveal how art both reflects and interacts with the world. Open without being ideological, the show includes a number of pieces specifically about wars and current events. But these are accompanied by other types of expressions: for example, works by Song Dong, Theaster Gates, Susan Hiller, and Zanele Muholi, that focus on different aspects of the art/life continuum. Starting at the Fridericianum and moving outward to public spaces, parks, and train stations, the exhibition's opening days attracted thousands of colleagues and friends from all over the world (which was, of course, another reason to go).

But in fact it was really the invitation of my friend Walid Raad that persuaded me to make the trek to Germany. Like me, the Lebanese-born artist lives in New York, and we teach at adjacent universities. We get together when possible, and recently I started pestering him about doing an interview—specifically, a session where he and I discuss the work of artists (like him) who do extensive scholarly research in order to prepare for visual projects. To flesh out my understanding of his process, he was anxious for me to see his exhibition in Kassel, the culmination of five years of thought and refinement. Entitled "Scratching on Things I Could Disavow: A History of Art in the Arab World," the show was accompanied by a series of live performances by the artist which were among the hot tickets in Kassel during opening week. The works on view became, in this context, springboards for, and embodiments of, Raad's concepts and ruminations. This was a Duchampian act for the twenty-first century, but instead of a Large Glass and an accompanying book (Notes and Projects), we had a multimedia display (including photographs and video, drawings, texts, collages, sculptures, and models as well as paintings and prints) accompanied by the explications of the moving body.

Walid's performances were so popular, and so crowded, that extra shows had to be scheduled, which made downtime for an interview impossible. But his presentation—and it must be said that I'd seen a previous version, a slide lecture at the Institute of Fine Arts in March, so I'd had some time to think about the ideas—raised a lot of issues I'd like to discuss. Also, of course, since we are friends, I'd heard about these projects over the years as they unfolded in his mind and then transformed themselves into images. It is precisely this transformation that interests me about Raad, who has a tendency (he does have a PhD in Visual and Cultural Studies from the University of Rochester) to do enormous amounts of reading, looking, and archival research in order to arrive at a spare or surprising visual symbol: a field of blue, a green dot, a painted splotch of red. That *Ur-* image, whatever it is, then gives rise to other images, schemas, and words, often lots of them, like those delivered in Kassel. Installations and performances grow up around a visual nugget, in other words, reversing the usual order of concept-based work. Is this indeed conceptual art—or rather visual thinking? The difference seems important to me.

The other thing that interests me about Raad's art is its slippery slope between fact and fiction, which of course has become his trademark since the days of the Atlas Group. (This trait goes beyond art making. When I come away from a lunch with him, I am never sure if anything he's told me is literally true—though it must be said that I'm always thoroughly convinced while he's spinning his yarns. Over the years I've learned to take this ambiguity in stride.) Raad rode into the art world on the wave of Archive Art; one of the most interesting of the artists included in this trendy group, he used his youthful experience of the wars in Lebanon to drive a wedge between concrete evidence and the manipulation and reception of data. But there was a moment when the exigencies of this version of conceptual art began to constrict his creative process, and he started working with ideas that were more far reaching, amorphous, and profound. Instead of focusing on truth and falsehood, he began obsessing over Jalal Toufic's theory of "surpassing disasters." Described in the book *Forthcoming*, a "surpassing disaster" is one that literally affects tradition by making it "withdraw," by rendering artworks "unavailable to vision" and to the perception of sensitive artists.[1] In other words, rather than deconstructing archival materials and intellectual strategies, Walid has decided to frame the history of Art in the Arab World by chronicling the inevitability of its material, aesthetic, and conceptual withdrawal. Having grown up during a time of civil war and terrorism, exiled by violence from his home and family at an early age, Raad's own surpassing interest is in the effects of deep trauma: not only on "truth" but on the human spirit. How can an artist express what happens to people, to places, to societies, to civilizations when their experiences are so profoundly negative that normal paths to communication, empathy, and sharing are blocked? The project in Kassel is about this state of affairs and its consequences.

Since we are discussing Walid Raad, of course, these consequences are never spelled out in a literal way. Topical political exegesis is not his style, though it is the focus of a number of projects on view in Kassel (like Rabih Mroué's fascinating installation and performance, *The Pixelated Revolution*, about cell phones and violence in Syria). Instead, political and social truths are transformed into images in Raad's work and spun as tales told by cooks or dancers and perhaps embellished by psychics. This is, quite literally, mythmaking with historical pretensions and a theatrical flair. It is important to note that when discussing this project in 2009, Raad mentioned that its final form might in fact be a play, a *pièce de theatre*, as the French would say. Seen in this way, the gallery becomes a world stage in the Shakespearean sense, a labyrinth of related projects that tell stories within stories, like the sprawling tales of the Arabian Nights.

The master storyteller William Kentridge also has a marvelous new piece (produced with Peter L. Galison) at Documenta 13. *The Refusal of Time* is a *tour de force* within the dilapidated spaces of the old train station. But Kentridge's all-engulfing style, his way of piling up films, animations, sculpture, and music in a noisy aggregate, bears no

---

[1] Jalal Toufic, *Forthcoming* (Berkeley, CA: Atelos, 2000).

resemblance to Raad's minimal arrangement of interpenetrating theatrical "screens" like those that dot the stage sets of Jean Genet. Upon entering the space, the spectator encounters a wall, a futuristic barrier of flashing lights that resembles nothing so much as a very high-end corporate presentation. Illustrated with what looks like a large-scale schematic drawing punctuated by video images, texts, and visual documents, the tableau charts new art initiatives like the Artist Pension fund. Tracking the Dubai Branch's complex relationship to the burgeoning infrastructures for the visual arts taking shape in the Arabian Gulf, the trail ends up at the doorstep of men trained in Israeli military intelligence. The "map," with its constantly shifting (and hard to grasp) images and its data impossible to read, creates a claustrophobic vision of the symbiotic entanglement between politics, conflict, and culture in the Arab world—and far beyond. It sets the stage for the other five projects on view, scenarios described in separate spaces, which Raad describes as "artworks and stories shaped by encounters on this ground with individuals, institutions, economies, concepts and forms."

These encounters take place as people living in this closed-circuit attempt to participate in their new culture. But their access—to their peers, their predecessors, their institutions, their customary modes of expression—is always denied. The "surpassing disaster" of war in the Middle East has withdrawn their tradition from them, and the viewer moves from scene to scene to experience this state of affairs. Artists' projects (like the Atlas Group exhibition on view) suddenly shrink to 1/100th of their original size. Colors are no longer available for aesthetic expression in the future, since they have taken refuge in corporate logos, and paintings lack reflections. The names of historical predecessors, earlier artists in Lebanon, don't show up in archives but can only be retrieved, inaccurately, by telepathy. A spectator attempting to enter a new museum of modern art in an Arab city is unable to proceed: he "hits a wall," so to speak. With his entry blocked, he declares the world flat and is removed to a psychiatric facility. All of these "scenarios," of course, are visualized by sculptures, or paintings, or prints. The inaccessible entrances are made manifest by shifting mirages of architectural spaces, the shrunken photos are too small to read, and the contrasts between splashes of spray paint and the flat hues of corporate prints become stark. The spectator "on the ground" begins to experience this world out of joint—which, surely, is Raad's point.

There's another performance work in Kassel right now, a joyful piece by Tino Sehgal. The spectator enters a pitch-black room, filled with singing, dancing, clapping, and people. In her review in *The New York Times*, Roberta Smith called Sehgal's work the "beating heart" of Documenta 13, and I can see why. At the risk of spoiling any future viewer's experience, I just want to say that the intensity of the human contact that occurs when the lights go up is both surprising and overwhelming. It is just that human contact which is unavailable to the poor souls in Walid Raad's airtight world. And since the circuits described in scene one encompass the globe, this projected future must belong to all of us, everywhere, no matter how hard we try to "disavow" it. The pilgrimage to Kassel suddenly makes us players not only within Raad's *pièce de theatre* but also within the relentless wheel of culture, the flat world from which it grows.

(And, by the way, I haven't given up on that interview. Stay tuned.)

WELCOME TO PHOTOVILLE!
by Shelley Rice and Lorie Novak
(June 29, 2012)

"WELCOME TO OUR little town in the shadow of the Brooklyn Bridge. What once thrived as a bustling harbor has been reborn as the glorious Brooklyn Bridge Park, and the temporary home of Brooklyn's newest settlement: *Photoville*. A photographic 'village' built entirely out of freight containers, in homage to the Brooklyn waterfront's storied past, *Photoville* was born out of a simple question: how to create a large-scale, mobile, photographic showcase, that challenges the role of visitor as a passive visual consumer."

This is the introduction to the small catalog accompanying the latest "destination" in New York photography, which runs from June 22 to July 1, 2012. A grassroots effort, made with love and a lot of volunteers, *Photoville* represents the kind of funky, local, and alternative event that New Yorkers like to create and can't wait to attend. Organized by United Photo Industries with the help of a number of sponsors and friends, the "pop-up village" consists of a 1,000-foot long "fence" (covered with pictures printed on photographic mesh by Duggal), a plethora of solo exhibitions in freight containers on the uplands of Pier 3 by artists like Wyatt Gallery, Bruce Gilden, Sim Chi Yin, and Li Hao as well as shows curated by *The New York Times*, Magnum, Conveyor Arts, and local art schools like SVA and the Parsons School of Design (among others). A beer garden, lectures, nighttime projections, workshops, food trucks, and even a dog run round out the list of "delights to suit all tastes and dispositions" at this unique photo venue in the midst of what has to be one of the most beautiful parks in the Big Apple. The weather was gorgeous this weekend, so we spent a lot of time looking at images, hanging out with friends, and just enjoying the sights on the East River.

Lorie Novak, my friend and colleague in the Photography and Imaging Department at New York University, is presenting an installation called "Random Interference" in one of the freight containers. Consisting of front sections of *The New York Times* collected over many years as well as a live randomized sequence of projected images, hers is a complex, thought-provoking, and timely contribution to the exhibition. Making an attempt to translate a three-dimensional installation into the virtual world of this blog, we originally presented the following artist's statement with an installation photo and a video from *Random Interference*.

Lorie Novak: Artist Statement

Random Interference explores the afterlife of images and the experience of looking at photographs as a disruptive encounter. Image fragments from my *Photographic Interference* project are randomly juxtaposed in a continuously changing sequence mimicking our experience of encountering photographs both online and offline.

In all my projects, I use different technologies of representation to recontextualize, recycle, and reuse media imagery, historical photographs, family snapshots (my own and those of others), self-portraits, travel photographs, and audio recordings. Pulling from these archives, I explore memory and transmission, how to visualize absence, and the sociopolitical meanings of photographs. I question how photographs affect how we know and what we know, how personal remembrances and cultural recall intersect, and how photographs influence storytelling and history. These issues have been at the core of my photographs, installations, and web work since the late 1980s. In my constructed photographs and installations, I use scanned newspaper and magazine images. I grab other photos from the Internet. Folders in file cabinets and folders in my computer contain hundreds of images. The images play like filmstrips in my mind.

In the late 1990s, I was clipping more photographs from the newspapers than usual. As it became clear in March 1999 that NATO was going to bomb Serbia, I decided to save the front section of *The New York Times* once the bombing started. My idea was to have a stack of newspapers that signified a war. When the cease-fire was signed, a true resolution had not been reached, so I kept collecting. The World Trade

Center was attacked, and I kept collecting. I have not stopped.

Temporarily relocated from my studio to a shipping container at Photoville are close to 5,000 sections of *The New York Times*. Photographs of atrocity are everywhere. It is hard to look and hard to look away. Images get under my skin. In making artworks that use and reference this media landscape, I want to cause a rupture in our expectations and speak to our difficult, confusing, and dangerous times where media and photography have simultaneously lost and gained credibility. I am both imagemaker and consumer.

JUST (A FEW MORE) KIDS: GEORGE DUREAU, ROBERT MAPPLETHORPE, AND COMPANY
(July 5, 2012)

George Dureau: Black, on view at Higher Pictures Gallery, New York City, May 31–July 13, 2012

IN 1978, MARCUSE Pfeifer organized an exhibition in her uptown New York City gallery entitled *The Male Nude: A Survey in Photography.* Hung salon style, overflowing from floor to ceiling with images by Imogen Cunningham, George Platt Lynes, F. H. Day, Baron von Gloeden, Minor White, and many others that had been hidden "in the closet," the show blew the lid off of American homophobia at around the same time that the Robert Samuel Gallery, devoted to a gay clientele and its interests, opened downtown. I wrote the introduction to the exhibition catalog, and because of this involvement I was privileged to spend months discovering both the hidden archive and the issues—formal, political, conceptual, aesthetic—it articulated.

The young Robert Mapplethorpe was included in *The Male Nude* show—it was one of his early exhibits. This was the first glimpse I had of him, and it was around the same time that I saw works by artists like Joel-Peter Witkin, Lynn Davis, and George Dureau. Davis and Dureau were big influences on Mapplethorpe, whose subsequent notoriety and success have obscured the very real context from which his pictures grew. As the press release of *Black,* a small but stunning exhibition of black-and-white photographs by Dureau from 1973 to 1986, makes clear, the two men were friends in the early 1970s. Born in New Orleans in 1930 (where he still lives at age 81), Dureau was already known as a painter by the time he met the young photographer; he had originally picked up the camera as an extension of his primary expressive medium, but his powerful pictures soon developed a life and a following of their own. One of his admirers was Robert Mapplethorpe, and a comparison of their works is useful for understanding not only the similarities and differences of their *œuvres* but also the language of the body that was current during this breakthrough historical moment.

Both of these men were attracted to the Black body, and the exhibition focuses mainly on this aspect of Dureau's work. And both were obsessed with the relationship between timeless, classical beauty and the documentary particularities of photography—a relationship that also was central to the photographic aesthetics of Walker Evans, Lisette Model, Aaron Siskind, and others working around this time. For Mapplethorpe, these poles were perceived through the lens of Edward Weston. Transformed into "quintessential" forms, decontextualized and monumentalized, Weston's sitters morphed into absolutes, into formal essences that linked their limbs to the "universal rhythms" of nature, technology, and the clouds. Sensual rather than sexual, focused most often on the female rather than the male body, Weston's example provided the hurdle over which the militantly gay Mapplethorpe could jump. Stark, sexual, filled with the promise of power, his sitters wrested themselves from the natural continuum of time and space to become iconic containers of male desire, abstractions both stylized and impersonal. Real people, frozen by the camera's click, retreated into a cool classicism implied not only by their physical perfection but also by their transcendence of particularity.

Dureau, on the other hand, was a people person, not an aesthete like either Mapplethorpe or Weston. His pictures breathe, they pulse, they are hot with the blood and sweat of the sitters who joined him in his apartment on Esplanade Street in the city where he was born, and sometimes posed with props that were part of his personal effects. Edward Lucie-Smith, who wrote a wonderful introduction to a book of Dureau's photographs published in the 1980s, compared the artist's ability to transform these autobiographical encounters into photographically classical pictures with the writing strategies of Baudelaire, most notably in the *Tableaux Parisiens* of *Les Fleurs du Mal*.[1] Like the poet, Dureau sought out the seamy underbelly of city life and stared at its personification through the lens of a Hasselblad camera. His subjects are often street people, dressed or nude friends, handicapped or

---

1 Edward Lucie-Smith, "Introduction," in George Dureau (ed.), *New Orleans: 50 Photographs* (London: GMP, 1985), p. 1.

deformed men who might inhabit the dark side of the New Orleans scene. Whereas Baudelaire could take a poor girl, a bum, an old woman, or a melancholy clown and transform these figures into archetypes of the forsaken, elevating them to myth through the language of lyric poetry, Dureau's eye stared so lovingly, with so much intimacy, respect, empathy, and desire, at the people—white or black, fat or thin, beautiful or deformed—who inhabited his daily landscape that their portraits now glow with what James Agee once called "the cruel radiance of what is."[2] All of the intensity of psychological and emotional experience—not abstract or mythic truth but subjective, personal, particular truth—pour into the timeless formality of these poses, to spectacular effect.

Higher Pictures' press release points out that this is the first New York solo exhibition of this extraordinary body of work by this extraordinary artist. What on earth have we been waiting for?

---

2   James Agee and Walker Evans, *Let Us Now Praise Famous Men* (Boston, Houghton Mifflin, 1969), p. 11.

FOUND MEMORIES: THE QUICK AND THE STILL
Directed by Julia Murat
(July 12, 2012)

THE YOUNG BRAZILIAN filmmaker Julia Murat explains that the original idea for *Found Memories* came to her in 1999, while she was working on a film being shot in a village with a closed cemetery. The coffins of those who died in the vicinity had to travel seven hours by boat to be buried. This Faulkner-esque quandary intrigued her and made her wonder what kind of story she could tell about a town where a locked graveyard made it impossible to die.

A sealed cemetery is indeed central to this mesmerizing film, which is about life and death but also, and ultimately, about time. It is set in a fictional village named Jotubaba, in a region of Brazil that bustled with the coffee trade in the nineteenth century but is now only a ghost of its former self. Trains have ceased to run on the overgrown tracks; the town is impoverished, cut off, and populated only by old people bound together by their land and their daily routines. As the film begins, Madalena (Sonia Guedes) makes bread before dawn (in a darkness illuminated only by Carravagio-esque gas light) and follows the old train tracks to deliver her rolls to Antonio's (Luiz Serra's) coffee shop. The two of them drink coffee and banter, go to mass, and then break bread with their neighbors. In the afternoon, the men play games, and Madalena walks home, to write yet another letter to her dead husband before she goes to sleep.

This sequence repeats itself a number of times during the film, with slight variations. The days blend into each other, and ritualized time seems frozen on eternal return. It must be said that the English title, *Found Memories,* is a weak translation of the original Portuguese *Historias Que So Existem Quando Lembradas*: "Stories That Only Exist When Remembered." This more nuanced title moves the film toward the retrospective, emphasizing the townspeople's insistence on clinging to the traditions that contain their memories of the past and those who have peopled it. It also highlights the importance of the arrival of young Rita (Lisa E. Favero), an itinerant photographer fascinated by the decadence of the old plantation towns who, by following the train tracks, ends up one day at Madalena's doorstep. Rita moves in with Madalena for a short stay, and in so doing she becomes the witness, the key to the preservation of the town and its people: their images, their stories, and ultimately their social fabric. Armed with an IPOD and a digital camera, she quietly shatters the complacency of Jotubaba while fitting herself seamlessly into its routines. Her presence brings music, dancing, technology, youth—in short, movement—into the town, a gift that is beautifully embodied by subtle shifts in the film's visual montage.

As this shift makes clear, visual language is an essential part of the storytelling in *Found Memories*. The beginning of the film is especially slow and static; the camera lingers on long shots that frame painterly, highly composed scenes, and it never budges when small people pass in front of the lens to momentarily populate their environment. The camera never moves while Madalena walks on the tracks; it frames her encounters with Antonio from afar, in classically balanced compositions that imbue a decaying wall and bench with the stillness and weightiness of a Vermeer. My favorite shot is an early exterior view of the cemetery where Madalena's husband is buried, and from which she is excluded by a rusty lock. Seen from afar and wide-angle, the vista is filled with flowers. But the daily tasks—sweeping, pruning, and planting—that mark Madelena's days and link her life to her husband's memory are small gestures in a much bigger and more impersonal picture.

The camera does not begin to move until Rita enters the picture, when cuts, jumps, and varied points of view suddenly enliven our field of vision. Rita, however, arrives not only with her contemporary attitudes and equipment but also with a primitive pinhole camera; as Madalena laughingly remarks, she carries fancy machines with flashing lights and also a can. Asked why she is so fascinated by "old stuff," Rita sighs and admits that she was born into the wrong time, but we never get answers to the riddle of her life. She comes from nowhere, belongs nowhere, so she and her camera function like spiritual messengers, harbingers of both life and death for the town. Her pinhole photographs, shadowy, static, and full of ghosts, are the still points in the turning world of the cinematic narrative. People might "forget" to die in the village, as Antonio says, but they become phantoms when frozen by her long exposure times. In looking forward, Rita also points backward; in moving, she recreates stillness. This temporal push and pull, on both narrative and formal levels, drives the story along to its conclusion.

Found Memories was selected for the New Directors/New Films series shown at Lincoln Center and the Museum of Modern Art last spring, and it opened this summer in New York on a limited release. It is a film about tradition and modernity, about stasis and change, about the waxing and waning of fortunes, history, and the generations. But it is also a film about pictures, what they mean and how they embody our relationship to life, love, land, and time. A purely Brazilian tale, it nevertheless speaks to us all about the simple pleasures, hardships, and paradoxes of lives lived well or badly—but always, by necessity, together. I cannot say enough about this stunning first film by a young woman whose soul must be both old and wise.

PEOPLE IN GLASS HOUSES...
by Shelley Rice and Pepe Karmel
(July 20, 2012)

SINCE THIS BLOG began, I have been harassing my friend and New York University colleague Pepe Karmel, well-known art historian, curator, and critic of contemporary art, to make a contribution to the ongoing discussion. Happily, The Philip Johnson Glass House staff decided to enlist him too, so we have all joined forces. The Glass House, completed in 1949, was Johnson's private residence, and it is considered to be one of his greatest architectural achievements. Inspired by Mies van der Rohe's Farnsworth House, the building has exterior walls of glass and no interior walls. It sits on forty-seven acres of land in New Canaan, Connecticut (which are home to supplementary buildings and works created by the artist over a period of fifty years), and the entire campus has been named a National Trust Historic Site by the United States Government.

Before practicing architecture, Johnson was the founding Director of the Department of Architecture at the Museum of Modern Art in New York, and curator of the famous 1932 exhibition, "The International Style." As a trustee and patron of MOMA for many years, he donated more than 2,000 works, by artists as esteemed as Jasper Johns and Robert Rauschenberg, to the institution. Johnson's close ties to the art world, and to its most important movers and shakers, inspired him and his partner, David Whitney, to use the Glass House as a meeting place for the great cultural players of his time. Conversations with people like Andy Warhol, Frank Stella, and Robert A. M. Stern became legendary, and Vincent Scully called these gatherings "the most sustained cultural salon that the United States has ever seen."

After the deaths of both Johnson and Whitney in 2005, The Glass House continued to host these conversations. In 2010, partnering with graduate students from the School of Visual Arts in Manhattan, the staff created an expanded digital forum. Accessible at https://theglass-house.org/?s=conversations, the site proposes provocative questions or debate topics, and by now 20,000 people from 150 countries have participated in the ensuing exchanges. The question posed to Pepe Karmel by Glass House Conversations recently is indeed a hot button, and often controversial, issue:

Is the United States still the leader in innovative new art as it was in the latter half of the twentieth century?

Here is Karmel's reply, as it was posted on the Glass House Conversation website.

If there is an avant-garde today, its very nature contradicts the assumptions implicit in the question. Why should we assume that the most important new art of a given era will be associated with a single nation? Is it actually the case that the United States was the "leader" in new art during the second half of the twentieth century? Is "new art" necessarily innovative?

The idea that, at any given moment, one nation is going to be the home of the avant-garde is a translation into artistic terms of Hegel's idea of the world-historical figure. In canonical art history, Italy carries the baton from the Renaissance until the eighteenth century, France is the leader from 1775 until 1945, and the United States has the historically important avant-garde from 1945 until recently. This is demonstrably wrong. What about Netherlandish art in the seventeenth century? German and English art in the late eighteenth and nineteenth centuries. South American, non-Western, and, yes, French art after 1945?

Specifically, I would argue that the dominance of US art after 1945 is in large part a chauvinist illusion. After the triumph of Pop and Minimalism in the 1960s, US art historians rewrote art history (in the 1970s) to eliminate pretty much all important art made elsewhere. Arguably, much of the most innovative art produced between 1945 and 1970 was made in and around New York. But that doesn't entitle us to ignore the rest. Nor does it entitle us to pretend that the dominance of New York lasted beyond this twenty-five-year period. Certainly, in the 42 years since 1970, as much or more important art has been made elsewhere as has been made in New York.

Finally, we need to question the concepts "innovative" and "avant-garde." They are rooted in the same Hegelian model, which assumes that the "essential" events in art history are formal innovations (Cubism, geometric abstraction, Abstract Expressionism, Minimalism) that supposedly follow a coherent logic of development and that everything else is a sideshow. In an era when Marcel Duchamp is a much more important influence than Pablo Picasso, is there any credibility left to this position? There have been few–or no–significant formal innovations since 1970. Not in the United States, not elsewhere. Some critics and scholars take this to mean that the history of art came to an end in 1970 and that everything since then is an epiphenomenon. That seems absurd. Much terrific art has been made since 1970. It is distinguished, not by formal innovation, but by the way it crystallizes and expresses important experiences of life in our contemporary world. From this perspective, much of the important art of our time is being made in the former "Third World," and addresses the experience of post-colonialism, triumphant in China, catastrophic in much of Africa, and different in different countries. If this means that the avant-garde has departed US shores, so be it.

STORIES PLAYED ON THE SAME KEYBOARD: LA JEUNESSE D'ALAN
AN INTERVIEW WITH EMMANUEL GUIBERT
by Shelley Rice
(July 30, 2012)

WELL-KNOWN FOR his drawings, cartoons, and animated characters like Ariol (the small gray donkey created in collaboration with Marc Boutavant in 2000), Emmanuel Guibert is the author of a number of books, among them *The Photographer* (with Didier Lefèvre) and *Alan's War*.[1] Emmanuel fascinates me because he explores the boundaries between photography and drawing, memoir and fiction, using elements from different sources in order to tell tales about love and war, childhood, and friendship. His intense interest in the stories of others, and his uncanny capacity to highlight and empathize with universal human experiences—whether profound or mundane, traumatic or serene—are hallmarks of a body of work that might chronicle centuries and continents but that always communicates through the tiny details of everyday life. I met with Emmanuel on Sunday, July 16 in his studio in Paris, to discuss his new book *La Jeunesse d'Alan (Alan's Childhood)*, which will be published in France by L'Association on September 14, 2012.

Emmanuel: So, Shelley, what would you like me to talk about?

Shelley: First, can you give me an overview of this project, since this is the second book you have written about Alan Ingram Cope and we need to inform our readers about its history.

E: Alan and I met in 1994 on a tiny island off the coast of France called the Île de Ré. I asked him for directions on the street and after that we

---

1   Emmanuel Guibert, *Alan's War: The Memories of G.I. Alan Cope* (New York: First Second, 2008).

became friends. We stayed friends for five years, from the moment we met until the moment he died. In the meantime, I taped hours and hours of conversation between the two of us to gather this patrimony, which would allow me to turn this man's experience into biography.

S: But why him?

E: Complete chance, just because we had some sort of crush on each other. I felt he was a very interesting person and I wanted to spend time with him. It just started like this. He was retired. He invited me to his home, he introduced me to his wife, his dog, and then his life. He showed me some pictures, then some books, and very soon I found myself meeting with him in the little garden he had near his house on the Île de Ré to talk and tape conversations. The conversations became stronger after a while as he opened his memory and his philosophy of life to me more and more. I was thirty at the time, and it always interesting for an inexperienced man to speak with someone who could see his life in perspective—a view of life that can be both an overview and a close-up, something only possible for an older person. It was fascinating for me. The main thing I can say is that he was one of the people in my life with whom I've spent the most memorable moments.

So I started very soon to turn his testimony into drawings, because I thought it would be interesting for him to see his memories coming back as drawings done by someone else, to see if that worked, and if he would allow me to interpret his memories. They couldn't fit exactly because I hadn't lived what he had lived, but I listened carefully to him to catch all the words and the images linked to the words. I knew that we could go quite far together if he would accept my interpretations, and I was relieved because the first time I came with my drawings he was very enthusiastic. We both felt that this was a way for our friendship to go on. We worked together for five years, from the time he was sixty-nine years old until his death at seventy-four. I worked hard to make sure he could see the first book but unfortunately, he died six months before it was released.

S: Can you talk about the first book and why you chose that aspect of his life—his experience as an American soldier in the Second World War—for the initial volume?

E: We had the opportunity to be prepublished in a magazine (*Lapin*), every three months, with no limit to the number of pages…

S: Wow, that's like Balzac…

E: So I started to create episodes about this childhood, but after a while, he said: "We have this regular appointment with readers. Maybe we should tell them something that can be like one story, like a *feuilleton*…"

S: Like Balzac!

E: He said the best thing to do might be to tell the story of "his war," because it has a beginning and then it is a voyage: you are in a vehicle, you are sent abroad, you cross Europe and end up at the border of Czechoslovakia…. This is really a story to tell in a magazine. So I stopped working on his childhood and started working on the war. While he was alive of course I always had the gold mine of his memory, and the opportunity to call him up and ask him questions: "What was the weather like on this day and what kind of jacket were you wearing back then?"

S: And he remembered?!!?

E: Yes, because he was an elephant! He was incredible. Maybe, at the origin of this project, there is the decision to pay a tribute to his incredible memory, because most people are not able to answer questions about the days of their lives. After his death, I decided that was the moment for me to travel to find his traces, to follow in his footsteps, and meet some people who had known him. So I went to America and to Germany, which he had occupied with Patton's army. It turned into an inquiry. I sent shot-in-the-dark letters to people wherever and got answers or not. In 2009 I was in Ohio with an old flame of his, his girlfriend when he was twenty and she was sixteen. Almost every week, even now, I receive photographs from a historian in the Czech

Republic, who read the book when it was translated into the Czech language. (*Alan's War* has by now been translated into ten languages.) The mission that took Alan from Germany to Czechoslovakia during the war is not well documented, but it is the specialty of this historian. I went to visit him and he opened his archives to me. He wanted to help me (even though of course the war is over for me now!) to find Alan, and the fact is that we didn't when I was with him. We found pictures of people in the book: I recognized the top sergeant and others. But it was only a few months later, after I came home, that I received from him a picture of Alan himself.

I meet people here and there who are often moved and interested by the fact that a young person is dedicating an important part of his life to an older one. That always attracts attention because we carry within us an urge to listen to those who have more experience. A lot of doors opened to help, to provide clues and images and memories, so the fact is that this project becomes more and more interesting as time passes.

S: Since you brought up photographs: Alan talked to you for a long time but he also gave you pictures from his past. What's the relationship between images and words in this project? How do these photos function as memory tools within the context of the books?

E: Some of them are published in the books, or interpreted, redrawn to be presented in the books…

S: And how do you make those decisions?

E: I wanted the reader to see his face, his actual face in a photograph, at least once in the book. In the American edition, I included a photo album at the end of the book since I know Americans have all seen and owned pictures like these. But in the rest of the book there are no actual photos because the drawings refuse to be associated with them. I tried, but it doesn't work. You have to have a graphic style that is very particular to allow a drawing to be near a photographic image: most of the time they don't want to be side by side and they fight against each other until one of the two is dead.

S: But you know that Barthes called photographs "counter-memories."[2] He insisted that they stop the process of memory. As an artist, you are trying to delve into the process of memory, so these two types of images are fighting against each other not only visually but also philosophically.

E: Exactly, but the fact is that these photographs are not part of my memory. They are part of his. If you accept the fact that now I've been living with them for almost twenty years, you realize that they have now become part of my life too. This also is something very interesting, and it is something that I will have to explore in later years. The time has not yet come, since I am still in the process of treating his testimony. I have told the story of his war and his childhood, but his teenage years are still to come. Until that is done, I'm not thinking too much about everything that is happening to ME by working so long on such a subject. After I have finished telling his story, that will be the moment to ask myself "what have I done, and why?" And when that happens, I will be probably be about the age he was when I met him!

S: Yo!

E: But about the pictures: I have a few anecdotes to tell. For instance, I would go to California with Alan's photo album in hand. In this album, there is a picture of a house on a certain street. I knew he lived in this house, I know more or less when, but I don't have the number of the street address and you know streets in California can go on from San Francisco to San Diego! So, I would spend days going up and down a street looking for this house. I knew that I might not find it. There was always the risk that the building would be gone, or changed, or that trees might have grown. But I do this only for the emotion I have when (if!) I do find it. If I do find the house, that's fabulous, and I just sit in front of it staring in amazement...

S: Have you ever gone in to meet the people who live there now?

---

2 "[Photography] actually blocks memory, quickly becomes a counter-memory." In Roland Barthes, *Camera Lucida: Reflections on Photography* (New York: Hill and Wang, 1980), p. 91.

E: No, I haven't done that yet, because I haven't yet drawn these houses in the books. When I do, the books are going to come back to these places in California. They will be in libraries and bookstores, there will be blogs, and people in the neighborhoods will know.

S: And then the people living in the houses now will invite you to tea!

E: Yes, maybe, and then that invitation will become part of the story too. It's like the chance meeting I had with Alan on the streets of the Île de Ré. I prefer to wait and let things happen. Sometimes when I do find people and see places, it is precious for me because I can draw exactly what is there, and often people have closets full of documentation that they generously offer to share with me. And the story grows.

The book I have just finished, of course, is about Alan's early years. The war book was about the experiences of a soldier who never really faced fire, who traveled through Europe seeing countries and meeting people. *Alan's Childhood*, on the other hand, is about everyday, simple anecdotes, his family, and the people in his young life: his uncles, grandparents, friends, his drawings, etc.

S: I have the sense that this new book is very much a look at *la vie quotidienne* of a young person living in California at that time.

E: Yes, but Alan's childhood coincided with the Great Depression since he was born in 1925. His father lost his job, his grandparents moved in with them because they couldn't afford a home, there were earthquakes…

S: So there were natural disasters and human-made disasters…

E: Yes, all mixed up with the simplest things of childhood. One thing I have learned from listening to older people is that even though a person may have lived very dramatic moments in his adult life, the things that stay closest to the bones are the facts of childhood. What remains in a lifetime are the first memories from which all the others grow, early memories that Alan sometimes told me with a trembling voice—a voice never present when he talked about the war or other aspects of his later life, some of them very dramatic. I try to capture that intensity in the new book. I tell my readers simple stories, many of which they have already lived themselves. But when your work is very simple it is also very risky, because the frontier between art and the mundane is very, very thin. But that is where I like to be: someplace we have all experienced.

Alan had a particular gift for telling those stories, which is part of my admiration for him. When I was with him, sometimes I would have this hallucination that he was shining with the capacity to resurrect episodes so one could SEE what he was saying. But when you see what someone says, you build the picture only from your patrimony. The images you are able to put together to illustrate what someone is telling you are not theirs; they are those that you have created yourself by connecting deeply with another. That is the miracle, that is what I call friendship. I make books to prove that it is possible for one person to listen so carefully to another that there will be coincidences in their visions because there is in fact a certain logic to life. All of these human experiences, we have them in us, which is the reason why stories can pass from one person to another. They all play on the same keyboard.

ANNE SINCLAIR, DIANE ARBUS, AND ME
(August 13, 2012)

THIS IS A postcard from Paris. I'm sitting in an apartment rented from a friend on the Left Bank and reading yet another book purchased at La Hune. (The French publishing industry anticipates an economic upturn the minute I arrive in town.) This time the book is Anne Sinclair's *21, rue La Boétie* (Paris: Bernard Grasset, 2012), a memoir chronicling her research into the history of her family and especially her grandfather, the famous art dealer Paul Rosenberg. Interweaving family stories with political atrocities and deceptions, Sinclair describes the lives and relationships of gallery artists and the fate of their works under (and after) the Nazi occupation. Rosenberg's fight to preserve his family, his collection, and his business interests under impossible circumstances is set against personal stories of war, exile, disappointment, and love. Sinclair is a clear, impassioned writer and an experienced journalist, so her cautionary tales of prejudice, cruelty, and deceit keep wiggling out of the past tense and surfacing into the murky political waters of the present.

A historian of modern art first and foremost, I am of course interested in the subject of Sinclair's book, especially since Rosenberg's influence as an art dealer—of Picasso, Braque, and Matisse, among others—spanned two continents and substantially impacted taste, the market and collections in the United States. A champion of the continuity between the past and the present, historical masters and the avant-garde, he fought to establish contemporary art in the highest precincts of American culture. His presence in New York after 1940, of course, was not simply a lifestyle choice, but an imperative dictated by the murderous anti-Semitism of the era. This same imperative dictated that Sinclair would be born of French parents not in Paris but in the Big Apple, a few years after the end of the war and a few years before me.

My family arrived at Ellis Island from Europe—Eastern Europe, mainly Romania it seems—a long time ago (in American terms, which means the nineteenth century). All four of my grandparents were born in the United States, making me the Jewish equivalent of a Native American, or a Daughter of the American Revolution. By the time I was born in the Bronx, the family history beyond the Port of New York was fuzzy indeed—though ironically it was a famous Jewish art dealer who provided me with much additional information when I was in my late 20s. While I was studying art history, Leonard Hutton was revered for his collection of German Expressionist and Russian Revolutionary paintings. I spent a lot of time in his gallery on the Upper East Side of Manhattan during my student days, not yet aware of his personal history or our family ties. Hutton was born Leonard Hutschnecker in Germany. Like Paul Rosenberg, he too fled Hitler, and arrived in New York Harbor in the 1940s with a minimum of money, no friends, and nowhere to stay. Thinking fast, he grabbed a phone book and found only one Hutschnecker listed in the whole city. He called that number, explained his problem, and asked if perhaps the New York Hutschneckers might be willing to help him get started since the odds were that they were his relatives. The family in question agreed and helped him get settled in America. He, in turn, swore he would construct a genealogy, a family tree to honor everyone from the bloodline that had saved his life.

Which is, oddly, where I come into this story. I was reading an article in *The New York Times* one day during the late 1970s; it was about Arnold Hutschnecker, a famous psychiatrist who treated, among others, Richard Nixon. My maiden name was Shelley Hutch, but my father was born Harold Hutschnecker. He changed his name to Hutch before his marriage, around the same time (and for the same reason) that Anne Sinclair's father changed his name from Schwartz to Sinclair. Seeing the article about Richard Hutschnecker, I had exactly the same impulse as Leonard had years before. I called the psychiatrist's office and announced that I certainly must be his relative. To my shock, the nurse called the famous doctor on the phone, and he arrived breathless, saying he had in fact been waiting to hear from me. He and his brother knew my grandfather and knew about my father. They had been hoping that they would be able to learn more about—and meet— the latest generation of the Hutch family. But, Richard said, he wasn't the one who kept the records of the family—I really needed to call his brother, the art dealer Leonard Hutton! He told me that Leonard would be thrilled to hear from me. My visit would allow him to fill in the gaps left in the family archive.

So in the late 1970s, my family expanded to include the amazing (and now deceased) Leonard Hutton Hutschnecker (along with his wife Ingrid), who around that time had decided to readopt the family name shed during and after World War II. Indeed, it was true, Leonard had kept his promise: he had constructed a huge family tree, tracing Hutschneckers all over the world, as far as Russia, Switzerland, and even South Africa. He was thrilled but not surprised to have found an art critic in the family. At the time I was writing columns for newspapers like *The Village Voice* and magazines like *Artforum* under the married name I still use. Considering that everyone else in my immediate family was an accountant, I seemed like a black sheep. But in the family as a whole, the global family, creative people (especially theater people and interior designers) have predominated. What a relief!

I am recounting this story not only because it is a good one but also to make clear—yet again, and in a personal way—the tremendous impact the Nazis and the Second World War had on the circulation and the future of art, artists, and intellectuals. This is precisely the general theme of Sinclair's enlightening book, the tight lines between the personal, the cultural, and the political, and the ways in which these various threads continue to surface (for better or worse) in contemporary life. She is strongest on her family history, and in describing (and sometimes questioning) her grandfather's efforts on behalf of art, artists, and social justice; she is weakest when discussing New York and its cultural history, which Rosenberg entered in mid-stream, hardly a pioneer. Picasso was shown in the city by Alfred Stieglitz before the Armory Show of 1913 and World War I; he didn't need to wait for Paul Rosenberg to give him his first exhibition in the Big Apple around the middle of the twentieth century, even though Sinclair's grandfather certainly helped to solidify the European modernists' acceptance and placement in major institutions and collections. This is one of the curious anomalies of the new book. As she admits, Anne Sinclair initially saw New York through the eyes of a child. In *21, rue La Boétie*, she has attempted to retain her youthful enchantment with the city while telling a very grown-up story—a balancing act that doesn't always ring true, especially since she herself mentions her ordeal of 2011, when she and her then-husband DSK (Dominique Strauss-Kahn) were essentially imprisoned within the city limits of New York while he awaited (never filed) legal charges for the sexual assault of a hotel maid.

It must be said that much of my knowledge of Anne Sinclair, ironically, dates from this period, when television newscasts showed nightly images of the couple bombarded by reporters on the street when they dared to venture outside of their Tribeca townhouse. That image of her—as stoic and supportive wife—needed some fleshing out, with information about her professional accomplishments and her distinguished lineage, which is why I bought this book in the first place. But I must confess that my initial motivation for writing a blog post was more concrete and more immediate than these intellectual concerns. I became obsessed by the black-and-white photograph of the young Sinclair and her grandfather printed on the cover of this memoir. In the picture, Anne is perhaps four years old. Facing the camera in what seems to be a park, she is holding the kind of bucket used in a sandbox and grasping her grandpa's hand. And, most importantly for me: she is the spitting image of me in a number of family photographs retrieved from my parents' haphazard archives and scrapbooks. A cute, chubby-cheeked, and dark-haired girl, she is wearing the same coat and the same beret I wore as a child.

For some reason, this fashion coincidence freaked me out. It was as if I was confronted by a mirror image. The repetitiveness of family snapshots, their conventional structure and style, hit home even across the Atlantic. The shock of recognition, in fact, was almost Barthesian: the photo confronted me head-on with what Roland Barthes called the madness of history. There's a section in *Camera Lucida* where the author talks about "history" being the time when his mother lived before he was born, without him. Whereas this "historical" time was a void for Barthes, I had the opposite reaction to Sinclair's image. A plenitude of historical detail flooded into my head when I realized the implications of this family snapshot. I don't know this person, she is French and living a very different life from mine. So how is it that she is wearing my coat, and why do we look so much alike?

It took me a while to realize that while we inhabit different worlds today, by accidents of history Anne Sinclair and I were two well-dressed Jewish girls about the same age during the same historical moment (the early 1950s) in New York City. We surely played in the same parks, perhaps even in the same sandboxes, and obviously, both of our families bought into the vogue for safeguarding family memories in snapshots made simple by new technologies. And yes, I probably am not imagining it, our mothers could easily have purchased nearly identical coats for their young (and pampered) daughters. My coat, as I recall, was slightly fuller at the bottom, but the wool tweed and the collar were absolutely the same, and I can never forget that great hat (which I must admit looks as cute on her as it did on me). In the years after this picture was taken, Sinclair would, of course, go back to Paris and make a name and a life for herself in France, while I would do the same in the Big Apple, and there this story might have ended. But the photograph grabbed my attention and made clear connecting links buried in time, space, and family archives—as well as in the annals of commerce. For my mother only bought coats at Russeks, the defunct Fifth Avenue store owned by the Nemerovs, the family of Diane Arbus. If we did, in fact, wear similar coats, perhaps the Sinclairs shopped there too. It is, indeed, a very small world.

GERHARD RICHTER: THROUGH A GLASS, DARKLY
Centre Pompidou, Paris
(August 22, 2012)

UP FRONT, I want to say that I decided to write about Gerhard Richter because I am in love with *Motifs,* the artist's book he conceived to accompany the retrospective *Panorama,* now on view in Paris. Organized by the Tate Modern (London), the Nationalgalerie, Staatliche Museen (Berlin), and the Centre Pompidou, the show is intended to celebrate the 80th birthday of this German master by exploring the complexity of his *œuvre* both chronologically and thematically. While I'm wearing my heart on my sleeve, I should also confess that I love the exhibition—and not because I am a die-hard fan of Richter's, a "groupie" like some people I know.

It was, in fact, a challenge to bring me into the Gerhard Richter fold. I've never been convinced by the strident—and too narrow, from my point of view—arguments of my peers on his behalf. First, there are the conceptual, indexical, archival types, who surround me in Manhattan of course and who pontificate endlessly about Richter's *Atlas* as if it were the Holy Grail of contemporary visual representation. Then there are those who swoon over Richter "*L'Artiste*," the painter in the old, male tradition who provides the world with a constant supply of abstract works embellished by squeegees and splashes galore. It's not that I don't appreciate these pictures (and these positions), but they've never succeeded in explaining to me (as a famous French intellectual friend of mine recently said) "why I need to see the works of someone who continually reproduces the whole history of art." The exhibition currently on view at the Centre Pompidou does, in fact, explain just that, by brilliantly linking the various aspects of Richter's *œuvre*— abstract paintings, photorealist works, glass sculptures, and everything in between—in ways that emphasize and communicate this prolific artist's overarching aims.

"I pursue no objectives, no system, no tendency; I have no program, no style, no concern. I like the indefinite, the boundless. I like continual uncertainty." This citation, used often throughout the show and its accompanying literature, becomes a rallying cry that allows the viewer to relax when confronted with such a diverse range of work. The decision to organize the *œuvre* chronologically and thematically rather than into discrete formal units (sculptures, works based on photos, abstract paintings) allows meaning to circulate around and between objects, making it very clear that Richter's ultimate aim is in fact to emphasize (continually, incessantly) that we humans always see the world through a glass darkly, a glass that can and will shift and change size, shape, perspective at any moment. The townscapes of Dresden—painted when the city had been rebuilt after the devastation of World War 2—are described in such fluid strokes that the destruction seems to manifest itself again through the renovation. Picturesque landscapes of barns and forests and meadows in Italy or France—painted realistically, impressionistically, or with abstract strokes layered on top of representational depictions—are all described by the artist as dreams ("a type of yearning, a yearning for a whole, a simple life, a little nostalgic"), while his layered abstractions are perceived as "more real…my presence, my reality, my problems." Painted references to traditional religious symbols—skulls and candles and angels—take their place next to works mediated by public or private pictures of family, politics, and war. Objects, places, people and paint strokes, photographed and projected, change scale; blown up, mirrored, juxtaposed, they morph into something else entirely. This is, in other words, a body of work bound together by Richter's inability to believe what he sees, to believe in the ultimate and unchanging truth of the visual information he creates or receives through his eyes: whether those eyes are seeing a magazine, a political or iconographic sign, a loved one or the landscape around him. The blurs, the breakups, the pictorial transformations are ways of visualizing this "continual uncertainty." The mental images mediating our experience of the world and obsessively engaged by Richter are nothing more than the screens through which we perceive—and ascribe meaning to—the continually shifting shadows on the walls of Plato's Cave.

One of my favorite such transformations, which involves some very contemporary working methods and media, resulted in the creation of *Strip* in 2011. In the process of making this work, painting moved through photographic reproduction into digitization—a movement in the opposite direction from many of Richter's well-known canvases, like *Betty* or *Aunt Marianne,* where a photographic image is reproduced in oils. To produce *Strip,* Richter began with a photo of *Abstract Painting (724-4)* of 1990. This original image was then divided (using computer software) vertically into 2, then 4, then 8, 16, 32, 64, 128, 256, 512, 1,024, 2,048, and 4,096 bands. The process (comprising 12 stages of division) produced 8,190 strips, each with the same height as the original image. At each new division, the bands became thinner and thinner, more and more minimal in detail. Eventually, these bands were used to create *Strip,* the huge, abstract laser print on paper that is one of the latest works on view in the exhibition.

Which brings me to the discussion of *Motifs: Division, Mirror, Repetition,* the bookwork Richter conceived as an accompaniment to the show. It is clear from the central importance of *Atlas,* and the existence of other volumes discussed in the catalog, that Richter enjoys working through ideas by making books, and these are often composed of photographs that are repeated, reversed, or transformed. As the subtitle makes clear, *Motifs* is such a project, based on the transformation of *Abstract Painting (724-4)* into *Strips.* In the bookwork, the entire process of division is documented, and the bands produced by the twelve stages are mirrored and repeated in ways that give rise to the abstract motifs that are the central surprise of the book.

They are surprising for several reasons. First of all, as one flips through the 238 color images that comprise the volume, one watches subjective, expressionistic splashes and drips of paint, with all their physicality, transmute into cool, clean digital color bands. Expressionism and minimalism, handwork, and computerized reproduction, no longer opposites, become part of a continuum that, once again, allows Richter to undermine the categories that define our ways of seeing. But the most beautiful surprises in the book are precisely the abstract motifs that emerge as the strips are mirrored, repeated, and juxtaposed. In the center of the book, between expressionism and minimalism, these motifs propose another universe of forms. They echo the patterns of Tibetan painting, Islamic decoration, South American weaving, and

Indian metalwork; like jewels, like lace, like flowers, they emerge from the fractured images of the painted surface, and echo the colors and forms of global culture. They are, in a word, wondrous—and from my point of view, they move Gerhard Richter's work forward in more ways than one. The last room in the Pompidou exhibition is entitled "Continuing to Paint," and the wall label discusses the paradox of painting in the digital age. Evidently, Richter has figured out a way to keep his medium relevant and expansive. This master might be eighty years old, but it seems he is still standing in the vortex of contemporary expression—peering, as usual, through a glass darkly at the diverse shadows animating our visual environment.

ON MEANING, CHRIS KILLIP AND A GIRL CHEWING GUM
Le Bal
(August 30, 2012)

THE BRITISH PHOTOGRAPHER Chris Killip made the decision to begin both his exhibition *What Happened: Great Britain 1970–1990* at Le Bal in Paris (organized with the Folkwang Museum in Essen, Germany by curator Ute Eskildsen) and his book *Arbeit/Work* (Steidl, 2012) with the following statement:

> "One night in 1994 my friend John Clifford, who owned the best bar in Cambridge, took me into the middle of Boston to where the civic center and other administrative buildings now stand. These buildings were built in the 1960s on top of the tough working-class district of Scully Square, where John and his brothers were born and raised. John pointed out to me streets that no longer existed, telling me who had lived where and in which house. Who had died in Vietnam, who had worked for the mob, who had gone to prison or ended up in politics. When I interrupted his narrative to tell him how great it was that he was telling me the history of this place, he spun round, gripped me by the throat, and pushed me against the wall. With his raised fist clenched he said, 'I don't know nothing about no fucking history, I'm just telling you what happened.'"

After seeing the exhibition, and watching the accompanying twelve-minute film from 1976, *A Girl Chewing Gum* by John Smith, the viewer begins to understand the relevance of this powerful anecdote. Personally, I had the sense that the entire show was a kind of personal struggle with meaning—in both art and life. Killip's documentary photographs, about inhabitants, workers, and others in Britain on the Isle of Man, Bury St. Edmunds, Huddersfield, Lynemouth, and areas of the Northwest of England, portray, as David Campany wrote, people "exiled within themselves, incapable of finding their moorings, merging into a collective drift" as they are increasingly disenfranchised by the changing economic circumstances of a rapidly deindustrializing nation. The meaning of these peoples' lives within the national economy takes a hit right in front of our eyes, but so does the concept of photography that allows an artist to interpret the conditions and destinies of others. This show and book are as much about Killip's attempts to define his relationship with his subjects as it is about the subjects themselves.

It is useful to understand that Killip's influences include Paul Strand and August Sander, as well as Bill Brandt, Robert Frank, and (especially, from my perspective) Walker Evans. Like Killip, Evans walked a thin and often tense line between the socially prescribed meanings of things and those in which he believed. Campany makes a case that Killip's work has never been "of its time," and in a sense, this connects him deeply to his forbear. Working in America in the 1930s, where everyone "knew" how to define and pity a victim of poverty, Evans struggled to transcend the popularly accepted, simplistic, and ultimately degrading definitions of those struck hard by the Depression. Committed to treating all humans, rich or poor, as complex beings and emotional equals, adamant that he would never allow political ideologies or economic hierarchies to stand between him and his subjects, he entered into continual conflict in his job at the Farm Security Administration because his superiors felt his work was "not political enough."

Looking at the muscular black-and-white images in *What Happened*, it is easy to see Killip fighting the same fight, but this time his invisible adversaries were (are) the proponents of "Concerned Photography" in (and after) the 1970s. Those were the years when the International Center of Photography opened its doors, and the years when the liberal print media (and it *was* liberal sometimes in those days!) expected photographers to understand and to fight for the poor or for those disenfranchised by race, creed, or religion. Nowadays, when every writer can be considered profound by adding "atrocity," "violence," or "trauma" to the title of some academic text, and every photographer can become a politically correct activist by (once again) defining and visualizing victims, Chris Killip is trying to look clearly, respectfully, and without prejudice at the lives of those who are struggling to survive a shifting and often merciless economy. "To the people in these photographs I am superfluous," he wrote in 1988 in *In Flagrante*. He refuses to see himself as anyone's savior, or anyone's judge; the only activism he admits is his own aspiration to understand and record the life around him. Given the trendiness of political correctness in the theory and practice of photography in the United States (where Killip teaches at Harvard), it is easy to see that he too is shadowboxing the adversary of popular stereotypes and preconceptions, both human and photographic. It took a long time (around thirty years) for anyone to acknowledge that Walker Evans had anything important to say, about the Depression, America, and the impact of money and machines on people's lives.

One of the first things to notice is that Killip, like Sander and Evans before him, has made the decision to shift the focus of his photographs away from the individual and toward a more socially contextual approach to human subjectivity. His early work, on the Isle of Man, consists mainly of portraits, with a strong Strand influence, of people who in the 1970s worked in traditional ways in occupations and on territories long considered to be their birthright. The instability of the economic context, the massive shifts in ways of working, and economic possibilities and liabilities, begin to impact the solidity of this long-established situation, and the pictures continually emphasize the malaise of sitters trying to position themselves within a strange new world. A man, standing to the left with his back to the camera, seems flimsy enough to blow away in the wind as he faces a brick wall; although his stance is firm, his white hair flies like the garbage surrounding him on the street, and his body has no more weight than his dark shadow mirroring him on the opposite side of the picture plane. A shipyard that supports a community closes, forcing people to disperse; housing complexes filled with families and children are demolished from one photo to the next; traditional occupations like fishing suddenly become anachronisms. Demonstrators, punks, and revolutionary slogans make their appearance. Killip's insistence that people flourish or fail within a social world, that their sense of self is based on moorings that include work, place, and community, makes him sensitive to the conditions that create, and degrade, human behaviors. Never perceived as arbitrary or extreme, his subjects are reactive to the times in which their lives are embedded. Their responses are neither programmed, programmatic, nor predictable. They just are what they are: "what happened."

Which leads me to John Smith's film, *The Girl Chewing Gum*, a hilarious and smart counterpart to Killip's searching work. An extended look at an urban corner dominated by a store named Steele's, this animated black-and-white street photograph is narrated in such a way that the questions of meaning discussed above become central to the activities of the most banal English passersby. Alternately acting like a Gregory Crewdson-style directorial photographer, a choreographer, a traffic cop, a scholar analyzing the random actions or attributes of anonymous pedestrians, or an increasingly bizarre interpreter of the visible (or invisible) evidence (which at the end includes descriptions of a black bird with a nine-foot wing span and a man with a helicopter in his pocket), the narrator is constantly intervening in what we see and hear, embellishing documentary records in ways that sometimes establish and more often stretch credibility. The girl chewing gum is elevated to significant iconography in this context; English words when read backward transform into Greek ones, and disembodied pronouncements fly (through electrical lines, of course) between the city and a field with cows twenty kilometers away. This film is the best antidote I've ever seen to the pretentious certitude of aesthetic interpretation and academic analysis. Susan Sontag, eat your heart out: I want every student I teach to see John Smith's masterwork at least twice before picking up a camera or an art history textbook.

THE VIEW FROM LEFT FIELD

An exhibition curated by Shelley Rice and Mike Nash with Jonno Rattman and students in both the Art History and Photography and Imaging Departments of New York University
(September 6, 2012)

This text is an adaptation of the wall text and a sampling of photographs from an exhibition on view in the New York University Department of Photography and Imaging Galleries from September 4 through November 17, 2011. All photographs are from NYU's Tamiment Library archive of the Communist Party of America (CPA), and they were reproduced in the blog courtesy of the *Daily Worker*. Many thanks to both of these organizations for their help and support.

The View from Left Field was the name of the sports page of the *Daily Worker*, the official newspaper of the American Communist Party. New York University's Tamiment Library, under the direction of Mike Nash, acquired the archives of the Party in 2006. Included in this acquisition, among the records, documents, and publications that date from the 1910s to the end of the twentieth century, was the photo morgue of both the *Daily Worker* and its successor, *The People's Daily World*. The estimated 500,000 images in the morgue, filed away in boxes with written documents and currently being digitized for use by the public, include approximately 25,000 prints, 85,000 negatives, and 165,000 wire service images, as well as twenty-five boxes of large format photographs produced for display purposes. The *Worker* and *World* photograph morgue and the larger Communist Party archive are widely recognized as a nationally important collection, certainly the most important that the Tamiment Library has acquired in the past twenty-five years.

One of the most significant special collections in the United States documenting the history of the American Left and the labor movement, the Tamiment Library substantially enhanced its visual holdings with the addition of this repository of images documenting Communist Party history, the Cold War, and all of the twentieth century movements for progressive social change that shaped American society. The original photography in the archive represents the work of staff and freelance photographers associated with the newspapers. Documentary images depict people at work, social conditions, factories, strikes, parades, farms, fields, struggles for civil rights and liberties, wars, and revolutions. The fight for racial equality, whether by Paul Robeson, soldiers in the Spanish Civil War, or baseball players in America, runs throughout the visual narrative. Images of Soviet society and conditions in Eastern Europe during the twentieth century, rarely seen by Western audiences, are also an important component of the archive.

Throughout the Fall 2011 semester, students in my *Toward a Critical Vocabulary* seminar at New York University systematically examined a selection of twelve to fourteen boxes randomly pulled for this purpose by Michael Nash. Each box has one or more themes, whether that is the Vietnam War, agriculture in Czechoslovakia, May Day Parades, student protests, baseball players, or the Civil Rights Movement, and that theme is developed in folders filled with both photographs and printed, handwritten or typed documents. The students' goal was to select images of exceptional interest—in form and/or content—that could be scanned, printed, and exhibited in the 719 Broadway Gallery of the Photography and Imaging Department of NYU's Tisch School of the Arts. After choosing the pictures, the students worked on related research papers with Professor Nash, who filled them in not only on twentieth century history but also on the ideology of the party, thus helping them to understand the complex social history behind the images taken, collected and ultimately selected for publication in the Party's newspapers.

This is, in other words, a project designed as a learning experience. It is not the definitive research exhibit on this material. It is a student sampling of available resources, an assemblage of amazingly interesting and relevant pictures, and not a comprehensive survey of the Tamiment's archive. There are notable subjects missing from this show that are, of course, part of the library's collection: pictures of the Triangle Shirtwaist Factory Fire, records of major union strikes, demonstrations, and negotiations of the twentieth century, and documents of the Abraham Lincoln Brigade that fought against Franco during the Spanish Civil War, among them. Students worked with and studied the material Nash chose for them, and often made decisions based on visual rather than strictly chronological or historical criteria. They were impressed with the quality of the images, and disturbed by something else that was missing: the lack of attribution. These pictures might have been taken by members of the Photo League who worked freelance for the *Daily Worker*, or unknown talents, or perhaps by known artists and photojournalists living in New York at the time—but until we study this further we will never know. Much more research needs to be done to establish authorship, and this exhibition is designed to both celebrate wonderful material and stimulate continued engagement.

Since *The View from Left Field* is being shown in a Photography Department Gallery, my colleagues wanted the exhibited images to look their best. All of the original pictures were, therefore, beautifully scanned and reprinted by Jonno Rattman, a student in the class, and then matted and framed by Karl Peterson and the rest of the gallery staff. Needless to say, this is not how the "working" photographs look in the *Daily Worker* archive. There they are of diverse sizes and materials; technically, they run the gamut and are in wildly variable conditions. Some are original black-and-white prints, some are postcards, some are wire service transmissions or clippings from other newspapers and many are torn or faded or covered with publishing marks. As a historian, I personally prefer to see the pictures in their "real" rather than their "ideal" state, so we have compromised, and composed an archival e-book of the original images, front and back, with their captions and marks, to accompany the show. This makes it possible for historical researchers to get a better sense of the actual state of images now stored in folders and boxes.

We are hoping that this sampling of what I call "the world in a box" will help to inform photographers, the NYU community, historians, and the general public about the archival treasures stashed away in the university's library, a major resource soon to be made available online. The study of this collection will add a lot to our understanding of photographic history, American history, the history of journalism, and international relations (among other things), and it is a visual feast chock full of information about the daily lives of humans on earth during both the quiet and the tumultuous moments of the twentieth century.

The View from Left Field is dedicated to the memory of Michael Nash, who left us in July 2012. He didn't make it to the opening he was so anticipating, but we know he is with us in spirit.

HOME AGAIN!
(September 20, 2012)

I KNEW, FOR SURE, that I was home again a few days after my plane landed in New York. Riding the crowded, sweaty subway, beleaguered passengers were suddenly confronted with yet another beggar, a young, strungout white guy in jeans who moaned about the indignity of his situation and then proceeded to tell us (in way too much detail, and way too loudly) why he and his young family were in such dire straits and what we could do to help them. This is, of course, a familiar occurrence in the Big Apple; none of us thought much about it until another passenger, a Black woman who obviously rides this particular subway line regularly, began disputing the facts of the beggar's story by pointing how much he'd embellished or altered it since she heard it the week before. Calmly, the two of them negotiated the details and authenticity of his public "performances," while the rest of us howled with laughter (and of course, offered him some cash). Only in New York...

The other way I know I'm home, of course, is the overwhelming, daunting task facing me and everyone else interested in keeping up with the sheer quantity and diversity of cultural offerings in this town. When the *rentrée* begins here, the floodgates open; even though this blog will end in a few weeks, life never stops in the big city. There are some fine gallery shows by well-established artists like Robert Adams (Matthew Marks), Sally Mann (Edwynn Houk), James Welling (David Zwirner), Douglas Gordon (Gagosian), Cedric Nunn (David Krut), Lise Safarti (Yossi Milo), and Richard Misrach (Robert Mann Gallery); retrospective glances at the influences of Warhol (at the Metropolitan Museum) and Conceptual Art (coming to the Brooklyn Museum); group shows like that surveying the Gutai Art Association in Japan (at Hauser and Wirth) and the thought-provoking mélange of objects from diverse cultures called *Collectors of Skies* (curated by Valérie Rousseau and Barbara Safarova) at the Andrew Edlin Gallery. There was a wonderful reading from, and discussion of, *My Poets,* the new and surprising book about her personal creative process by writer and scholar Maureen McLane. For this blog post, however, I will single out a few of the things I've seen this month that I've especially enjoyed.

First on my list is the Frank Moore exhibition of paintings, videos, drawings, writings, and stage designs at the Grey Art Gallery and the Fales Library of New York University. An active participant in the downtown art scene until his early death from AIDS in 2002, Moore's eccentricity and utter originality shine through in this retrospective of his work about illness, toxicity, and the environment. Large-scale, almost magic realist paintings, colorful and bizarre, remind viewers immediately of artists like Frida Kahlo, whose image-world was both personal and extremely political in its pain and its naivety. Sometimes based on photographs of models, Moore's works morph immediately into surreal alternative universes, where hospitals become broken ice floes with patients and doctors stranded in isolation. Thanksgiving dinner is a blood (and not a turkey) fest shared by all races, colors, and creeds, and buffalo roam not on the range but on white bed sheets. Hieronymus Bosch-like characters make their way through landscapes littered with medical vials, mice, and pills, illuminated by piles of gold coins. In Moore's reality, every frame is a work in itself: pharmaceuticals, plumbers' pipes, and maps echo and encircle the iconography, breaching the boundaries between art and life so that bizarre and horrific images spill over to implicate those of us seemingly safe in the surrounding space.

I was also enthralled by the retrospective of Lin Tinmiao, one of China's foremost women artists, at The Asia Society Museum. Surveying her work since 1995, *Bound/Unbound* is comprised of installations, sculptures, and two-dimensional works, many of which have not been seen outside of China. Thread and hair, usually white, link the works in this show, and it is often hard to distinguish between them. Wrapped around objects, obliterating or enhancing photographed faces, morphing into bodies, body decorations, or covers, these tangled skeins are sometimes accompanied by video or sound. This is an uneven exhibition; works like *The Proliferation of Thread, Bound and Unbound,* and *Focus* are very strong statements, while others seem less powerful and more decorative in impact. Most extraordinary, from my point of view, is *Here? Or There?*, originally produced with her husband Wang GongXin for the 4th Shanghai Biennale of 2002. A room filled with mannequins, dressed in bizarre and beautiful costumes made by the artist that hover between the traditional and the space-age, opens outward toward video views that flash between old landscapes of China and the new, dissonant cityscapes into which the country is transforming. Watching this extraordinary spectacle, familiar yet foreign, fascinated by a vision of people, of society, of female experience I could perceive but never fully grasp, I was grateful once again for the window onto the world that contemporary art provides.

Speaking of which, there is also the debut show of Fazal Sheikh's latest work now on view at Pace/MacGill Gallery in midtown Manhattan. Entitled *Ether,* comprising over forty small pigment prints of images taken in the sacred city of Varanasi (Banaras or Banares on the banks of the River Ganges in Northern India), the images focus on sleep, dream, death, and birth in the place Hindus consider the auspicious site of the soul's emancipation from the eternal cycle of reincarnation. Often seen in groupings that juxtapose various bodily states or the five elements, the photographs document—but can never penetrate—the mysteries of the physical body as it enters the world, travels in dreams, or is transformed through death into earth, fire, water, air, and ether. With these quiet and beautiful images, Sheikh is paradoxically using photography's descriptive capabilities to highlight the spiritual side of our nature, the ineffable metamorphoses between states of being that can be neither perceived nor described. Like Zoe Leonard, who has created another in a series of site-specific and room-sized *camera obscuras* in Murray Guy's Chelsea gallery, Sheikh has decided to look beyond the purely political and ask different, less tangible, questions about sight, subjectivity, culture, and interconnectedness.

And then, last but not least, there was the revival of *Einstein on the Beach* at the Brooklyn Academy of Music. This is the third time I've seen this *magnum opus* by Robert Wilson and Philip Glass with choreography by Lucinda Childs—and the first time was the original performance at the Metropolitan Opera House in 1976. *Einstein,* for me, is therefore a homecoming of a different sort, a reminder of a Downtown New York legacy that sometimes seems quaint (there's a whole scene where a toy spaceship traverses the closed curtain) but that nevertheless has lost none of its original power. The train and the courtroom, the clocks and the night bus, the gestures and words endlessly repeated but always new: they *were* there, they *are* here, they are luminous. They are icons whose strength lies precisely in coalescing the fugitive visions glimpsed in passing within Leonard's *camera obscura* and making manifest whatever is monumental about our passage through space and time.

DOMESTIC TENSION: AN INTERVIEW WITH WAFAA BILAL
(September 27, 2012)

The Iraqi artist Wafaa Bilal is one of my colleagues in the Photography and Imaging Department at New York University. Though his studies were originally in photography, Wafaa has an open and flexible attitude toward media, and it is not only the politically charged content but also the form of his works—which are becoming increasingly well-known internationally—that will interest readers of this blog. This interview took place over lunch in Greenwich Village on September 19, 2012.

Shelley: Given the fact that your life has been so eventful, I think the best way for readers to understand your art would be for you to begin discussing your background.

Wafaa: I was born in Iraq in 1966, that's about two years before the Ba'ath regime took over. As a child, I grew up idolizing the regime, we were kids and we were swept away, of course, but slowly as I grew up I noticed, everyone noticed, that the regime became more and more oppressive. At the age of eighteen, I had a strong ambition to go to art school, but for political reasons, this was not allowed, and I was sent to study geography at the University of Baghdad.

S. What kind of political reasons?

W. Physical education and art were considered to be highly effective fields, and the regime made sure that every candidate for these fields was carefully screened. Considering my family's background in politics, I was rejected, so then I was sent to study geography. Even though you can see that is not at all my passion and I resisted, I had to do it, because if I failed college I would be forced into the military, and placed on the front lines, and this was during the war with Iran. So of course, I stayed in the program. But it wasn't so bad, I had access to a studio at the university and I could paint on a daily basis. I used that as a platform, I put up shows, and every show I organized had problems. Some works were political in nature and they were confiscated by campus security; sometimes I was dragged to the office for interrogation. But in 1990, right after the invasion of Kuwait, I was one of the students who stood up publicly and refused to volunteer for the Kuwait war, and at that moment I knew I was blacklisted and needed to run. In 1991, there was a bombing for forty days, and I used that opportunity to escape from Baghdad. I waited on the edge of my hometown of Kufa until March, when there was the uprising, one of the first Arab Spring uprisings when people took over. But the regime unfortunately crushed the entire uprising and we were on the run. I stayed in a refugee camp in Saudi Arabia for two years. After that, I was able to come to the United States, to New Mexico, and that's when I said: no more geography and geology, I will study art.

S. How did you get to New Mexico? That's not a self-evident choice…

W. I had a friend who was a translator for the United States military. He left the camp before me and his sponsor was one of the American officers who lived in New Mexico. I needed an address and that was the only one I had. But it ended up being good, the university was a great school for me, with great photo teachers. Five years later, I got my undergraduate degree and then I went on to the Art Institute of Chicago and studied Art and Technology for my Master's Degree.

In 2007, I started one of my major projects, called *Shoot an Iraqi*. *Shoot an Iraqi* came from my personal devastation after the loss of my brother, who was killed by a drone in Iraq in our hometown. I think at that moment my work shifted. From being about human rights in general it began engaging larger, more personal issues. It became intensely focused on my deeply felt responses to the war in Iraq and, and the same time, on the idea of engaging people beyond the confines of art spaces. This is when I started linking gallery spaces with the Internet.

I received the news about my brother's death in 2004, and for the next few years, I honestly did not know how to deal with my losses, or how to communicate that through art to the public. Only when I watched an interview with an American soldier who was sitting in Colorado, directing these drone planes and dropping bombs on people in Iraq, did I realize that he was completely disconnected psychologically and physically from his targets. That's when it hit me, that's when I knew the combination of media I needed to communicate my ideas. I wanted to create something that gave control to the viewers but also detached them psychologically and physically from the target. Then I thought: The target needed to be real, needed to be live, and its interaction with the viewers needed to last long enough so that people had time to connect to it. For this project, which was originally called *Domestic Tension* because the gallery thought that *Shoot an Iraqi* was too provocative, I lived for a month in a 32 × 15 foot space in the back of the gallery with a bed, a desk, a computer, a lamp, a coffee table, and an exercise bike. Several Plexiglas screens separated my "bedroom" from the rest of the gallery, where a paintball gun, outfitted with a robotic mechanism that fired in response to the commands of online viewers and gallery visitors, was stationed at the threshold. People could go on site, direct the gun, and shoot a paintball at me at any time for thirty days. By the end of the live event, more than 65,000 shots had been fired at me by viewers from 136 countries.

S. So where was this? Which gallery and when?

W. It was in Chicago, in the FlatFile Galleries, for thirty days from May 7–June 5, 2007.
At the beginning, I disconnected myself from the viewers: there was no sound, the picture was grainy, etc. But every day I uploaded a ten-minute video clip so people could see the emotional roller coaster I was going through on a daily basis. Because of that more and more people started coming, to see the site and to interact with me. Then the media picked up the story. The public got attached to the project first and then the media came around, which is the reverse of what usually happens. But it got much bigger when the *Chicago Tribune* wrote an article about it on the front page, about targeted shootings. It was such an important project for me because after *Shoot an Iraqi* I started thinking about making projects that are dynamic, rather than didactic.

I started involving the live body as a medium because of its immediacy, connecting people inside and outside of the gallery through the Internet and giving viewers some kind of control over the work. These ideas about dynamic encounters have a lot to do with earlier works like Happenings, by artists such as Allan Kaprow, of course. Like them, I want to make art that is open ended: nothing is predetermined by me but evolves with the participation of the viewers themselves. Without the participants, nothing will happen, and the project will be idle.

S. After the performance, I know that you published a book about your experience. Why did you decide to do that?

W. When *Shoot an Iraqi* was over, I ended up with massive amounts of documentary materials—videotapes, daily journals, etc.—and I decided I wanted these records to be archived so that everyone could have access to them. I wanted the project to continue beyond the thirty days. One of the writers, Kari Lydersen, who at the time reported on the project for the *Washington Post*, did an excellent job. I was so amazed by how she dealt with it that I approached her later, asking her to cowrite the book with me. We had a few offers from publishers but chose City Lights because we knew the quality of their work; the book continues even now to be well received by many people, including academics. We structured it by describing how I survived the thirty days without breaking down—but also by showing what things, which events, inspired the project in the first place. So there was a parallel structure: after a day in the gallery, the focus of the book would shift to Iraq. Going back and forth between art and life gave the reader a sense of what happened in the gallery space and also an open window onto Iraqi life, how my family lived, and the devastation we suffered losing both my father and my brother within two months.

S. I know that all of these things continue to be major parts of your work: expanding media, interfaces with the public, and your engagement with political issues of the day. How do you see the development of your art as moving on a parallel track with the development of your media?

W. That's a really good question. I always see the project as determining the medium, and not the other way around. Right now, new media work best for what I want to say—because most of the time I'm dealing with global issues, so it doesn't make sense to stay local in my art. As I said before, I'm building not objects but events, encounters— and encounters are very dynamic. I need a physical space, a gallery space, as a platform, but after that the medium becomes the story: the encounter between the platform I set up and the viewers of the event, wherever they are. Digital connectivity is not just a tool, it becomes the medium itself.

S. Would you like to update this interview by discussing some of your recent work, like the event you created in Tehran at the end of 2011? This project is a very good example of the interactivity you've been describing, and the interface of film and performance too.

W. One of the most recent projects was entitled *A Call* (which translates into Farsi as *Neda,* the name of the young Iranian woman killed on the street during the recent protests against the election in that country). I was invited by the Aaran Art Gallery in Tehran to commemorate the 30th anniversary of the Iraq/Iran War. I didn't know how this was going to happen, so I started talking to people, looking at the space.... One thing that triggered the entire project was the empty swimming pool sitting at the back of the gallery, which used to be a home....

S. Had you seen the gallery?

W. No, one of my students from Iran alerted me about the empty swimming pool. It hadn't been used for thirty years, so it had become allegorical. Since we were talking about the losses of this war, which continued for over eight years, I wanted to divide these losses into the ones who were lost and the ones who were left behind. The pool, of course, is underground. So, I separated the performers into two groups: the ones standing in the swimming pool and the ones above, the ones that left and the ones that are left behind. I used all local performers, eighty performers dressed in black and white. They descended from the second floor of the space, moving through the viewers to arrive at the swimming pool. Some stood in the pool, some were placed around it, and then they all stood and stared at the audience for thirty minutes. Standing motionless, looking at the viewers surrounding them, at a certain point they began to symbolize the *status quo* in Iran at that time. So the piece moved beyond being a commemoration of the 30th anniversary of the war.

One complication to all of this: I didn't get a visa to go to Iran. We tried everything, but nothing worked. So, I directed the entire piece through Skype from my living room in New York, with the gallerist Nazlia Noebgshari in Tehran holding a laptop, walking around, and showing me where everyone was walking and standing! On the day of the performance there were so many people who couldn't go—even the curators (Ava Ansari and Molly Kleiman from The Back Room) weren't able to be there—that we decided to do a live stream of the performance from Iran to the White Box Gallery in Manhattan. At that moment, everybody was connected: Iranians who were not able to witness this event could come to the gallery to see it performed, while the people in Tehran could look at us in New York commemorating this event. So the distance was erased through technology.

S. How did the Iranian government react to this event?

W. I don't think the gallery had many problems. No, as far as I know the only complaints were that the event involved too many people. The piece was very vague, so there was nothing to complain about, and that was deliberate. Political art does not have to be so direct; sometimes, it is much more powerful if it suggests multiple interpretations rather than meanings assigned by the artist. That's the good thing about creating an encounter: you trigger something and let it unfold, and you don't control the outcome. The gallerist said that everyone involved felt a lot of responsibility to do the best they could since I could not be there. The performance had two runs, and there was so much demand that the gallery decided to do a third show one week later.

LIFE WORLDS
WALTHER COLLECTION AND INTERNATIONAL CENTER OF PHOTOGRAPHY, NEW YORK
(October 9, 2012)

> We must return to the point from which we started: [...] not a return to the longing for origins, to some immutable state of Being, but a return to the point of entanglement...
> —Edouard Glissant, "The Known, the Uncertain"[1]

THIS GLISSANT QUOTE makes an appearance in Sarah Nuttall's superb book *Entanglements,* an examination of contemporary art and literature in South Africa.[2] The blurb on the book jacket fittingly describes Nuttall's text as an "exploration of postapartheid South African life worlds." Committed to illuminating the complex strands of difference and sameness, violence, victimhood, and resistance entangling all of her fellow citizens in their web, the author explores a rocky terrain of communication, misunderstanding, and mutuality that reveals itself even to transient visitors of this intensely creative nation. My own 2009 visit to South Africa—thanks to an invitation from the Roger Ballen Foundation—was, I must admit, one of the high points of my intellectual life. While participating in a two-day seminar at Wits University with artists, curators, critics, and intellectuals from Jo'burg and Cape Town, I was privileged to enter into a profound exchange about the nature and responsibilities of culture. Engaging in an open-ended, dynamic, and rich dialogue committed to "returning to the point of entanglement," the participants were intent on forging an artistic and political future *not* framed by what Nuttall calls a "persistent apartheid optic."

---

1 Edouard Glissant, "The Known, the Uncertain," in *Carribean Discourse. Selected Essays,* trans. Michael Dash (Charlottesville: University Press of Virginia, 1989), p. 26.
2 Sarah Nutall, *Entanglement: Literary and Cultural Reflections on Post-Apartheid* (Johannesburg: Wits University Press, 2009).

This was, and is, a tall order, and a continuing quest. I'm happy to report that another stage in the ongoing discussion is taking place right now in New York City, in the form of two major exhibitions at the Walther Collection and the International Center of Photography. As I mentioned, when visiting Johannesburg, I was grateful to participate in a workshop with people who, while living in a social and political environment that continues to be impossibly difficult, try every day to confront and express their problems directly, head on, instead of relying on "persistent optics" or tired ideologies. The complexity of the approach that arises from such an intense commitment is evident in both exhibits, albeit in different ways. *Distance and Desire: Encounters with the African Archive,* curated by Tamar Garb for the Walther Collection, will ultimately be a three-part show. On view now, in Part One, are works by Santu Mofokeng and A. M. Duggan-Cronin. Garb sees the African archive as "a contested compilation and collection of artifacts and representations that have accrued over time, and that are open to scrutiny and examination by a new generation of artists and viewers for whom the colonial orthodoxies and truisms that led to its creation are no longer operative or true." The "contested" part of this assertion becomes clear in the juxtaposition of these two projects, as well as these two exhibitions. A. M. Duggan-Cronin's *Bantu Tribes of South Africa,* an eleven-volume study published between 1928 and 1954, visualizes an ethnographic vision of indigenous tribes, frozen in an "immutable state of Being" in traditional costumes and ennobled poses in barren and empty landscapes. Hovering somewhere between proud African types and demeaning stereotypes of aboriginal people (depending on your point of view), these Bantu tribes were presented by Duggan-Cronin as representative of an authentic and timeless Africa even as the political struggle for and against apartheid wracked the urban centers of the nation—a struggle extensively described in *The Rise and Fall of Apartheid: Photography and the Bureaucracy of Everyday Life,* curated by Okwui Enwezor with Rory Bester, on display concurrently at ICP.

In other words, two distinct South African temporalities are on view in New York: the one, the stasis of the noble Black savage who exists in an eternally retrospective state, and the other, the quick tempo of enraged and embattled denizens trapped in a modern bureaucratic state that systematically dismantled their human rights after 1948. But even within the Walther exhibition alone, the definition and depiction of what it means to be an African is "at stake," as Marta Gili would say. Sharing the space with Duggan-Cronin's project is Santu Mofokeng's *The Black Photo Album: Look at Me*, created as a slide show in 1997 (and shown recently at the Jeu de Paume as part of his retrospective exhibition). The pictures (shown in three versions: as slides, as the silver gelatin exhibition prints Mofokeng produced from the deteriorating originals, a few of which are also in the gallery) are part of the artist's personal collection, salvaged from the albums and drawing rooms of neighbors and acquaintances and researched to identify sitters who posed for studio photographers between 1890 and 1950. Coextensive with Duggan-Cronin's project (as well as the early days of apartheid), these pictures represent the original studio portraits commissioned, paid for, and preserved by Africans who envisioned their ideal selves in modern European-style dress and fancy hats.

My colleague Dr. Jennifer Bajorek, who has contributed to this blog and who lectured in conjunction with the exhibition, told her audience that when Mofokeng showed his personal works (black-and-white documentary pictures describing township life, religion, and land, some of which are simultaneously on view at ICP), his subjects did not like them at all. He began collecting *The Black Photo Album* pictures in order to discover what types of images his neighbors in fact preferred, and thereafter only exhibited his own photographs interspersed with ones that had been commissioned by people in his community. The differences in the depictions are obvious, of course, but so are the time warps built into the project. Multiple temporalities converge when the records of the original sittings (represented by the faded original prints) jostle with the contemporary vision of an artist interrogating the meaning of his forebears' photographic experience. Unmoored from personal albums and sequenced within the narrative of Mofokeng's slide show, the portraits are interspersed with his queries and contestations: "Are these images evidence of mental colonization or did they serve to challenge prevailing images of 'The African' in the Western world?" is one of them. Of course, there is no answer to this question, the pictures represent neither and both, and the question floats into an existential void. This is the complexity—and irresolution—of entanglement. When the viewer understands that the photographs describe distinct, sometimes contradictory "life worlds" coexisting within the same historical time and space, he or she begins to comprehend the hall of mirrors that is South Africa today.

The same dense interactions are evident in *The Rise and Fall of Apartheid*, although that exhibition gives them a completely different spin. Whereas *Distance and Desire* is spare and focused on two extended projects, Enwezor and Bester have organized an enormous exhibition with a cast of thousands. Though no one agreed on the precise number of pictures on the walls at the Press Preview, there are at least 500 photographs, which are accompanied by magazines, videos, and "overtime" information available on computers in the galleries. At the Preview, Enwezor explained his interest, and excess, by explaining: "We've all looked at enough images of D-Day, I wanted people to see something else that was going on around the same time." Central to the organization of the show is the theme of bureaucracy: the ways in which this horrific system of government was "normalized" within the society through laws, paper trails, housing, transportation, and entitlements. Photographic evidence describes how populations forced to live in this increasingly oppressive nightmare internalized (or not) their roles—and developed methods for either maintaining the *status quo* or fighting back.

The show is divided into two parts. On the upper level of the museum, the viewer can follow the history of apartheid from 1948 (with the victory of the Afrikaner National Party) until 1994 (the rise of Nelson Mandela). Here we see many, mostly black-and-white documentary photos, accompanied by texts and timelines as well as videos and magazines. The vast majority of the pictures were taken by South African photographers like Peter Magubane, Jürgen Schadeberg, and Ernest Cole, but there are also some by outsiders like Margaret Bourke-White and Dan Wiener. The downstairs space focuses mainly on artistic expression, on the responses of creative imagemakers to this system of injustice. On display are works by South Africans like Sue Williamson, Jo Ractliffe, Guy Tillim, William Kentridge, David Goldblatt, and the collective Afrapix, as well as contributions by foreign supporters like

Adrian Piper and Hans Haacke. One of the major premises of the exhibition is that during this historical period, photography was deliberately transformed by its practitioners into an active social instrument. So the duality of the exhibition, its highlighting of both documentary description and artistic interpretation (with lots of links and overlaps between them), is designed to emphasize the multifaceted usage of visual media during an intense period of political struggle.

Another level of intricacy, however, is evident in the choice of subjects covered in the show. Enwezor has made no secret over the years of his disdain for the "persistent optic" of Afro-pessimism: the media's insistence on seeing the continent and its inhabitants as unmitigated disasters, mired only in violence, poverty, and corruption. This exhibition gives a much more nuanced picture of daily life under apartheid, and both Blacks and whites are visualized in multiple ways that are not exclusively political. Along with documentary records of government meetings and political figures, protests, violent encounters, and hardship, there are pictures of everyday life in both the African and the Afrikaner communities: living conditions, education, religion, parties, music (Miriam Makeba!), and magazines like *Drum*. Though separate within the context of the show (and the apartheid system), these social manifestations have an equivalent weight here. Their presence does not allow any South African, Black or white, to become "stuck" in the political stereotype of victim or aggressor. From Nelson Mandela and the thrill of victory in the 1990s to the disappointment of the current social malaises and divides expressed by young photographers, we are left not with a fairy tale but with a complicated evolution of many intertwined histories: their triumphs and failures, their possibilities and disappointments as well as their aftershocks and legacies.

Life Worlds will be the last article in my series for the Jeu de Paume. As I said during the video interview posted in the museum's online magazine, I accepted Marta Gili's challenge in order to revitalize the language of my contemporary responses to global art. During my travels, I've met no people more committed to the complexities of this language than South Africans. As I say goodbye to the blog and its readers, I am pleased that these artists and writers are front and center. My hat is off to them for all they've taught me—and all they continue to teach me in exhibitions like these, enriched with insight about every "entangled" contemporary society wrestling with difficult questions that have few, if any, easy answers.

FAREWELL FROM THE BIG APPLE!
(October 17, 2012)

SUMMER IS OVER, and the weather in New York is getting colder... Even dEmo's 24-foot rendition of David is wearing long underwear (designed by Missoni!) as he hangs out among the crowds in the Meat Packing District of Greenwich Village.

So it is time for my blog to come to an end.

For me, this assignment has been a wonderful opportunity and a great privilege. Many thanks to Marta Gili, Adrien, Marta Ponsa, and Maurice at the Jeu de Paume, to the friends and colleagues who've contributed so much to the success of this series, and to all of you who've been reading and commenting on what I've been writing for the past six months. May we meet again!

POSTSCRIPTS: PART 2

GIFTS, MISAPPROPRIATED: KARA WALKER'S *NORMA*
La Fenice, Venice, Italy
Originally published in Africanah.org, July 5, 2015

I WAS ONE OF the lucky ones: my Teaching Assistant, Allison Young, was working on catalog research for the 2015 Venice Biennale, *All the World's Futures*, when she happened to find out that Okwui Enwezor had commissioned Kara Walker to do the stage direction, set design and costumes for Vincenzo Bellini's opera *Norma*, already on the schedule for late May and early June at the famous Teatro La Fenice. A collaboration between the Biennale and the Opera House, the work was billed as a "special project" of the biannual exhibition and included a show of preparatory drawings on view in a special gallery in the extraordinary theater (which was rebuilt and reopened in 2004 after a devastating fire destroyed it in 1996). Being an early bird, Allison managed to hook us up, months ago, with two tickets for the event the night of June 3, and made us the envy of our friends. As she had predicted, the show was sold out very soon after we made our purchase, once the details of the production were made public and tickets were offered for sale.

As many of the readers of this magazine know, I am an art critic, not an opera critic—or even an opera fan. My interest in this production was simple: I wanted to see what would happen when a formidable African American concept artist like Kara Walker confronted and reinterpreted a cornerstone of European culture. Moving from the art world into the opera world is not unprecedented; most recently and probably most publicly, South African artist William Kentridge has been very active in the theater, designing *The Magic Flute* and *The Nose* as well as original signature works for the stage. But because Kara Walker is so deeply ideological, and so deeply identified with Blackness, its culture, and its history, I was curious to see what acts of appropriation—she calls them "misappropriation"—she would commit in re-presenting Bellini's "gift."

The answer was evident as soon as we entered the theater and saw the front curtain, the "grand drape" that hid the stage. On it, an obviously African woman—of monumental scale and naked above the waist—peered outward, toward the public, with a steady gaze. Simultaneously growing from and anchoring the swirling, stylized branches of forest trees surrounding her, her dark skin was embedded within two-dimensional patterns of light that echoed the patterns on her incised skin. In other words, a message about the primacy of the Black female body, in particular the African female body, and its profound relationship with nature, culture, and cosmic rhythms greeted spectators as soon as they walked into the theater. (This image was created by a projection, and it was also used on the poster announcing Walker's *Norma* to the public. It represents, obviously, the iconic Norma of the artist's imagination.) It was immediately clear that this African body would stand her ground; she was going to stare back at you, at the people sitting in the audience, unlike most of the nude female subjects—whatever their race—in European paintings and colonial photographs. This evening, in this theater, Kara Walker was saying, the audience would experience, eye-to-eye, a face-to-face encounter with the Other.

It was of course also clear that the Others in question would not be the tribe of Druids, colonized by the Romans long ago, who were the stars of Bellini's original script. Kara Walker, first and foremost, chose to highlight the fact that Bellini's *Norma*, while having a secure place in the canon of European culture, is a deeply political story about unequal power relationships: between conquerors and colonized people, as well as between men and women. But it is not a story about battles, or action, or male bonding; in fact, very little actually happens in this play. The action unfolds through the bodies, interactions, and emotions of the women on stage, who are snared within its political web. This overarching political scenario was made clear in Act I, Scene I by Bellini himself. The scene introduces the audience to the Druids, who meet in the forest with their High Priest Oroveso to vent their rage and express their desire to make war on the Romans who oppress them. Immediately after that, Roman Proconsul Pollione enters. Rather than political strategy, he discusses his love life with his aide Flavio. Pollione has fallen out of love with the High Priestess Norma, Oroveso's daughter, with whom he has fathered two children in a secret affair. The plot revolves around his disenchantment, and the fact that his latest passion is a young virgin priestess, the novice Adalgisa, who returns his love.

But this is not a simple soap opera plot, an everyday male midlife crisis, because Pollione is a colonial ruler, and his "marriage" to Norma unites him to his nature-oriented, mystical subjects, keeping peace and balance between two very different cultures and cosmologies. This aspect of the story is made very clear, very early in Bellini's drama. Norma has enormous spiritual (ergo, in this situation, political) power, a power respected by her people and by the forces of the natural world they worship. Norma's love for Pollione kept her social world in a tense equilibrium; peace depended literally on her female body, her patience, and her emotional balance. Pollione's betrayal—his love for the young priestess Adalgisa, and his obsessive desire to flee to Rome with her—would therefore by necessity have enormous diplomatic consequences, which everyone but him seems to understand instinctively.

Norma's fury at his decision to leave (and presumably desert her and his two children) reaches a crescendo when she realizes (in a discussion with the novice Adalgisa, who comes to her for counsel and advice about her suitor, totally in the dark about Norma's secret relationship with the Roman proconsul) that her lover has betrayed her with the young priestess. Emotions are unleashed: Norma's anger stirs up the dark forces of the natural world, and Adalgisa is so horrified by Pollione's duplicity that she rejects him. Pollione alone stays the course of his sexual obsession, obviously oblivious to (and uninterested in) the huge consequences—on the women, the temple, his children, and the political balance of the region—of his actions. Literally, the future of the community is dependent on these two women and their ability to rectify a situation within which neither has the power.

Act II is really about Norma's reaction to these events: the murderous, horrified, frightened, tender, and irrational emotions that a woman of her stature would have as she tries to retain the moral balance necessary to safeguard her family, her culture, and the natural and mystical forces she channels. The curtain opens on her failed attempts to murder her sleeping children, to protect them from living in disgrace without a father—or perhaps even as slaves in Rome if their father chooses to bring them there. The two women meet and reconcile; Adalgisa refuses to go to Rome with Pollione and offers to speak to him, to make him understand that he must return to Norma to keep their world in balance. Norma is assuaged, for a short time. A new commander is announced, who will replace the Proconsul when he leaves (we see very little of the Romans, they are like an omnipresent but invisible *deus ex machina*). Pollione refuses to return to Norma, and the High Priestess' fury causes her to urge her people to attack the conquerors—and to kill both Adalgisa and the Proconsul—when he is brought in as a prisoner, for profaning the temple. Pollione was caught trying to breach the Virgin Priestesses' sanctuary in order to steal away his young love, a crime of transgression punishable by death under Druid law. The peace has ended, shipwrecked on the bodies of women and the rash and impulsive actions of a man. Norma tells her compatriots that a guilty priestess must also die—and to their horror makes it clear that the condemned woman must be herself, she who had broken her vows long ago and set this chain reaction in motion. Moved by her nobility, in love again, Pollione begs to share her fate, and after ascertaining the safekeeping of her children, Norma leads him to the pyre and the curtain falls.

Watching this supercharged drama unfold, it was hard for me not to think about the recent film *Boyhood*, directed by Richard Linklater. That movie is ostensibly about a boy, his youth and growth, but in reality it is about his mother, the amazing Patricia Arquette, and the enormous trials and tribulations she undergoes, and burdens she shoulders, in order to simply raise her children in some kind of safe and secure environment. In the film, as in *Norma*, the personal becomes political—and the men, to a one, are deadbeats, whose actions and reactions create turmoil for those around them. This too was a primary thought for Kara Walker, who modeled Pollione on Pierre Savorgnan De Brazza, an Italian explorer—charming and reckless, accused by Africans of raping young women—who colonized Central Africa for the French government in the late nineteenth century. A foppish man, a functionary ("That's the thing that gives this colonialized country its tragedy," Walker wrote in her notes. "We are conquered by that? And Norma, her inherent flaw, seduced by Him?"), de Brazza, like Pollione, is, in Walker's words, "both laughable and extremely dangerous." In

Walker's version of the story, Norma's consort arrived onstage in flamboyantly North African clothing: khakis and boots adorned with an Arab turban and beard. Coming straight out of Lawrence of Arabia rather than Bellini, Pollione's colonial costume made the audience gasp audibly when he appeared. Like the African woman—the Norma archetype—staring out at us from the grand drape, the actor playing the Proconsul located the drama of Walker's opera by embodying it.

This conflation—of the Druids and colonized Africans, of Pollione and de Brazza—makes manifest Walker's reinterpretation ("misappropriation") of Bellini's *Norma*. The artist made it clear, as soon as the audience entered the theater, that her rendition of the opera is not about Druids, it is about Africans, and it is set in a Central African colony around the early 1900s. (Using Gabon masks and colonial photographs as models, Walker once again located the action by visualizing it.) The actors in her production, like Bellini's, are "hybrid fantasies of the Noble Savage, *Others*," and the sets are stylized forests and landscapes—pastiches of forms uniting Kara Walker's flat silhouette style, the European "misappropriation" of African art in modernism and the blocky, sculptural masks of Central Africa. This is most evident, and most successful, in the artist's amazing and protean stage set. Simple shapes, usually black in color though not always, outline the landscape. But the major landmass upon and around which all the action takes place resembles a Gabon mask of a woman's face. Colors might morph depending on the light; skies might flash red or forests run rampant in stunning silhouettes projected as backdrops, making the mood and the scene more complex and dynamic. Actions of groups or individuals give different meanings to the sinuous and *polysemous* shapes on the stage. But the African female body is, literally and always, the ground upon which all the action in this opera unfolds.

And this, of course, is the point: all family ties, all of Nature, the spirit world, and human politics ultimately rest on the challenges that face the two women on stage. One of them is young and fresh; the other is older, and deeply enmeshed in life's obligations. One of them—Adalgisa—seemed to this viewer to be more symbolically African than the other. She embodied, in her hair and clothing, a closer resemblance to the sculptural forms of a Gabon mask—a signifying chain that for me at least encouraged, in fact, demanded, a highly racialized interpretation of the story. The future of this colony evidently depended on what happened to the Black female body—but that body was lying on the ground being walked upon by men during the whole production, and was vulnerable to being forcibly grabbed even during prayer time in the Temple. This is powerful stuff, and Walker's transposition of the story adds immeasurable contemporary relevance to Bellini's original tale—making its tragic lessons available to the present, to the future, to us all.

For all of these reasons, Kara Walker's *Norma* is a great success and an eye-opening interpretation that both adds to and subverts Old World history and culture. Her decision to focus on the African context shatters the proscenium wall that separates European audiences from their own history and culture. Like Okwui Enwezor's Venice Biennale, Walker's opera insists on reinserting the disappeared ones into the histories (and futures) of the Continent and does so not by storming the house but by pointing out the shared dilemmas, common languages, and "intense proximities" (to quote Enwezor) that affect us all. The only negative thing I can say about Teatro La Fenice's production of *Norma* involves the costumes, which might have been based on African sculptures and colonial photographs but which were, in fact, confusing for the audience. Guards in skirts carrying spears were legible to me as stylized representations of nineteenth century tribal warriors only late in the play, when they assembled; before that time, they just seemed weird, a bit kinky. In the absence of (the politically incorrect) use of blackface, odd hairdos and outfits on white actors read less as African and more as some hybrid of a Noble Savage, a vacillation that dampened the tremendous signifying power of the other aspects of the production. Needless to say, "misappropriating" European singers and actors to represent colonized Africans is a challenge in this day and age, and to its great credit Walker's staging made that challenge abundantly clear. There are many lessons to be learned from this wonderful and complex work, and I can only hope that this artist's pointed and pertinent dialogue with our past, present, and future will continue to provoke audiences on the shores of a few other continents.

SHIFTING SPACES, IMPOSSIBLE BORDERS: ANA MENDIETA, LILIANA PORTER, AND CECILIA VICUÑA

Originally published in lemagazine.jeudepaume.org,
October 12, 2018

"My art began by disappearing.
I made an offering for the sea to erase.
The waves weave our breath, in, out.
Dissolving gives life to what comes next."

—Cecilia Vicuña[1]

THIS BEAUTIFUL EXCERPT from Cecilia Vicuña's Artist Statement was displayed on the wall next to Disappeared Quipu, her sculptural and luminous "poem in space" on view at the Brooklyn Museum in the summer of 2018. Describing, in both literal and metaphoric ways, the banished symbols of the ancient Incas, her installation paid homage to alternate modes of communication—handicrafts and textiles, sounds and images—which shaped the records and the narratives of this complex civilization not tied to written language. The knotted "quipu" strings central to the installation, which were banned in 1583, "began by disappearing," as she said, and their absence "gave life" to her understanding of the South American cultural heritage into which she was born.

Chilean by birth, Vicuña left her country to study, and then to escape Pinochet's dictatorship; she has lived in London, Bogota, and, since 1980, New York. Like the Cuban Ana Mendieta and the Argentinian Liliana Porter, she is a Latin American woman whose experience of the world has been shaped by travel, by relocation, by exile (both of necessity and choice). All three of these artists have lived multiple perspectives and realities. They have chosen to explore the interstices between fixed spaces, homelands, and national identities. In *Disappeared Quipu*, Vicuña is peering across time and space to understand the

---

1   Cecilia Vicuña, Artist Statement for the Exhibition *Disappeared Quipu* (New York: Brooklyn Museum, May 18–November 25, 2018).

Incas. She is rediscovering the language of the ancient textiles of the Andes in the collections of the twenty-first century Brooklyn Museum, bringing history forward and superimposing the geographies of the two Americas. It is the premise of this essay that this working method, this perceptual pattern, and indeed this interstitial vision of the world is becoming increasingly common in contemporary art. But it is especially pertinent to, and descriptive of, the art of Latina pioneers like Vicuña, Mendieta, and Porter.

> Now I realize you can live (in New York) a thousand years, but you will always be a foreigner. Not long ago, someone asked me when I finally became integrated here, and I replied that the interesting thing about living here is that you don't have to integrate. People have the right to continue being different, to live in their own unique, personal countries; here you can invent your own country....
>
> —Liliana Porter[2]

Liliana and Ana were friends: good friends, the kind who share dinners and acquaintances and personal stories and send postcards when they travel. Part of an active group of Latin American artists that included Louis Camnitzer (Liliana's first husband), Luis Felipe Noé and José Guillermo Castillo, Porter originally arrived in New York as a tourist on her way to visit the museums of Europe. Attracted to the city, she decided to stay. But there was a caveat. "The one thing I always knew that I wanted," she told Inés Katzenstein, "was to maintain my relationship with Buenos Aires—to not lose my identity as an Argentine, even if that definition is totally abstract, subjective, and very difficult to explain."[3] Though resident in New York State for over fifty years, her decision to be different—to remain deliberately foreign, to create her own "unique, personal country" in her mind, her life, and her art—has been determinant.

On some level, this deliberate disjunction is the centerpiece of her

---

2   Liliana Porter, *In Conversation with Inés Katzenstein* (New York: Fundación Cisneros, 2013), p. 57. Porter is currently the subject of a retrospective exhibition at El Museo del Barrio in Manhattan. The show opened on September 13, 2018, and will be on view until January 27, 2019.
3   Ibid., p. 33.

artistic practice. The idea of "inventing" her own country is paralleled by her understanding of her works, which she sees first and foremost as philosophical propositions, and later as material, formal statements. When teaching, as she told me in an interview in August,[4] the first thing she drives home to her students is that an artwork is not a reflection of, or even tied to, any reality—and that is its strength. It is an arena where a new reality can take shape, where a rabbit can levitate or Che Guevera can hang out with (a piece of cheese named) Joan of Arc, and from her perspective that new vision must take precedence over technique or medium. As she sees it, a piece of paper or canvas is not a mirror. It is a separate world with different rules, where anything is possible. Like an invented country.

* * * * *

There's a lot of unfilled space in Porter's works. Whether drawings, paintings, prints, photographs, installations, or mixed media works, they are notable for their emptiness. Inés Katzenstein postulates that this surface blankness is fundamental to Porter's expression because it allows her to concentrate on "relational events."[5] Subject matter—whether a drawn sickle or a photographed plastic Jesus, a figurine of a man or a bear or a painted house—is unmoored from its context, taken out of its natural habitat. Once repositioned in Porter's artistic arena, these images or objects (no matter how divergent in origin, culturally or geographically) seem to share the same space-time, to encounter each other as "virtual travelers…who coexist in a new continuum, a hyperspace where various times and spaces interact."[6] The empty space—whether defined by a canvas or photographic picture plane, a wall or a wooden cabinet—gives the illusion of expanding into depth, allowing the focus on disparate and sometimes minuscule images or objects (often small mass-produced bric-a-brac from flea markets or

---

4   The author spent the day in Porter's Rhinebeck home and studio in August of 2018, and all references to comments made in an interview come from her discussion during this visit.
5   Inés Katzenstein, "Liliana Porter. Photography and Fiction," in *Liliana Porter: Fotografía Y Ficción* (Buenos Aires: Centro Cultural Recoleta, 2004), p. 197.
6   Gerardo Mosquera, "Liliana Porter: Shaking Hands with Mickey," in *Liliana Porter Photographs* (New York: Foundation for the Arts, 1996), n.p.

shops), to become so intense that the difference between representation and reality seems to collapse. Katzenstein remarked that Porter's photographs create a "theatre of replicas,"[7] where these deracinated, pop cultural *tchotchkes,* alone and unprotected, seem to reach out across space, time, culture, and ideology to engage—with each other and with us the viewers.

This temporal and spatial displacement is key to Porter's vision. Her images may be charged and are often political in precisely their banality. In the context of her works, pop culture pictures of Jesus and Che lend their ideological weight to capitalist icons like Elvis and Minnie Mouse, effacing cultural, philosophical, economic, and social differences as they "pose" together or seem to embrace. Mickey Mouse engages the White Rabbit. A toy soldier shoots at an outsize piggy bank. A tiny man standing on a full-sized white chest seems (implausibly) to hack up its wooden surface with a pickaxe, while a minuscule woman begins to sweep endless amounts of red dust with her impossibly small broom. This *Forced Labor* series gives a hint as to the seriousness of Porter's thinking and the implicitly political nature of her art, however entertaining and surprising it may be. The scales of things are out of whack, but so are their geographies, cultures, religions, ideologies and identities, and interactions. Porter sees this in not only artistic but political terms, since in her mind her works visualize and propose the possibility of "the encounter with the Other."[8] Her cheap, disposable, mass-produced "characters" (as Gerardo Mosquera calls them[9]) "cross through impossible borders, like an Alice in Wonderland."[10] Small wonder that Liliana most often cites Lewis Carroll and Jorge Luis Borges as her major influences. Moving from popular culture to the world of art, creating an environment within which dialogue uncannily takes place in spite of radical differences, Porter's subjects inhabit her "invented country."

On the night of her opening at El Museo del Barrio in New York in September, my first stop was the Delacroix exhibition at the Metropolitan Museum. That show ended with a grand finale, the remnants of the damaged *Lion Hunt* (1855*),* which was extraordinary in its

---

7   Katzenstein, "Liliana Porter. Photography and Fiction," p. 201.
8   Porter, *In Conversation,* p. 90.
9   Mosquera, "Liliana Porter," n.p.
10 Porter, *In Conversation,* p. 82.

grand scale, its passion, its rampant destruction, and its densely woven colorful surface. Moving uptown to Liliana's show, I looked at *To Sweep*, a large white canvas whose only imagery is in its midsection—where a brush, similar to one used to clean bathtubs, has swept across a plethora of tiny plastic objects like the gale winds of a hurricane, crushing horses, carriages, and other more mundane *tchotchkes* in a barrage of paint. Empty where Delacroix's painting was packed full, its "contents" minuscule, plastic, hard to discern, and sometimes domestic instead of monumental and dramatic, Porter's work blew my mind. It was the exact corollary to Delacroix's painting, a visualization of destruction, a narrative told from another (more feminine and ironic) point of view, in ways that implicated not the beasts but the most banal among us.

Ana Mendieta
Cuba New York Rome
She found her roots here.

Memorial Plaque at the Rome Academy,
Composed by Ana's sister Raquel[11]

Home—and its elusiveness—is an important subject in the art of both Liliana Porter and Ana Mendieta. For Porter, it is an anchor, and unreachable. Her tiny painted figures sometimes try to traverse vast landscapes to arrive at aspirational, impossible domestic destinations. Like the thought of Buenos Aires, home is always there for Porter, hovering in ways that seem increasingly abstract. She created a large painting of a small cottage against an almost white background in 2007, and then reused it in various formats (installations, photographs), allowing the structure to function within a hall of mirrors not unlike Duane Michals' photographic sequence "Things are Queer" from 1973. Entitled "The Resemblance," the painted house seems to float in the pictorial landscape within which it is embedded. Its scale creates a sense of intimacy and proximity, but at the same time, its environment gives the illusion of expanding, making the cottage feel recessive,

---

[11] In Jane Blocker, *Where is Ana Mendieta? Identity, Performativity, and Exile* (Durham and London: Duke University Press, 1999), p. 106. Just an aside: this is truly one of the great books of contemporary criticism.

distant, almost out of reach. The small building, and the spatial dissonance that surrounds it, was on my mind the day I visited Porter's studio in Rhinebeck, New York. As I was looking out the window of her home, I spotted that identical structure: small, white, and yes, simultaneously near and far, its distance really, literally, inexplicably hard to gauge. I gasped; Porter laughed. I wondered whether art had imitated life, or instead just played tricks with my eyes and my mind.

Liliana likes to collect and save things, not only the bric-a-brac that populates her works but also her correspondence. Included in her archive are several postcards from Ana—postcards presumably composed in Rome while Mendieta was living and working there, but sent through the United States Postal Service. (Older Americans will remember that in the 1970s and 1980s travelers often bought and wrote postcards abroad but sent them home with friends to be mailed, thereby avoiding large postal fees and delays.) Only one of the three touristy commercial cards Porter showed me has a direct relationship to Italy. There's a postcard of a tropical parrot jungle scene, one from the Amstel Hotel in Amsterdam, and one depicting the sculpture "Love and Psyche" that resides in the Capitoline Museum in Rome. All three describe her voyages, her work, insights about her relationships, feelings, and daily life. An American citizen by this time, Ana used the mail to assert her dislike of New York's increasing commercialism from her studio in Rome, by writing to her Argentinian friend living in Manhattan. Mendieta chose a mobile life, of shifting spaces and elusive boundaries, and she inhabited, loosely, the cracks between the near and the far. Like Porter's voyagers, always both close by and out of reach, Ana's travels were a means of putting down roots in the interstices between places—of displacing the emotional targets and traversing impossible borders. They were, as Jane Blocker has observed, a way to "make exile her home."[12]

* * * * *

Whereas Porter uses her art to create an arena for encounters, Mendieta's visualized absence. This is true from the earliest works, performances documented by photographs and films, where clues are

---

12   Blocker, ibid., p. 78.

strewn around her room or in the street, pointing to some violence that must have occurred—out of the frame, in the past. Ana chose to use photography to manifest what Roland Barthes called, in *Camera Lucida*, the *noeme*[13] of the medium: the fact that what you perceive as you look at any given picture was once present and is no longer. A photo, seen from this point of view, can only attest to absence; it is the evidence that what is in front of your eyes "has been." For Barthes at the end of his life, the medium was first and foremost about Time and its mysterious, uncanny displacements. For Ana Mendieta, who was sent away from her country and her family in Cuba for political reasons when she was twelve, whose teen years were spent in foster care in the United States deprived of everything (including her native tongue) that was familiar, temporal disruptions were a potent subject.

Critics like the brilliant Jane Blocker see Ana's *Silhuetas*—the earth drawings or sculptural carvings that Mendieta loosely traced from her body in Iowa, in Mexico, in Cuba, and elsewhere, known to us primarily through photographs—in this vein. They are spectral doubles of the artist, shadows that allude to her presence while signifying her absence. "In these shadows," Blocker writes, "she is always already somewhere else. They cannot tell us who she was, only where she has been. They force us to ask, 'Where is Ana Mendieta?'"[14] Those who have written about the artist often trace the origin of her work to the trauma she experienced in her exile, as if her life began in the shock of a new culture at the of age twelve. But perhaps that shock also functioned in another way, more constructive, as an opening toward an expanded perspective. Perhaps it provided her the opportunity to choose not to integrate, to "invent her own country," to imagine a conceptual territory born out of multiplicity and enhanced by accretion rather than rupture. Porter feels strongly about this, seeing parallels between her attitudes and Mendieta's. "While she was growing up in the United States," Porter told Sean O'Hagen in an interview, "Ana voluntarily kept her identity and her culture while simultaneously integrating to the new codes. She spoke perfect English. Her art reflects all of these issues and circumstances."[15] For Porter, Ana's life was not an either/

---

13 Barthes, *Camera Lucida*, p. 85.
14 Blocker, *Where is Ana Mendieta?* p. 99.
15 Liliana Porter, "Questions re Ana Mendieta," email interview by Sean O'Hagen of *The Guardian*, September 10, 2013.

or; it was synthetic, aggregated, and layered like a collage. As Liliana assured me, Mendieta knew how to use her Latin American heritage to her advantage in the international art world she traversed.

Viewed in this light, the traces (performances, drawings, sculptures, photographs, and films) designating where Ana "has been"—spatially, temporally, geographically, culturally—together create a network linking her body to myriad cultures, to history, the future, the earth. In this outreach, her works can be seen as the precursors of Cecilia Vicuña's *Disappeared Quipu*. They were not an attempt to find a lost past, become a feminist goddess, or merge with a nature devoid of culture. Never nostalgic, her art "skipped across time and through time, giving a physical shape to time. By inscribing her shape into the archaeological landscape, it was as if the artists had subtly merged with that place and its past. She was operating as an artist in the present tense with contemporary gestures and artistic methods, yet she was magically connected to the past, the ancient culture. The image was physical. It was temporal. It was of the earth. It was in the mind."[16] It was multifaceted and multilingual; its meanings were as elusive and as transient as the *Silhuetas* washed away by the sea or obliterated in fire and smoke. Like Vicuña's Quipu strings, Ana's traces "began by disappearing." They "gave birth" to her body's mobility, its rootedness in an expanded and virtual time and space. Seen from this perspective, Mendieta's painful experience of exile was what allowed her, like Liliana and Cecilia, to become unstuck without being unmoored, to live permanently in the cracks between places and languages, cultures, and historical moments. Her art was her postcard, sent to describe this shifting space, with its elusive borders, to those of us who stayed at home.

> The constant displacements, the continual disappearing acts that left their evidence of having been, all those open wounds silhouetted over and over again. Things burn themselves out. The films force us to endure that process, exiled from completion.
> —Rachel Weiss[17]

---

16 Howard Oransky, "Foreword," in *Covered in Time and History: The Films of Ana Mendieta* (University of California Press for ex. cat., the Katherine E. Nash Gallery, University of Minnesota, 2015).
17 Rachel Weiss, "Difficult Times: Watching Mendieta's Films," in ibid., p. 63.

When I knew Ana, in the 1970s, she was not usually identified as a filmmaker, though many of us knew that she made films. Not being particularly close to her, knowing her through Mary Beth Edelson, Carolee Schneeman, and others in the active art world feminist movement, I most often encountered her depictions of solitary performances. Through the medium of photography, I saw the records—of blood on the walls and sidewalks, of carvings, drawings, and sculptures etched on land, in sand and surf, and on the walls of caves. I saw her flesh covered in grass, feathers, blood, mud, and rocks. I saw, in other words, the myriad traces left by her passage through locations in different countries, on different continents, at different times. Transient séances, immobilized and preserved through the stop-time of photographs, became as mobile, portable, and spectral as the artist herself.

What this means, of course, is that Ana has, recently, posthumously, crossed another border: she has augmented her repertoire, adding filmmaker to her usual titles of photographer, performance artist, and sculptor. This is important, for it forces us to rethink and review her work within an expanded framework, one that incorporates movement and time more evidently, more forcefully. Being recognized as a filmmaker, within the context of performance and installation, was very difficult during the years Ana was alive. There was little framework for critical assessment and exhibition of moving images or installations until the year before her death, when the Stedelijk Museum in Amsterdam mounted *The Luminous Image* exhibition of video works. The traveling exhibition *Covered in Time and History*, therefore, is significant in this repositioning of Mendieta's achievements, not only in its assumption that these works are important but also in the effort that was put into the films' conservation and restoration. The exhibition, in fact, demands that we reevaluate her entire *œuvre*—after her death, when she doesn't have a voice.

I am treading lightly here, since I don't really know how exactly Ana saw these unedited films within her body of work, whether (as some suggest) they were simply sketches for her or whether she aspired to have them recognized as independent statements. Suffice it to say that she did enough of them to have their placement within her body of work make a difference in how we perceive her as an artist, and she made them continually, throughout her career. She began with her difficult early works, about rape, blood, murder, violence, voyeurism, and apathy. Passing into her landscape works, she moved away from menace and toward connection. As Rachel Weiss writes in the catalog, "The site of intensity relocates to the landscape, which develops a fluid interface with the body. The membrane of the self, so harsh at first, becomes transactional."[18] The films show that transaction as a process, as Ana and her surrogate *Silhuetas* are buried under, flow with, or are dissolved into the natural world—presumably allowing her, and us, to experience unions more primal than those of citizenship.

The continuity of these transactions is the films' *forte*, but their temporal flow leads us down unexpected pathways. Unlike the photo works, which freeze a moment, creating a fixed symbol that summarizes the performative experience, the films exist in what we perceive as "real" time. There is, therefore, the anticipation of a narrative arc and resolution; unlike photographs which preserve the past, films move toward a future. But this promised resolution never materializes, it is withheld in these works, devoid of editing and manipulation. The critic and curator Rachel Weiss has called attention to the claustrophobic nature of much of Mendieta's camera work. She writes that Ana's "Cyclopean vantage point"[19] establishes a closure within the open landscape, creating a spatial disjunction uncomfortable for both us and the artist. The writer sees this disjointed space as disruptive, especially in those films where viewers simultaneously perceive both Mendieta's merger with nature and her physical discomfort or obliteration within it. For Weiss, the human-nature truce articulated in the films is "provisional," and the artist's resulting isolation, her "exile," is akin to "being in a social body that she can never be within… The hope of union, expressed as a dynamic between self-nature, gradually becomes a diary of the accumulating fact of non-union." [20] As she sees it, the films make clear that Ana's physical body and its surrogates—buried, flooded, scratched, washed away, or burned in effigy—cannot achieve the merger to which the artist seemingly aspires, a merger perhaps implied symbolically in the photographic and sculptural works. "These films hurt," Weiss writes, and not only physically. They hurt

---

18   Ibid., p. 60.
19   Ibid., p. 61.
20   Ibid.

because in the end they are about "the abandonment of the ministrations of myth.... They kick us out of the garden." [21] Short, inconclusive, they end when Ana disappears or walks away.

I wonder how Mendieta would feel about this interpretation. Her works appeared during the early heyday of feminist art, and they were originally celebrated within the context of the Goddess movement (with which she had serious disagreements). Her silhouettes on rocks, soil, and sand were perceived as "Herstories," inspirations for women trying to express the ancient source of their power and heal the wounds of separation afflicting both nature and culture. But now we are in a different time, and the placement of the restored film as front and center in her *œuvre* adds a new wrinkle to this tale—a wrinkle that resonates, perhaps, with Liliana's delight in non-integration. Rather than confirming Mendieta's merger with universal rhythms, the films instead make manifest her separation and her solitude.

When Ana died in 1985, after falling (being pushed?) from the window of her husband Carl Andre's 34th-floor apartment in the East Village, she landed on the roof of our local deli, right across from the Tisch School of the Arts where I was then and am now a professor. In the middle of Manhattan, far from nature, her body, according to witnesses, eerily resembled certain of her photographs. Bloody, broken, covered with a sheet, it left its traces on the rooftop's surface. Life, we fearfully understood, had in the end imitated art. But this time, our gifted and spirited friend could no longer get up and walk away.

---

21   Ibid.

ACKNOWLEDGEMENTS

IN CLOSING, I want to thank Mary Bahr and Ulrich Baer for offering me the opportunity to collect these articles into a book and for working so hard and fastidiously to get this project done. A shout-out also goes to Marta Gili, who invited me to write for the Jeu de Paume's magazine, and Quentin Bajac, the current director who supported this collection with enthusiasm. Needless to say, the friends and colleagues who contributed to the blog are a big part of its success—hats off to the intelligence and creativity of my social network! Big thanks are also due to Erin Donnelly, who retrieved and retyped my articles from the *Soho Weekly News*. Francesca Woodman's beautiful and mysterious photograph, which graces the cover, spans the years between the Then and the Now of my career. Its inclusion is bittersweet for me, since Francesca was part of my friendship circle in the 1970s while I was writing for the *Soho Weekly News*. Her image would not be here without the support of the Woodman Family Foundation and the Center for the Humanities at NYU, which awarded me a Book Subvention Grant for the licensing fees. Many thanks to them both.

I have long hoped to preserve my journalistic essays, knowing full well that ephemeral commentaries, with all their glitches and missteps, are important traces of culture and history "in the raw." The work that I have done for popular audiences has had a major impact on my teaching at NYU; as my students will attest, the greatest (and most exciting) challenges they face are the response papers I oblige them to produce after forays into museums or galleries, theaters, or cinemas. Ultimately, what they take away from my courses, whether historical or contemporary, is the certainty that visual culture is meaningful, that it holds the key to understanding and shaping our social and symbolic life. This book is for them, and their friends and loved ones. It is my hope that *Image Making* will continue to elucidate meaning, to serve as a guide for those committed to the joyful generational task of creating the world anew.

www.ingramcontent.com/pod-product-compliance
Lightning Source LLC
Chambersburg PA
CBHW031616210526
45464CB00004B/1600